The Political Economy

Series editors
Rory Miller
School of Foreign Service
Georgetown University
Doha, Qatar

Ashraf Mishrif
Institute of Middle Eastern Studies
King's College
London, UK

This series explores the nature of Middle Eastern political regimes and their approaches to economic development. In light of the region's distinctive political, social and economic structures and the dramatic changes that took place in the wake of the Arab spring, this series puts forward a critical body of high-quality, research-based scholarship that reflects current political and economic transitions across the Middle East. It offers original research and new insights on the causes and consequences of the Arab uprisings; economic reforms and liberalization; political institutions and governance; regional and sub-regional integration arrangements; foreign trade and investment; political economy of energy, water and food security; finance and Islamic finance; and the politics of welfare, labor market and human development. Other themes of interest include the role of the private sector in economic development, economic diversification, entrepreneurship and innovation; state-business relationships; and the capacity of regimes and public institutions to lead the development process.

More information about this series at
http://www.palgrave.com/gp/series/14415

Ashraf Mishrif • Yousuf Al Balushi
Editors

Economic Diversification in the Gulf Region, Volume I

The Private Sector as an Engine of Growth

Editors
Ashraf Mishrif
Institute of Middle Eastern Studies
King's College London
London, United Kingdom

Yousuf Al Balushi
Supreme Council for Planning
Muscat, Oman

The Political Economy of the Middle East
ISBN 978-981-13-5488-5   ISBN 978-981-10-5783-0   (eBook)
https://doi.org/10.1007/978-981-10-5783-0

© Gulf Research Centre Cambridge 2018
Softcover re-print of the Hardcover 1st edition 2018
This work is subject to copyright. All rights are solely and exclusively licensed by the Publisher, whether the whole or part of the material is concerned, specifically the rights of translation, reprinting, reuse of illustrations, recitation, broadcasting, reproduction on microfilms or in any other physical way, and transmission or information storage and retrieval, electronic adaptation, computer software, or by similar or dissimilar methodology now known or hereafter developed.
The use of general descriptive names, registered names, trademarks, service marks, etc. in this publication does not imply, even in the absence of a specific statement, that such names are exempt from the relevant protective laws and regulations and therefore free for general use.
The publisher, the authors and the editors are safe to assume that the advice and information in this book are believed to be true and accurate at the date of publication. Neither the publisher nor the authors or the editors give a warranty, express or implied, with respect to the material contained herein or for any errors or omissions that may have been made. The publisher remains neutral with regard to jurisdictional claims in published maps and institutional affiliations.

Cover illustration: © titoOnz / Alamy Stock Photo

This Palgrave Macmillan imprint is published by Springer Nature
The registered company is Springer Nature Singapore Pte Ltd.
The registered company address is: 152 Beach Road, #21-01/04 Gateway East, Singapore 189721, Singapore

Preface

This book brings together resources and knowledge from different fields related to economic diversification and sustainable development in the Gulf Cooperation Council (GCC) countries. This edited collection of research papers presented at the Gulf Research Meeting held at the University of Cambridge in August 2015 provides an interdisciplinary approach to address one of the most highly debated and discussed topics in Gulf studies—that is, economic diversification and contribution of the private sector to economic development. The book intends to have a wider coverage and more updated knowledge in this important subject, as well as critically evaluate the current diversification strategies across the Gulf region. The overarching focus is on analysing the efforts to shift Gulf economies away from heavy dependence on hydrocarbons towards a more diversified economic system, where the private sector becomes the engine of growth.

This publication has two main objectives. The first is to underscore the need for economic diversification in order to minimise the negative impact of oil price fluctuation. Diversification is no longer a policy option but a must for GCC countries because of structural weaknesses in their economies. Diversified economies tend to be more stable and have the capacity to create jobs while being less susceptible to the boom and bust cycle of oil and gas prices. The sharp drop in oil prices from more than US$100 per barrel in 2014 to less than US$30 per barrel makes the timing of this publication perfect. Such drop has put diversification at the very core of economic development strategies.

The second aim is to underline the extent to which the private sector can participate in economic development. While the aim of GCC countries is to bring about structural changes in their economies, this publication explores ways through which the private sector can become the engine of growth. Of course, we recognise that the private sector is relatively small and plays a minimal role in GCC economies and, for the most part, continues to depend on its activities on the performance of the hydrocarbon sector. If the private sector is to play a greater role in the development process, structural changes should aim at creating conditions favourable for the private sector vis-à-vis the public sector. This requires limiting the role of the government to strategic guidance and diverting production activities from the public sector to the private sector that is often characterised by efficient allocation of resources and high productivity. Such changes should also produce a system that liberalises the regulatory framework, supports the development of the banking sector to enable small- and medium-sized enterprises (SMEs) access to finance and encourages private investments in the non-hydrocarbon sectors. A balance should be also struck between the nationalisation of the labour market and the needs of the private sector in the context of high unemployment and low productivity among the national workforce; such a balance could reduce the risk of low competitiveness in GCC markets due to low productivity and efficiency. This underscores the close link between the quality of the education system and entrepreneurship on the one hand and the performance of workers and ability of SMEs to competently utilise the financial and technical support provided by the government on the other.

In order to achieve these objectives, this book is divided into ten chapters; each chapter addresses one of the key components of diversification and private sector development. Chapter 1 provides an overview on economic diversification in the Gulf region and critically analyses diversification strategies of each member state of the GCC. Chapter 2 looks at the status of the private sector in Kuwait. Chapters 3 and 4 examine ways for the private sector to participate in economic development through either an integrated system in which private enterprises provide key services to state-owned enterprises in infrastructure projects or public-private partnerships. Chapters 5 and 6 highlight the importance of the regulatory framework and business environment, particularly in terms of promotion of foreign direct investment and improvement in the quality of education and labour market, which are critical to private sector development and needs. Chapter 7 examines how the organisational efficiency strengthens the role of the private sector in GCC countries. Chapters 8 and 9 assess GCC diversification strategies in the agriculture and tourism sectors, while Chap. 10 investigates the impact of GCC regional integration arrangements on private sector development through the internationalisation of Gulf SMEs in the regional market and on economic diversification.

London, UK   Ashraf Mishrif

Muscat, Oman   Yousuf Al Balushi

ACKNOWLEDGEMENT

We are delighted to have put together this highly valued work on the role of the private sector in the economic diversification in the Gulf Cooperation Council (GCC) countries. This original research and invaluable insights brought forward by leading experts from various disciplines and professions make this volume truly interdisciplinary and offer a realistic vision on the current stages of economic development in the Gulf region.

The production of this work is made possible with the generous contribution of the authors, who committed their time and efforts to present their work and share their views on this timely topic. We are extremely grateful to all the contributors of this volume, without whom this book would not have been available.

Special thanks go to the Gulf Research Centre for organising the workshop Economic Diversification: Challenges and Opportunities in the GCC held at the University of Cambridge, United Kingdom, in August 2015. We appreciate their generous financial and administration support and their commitment to advance knowledge in humanity and social science in the Gulf region. We also appreciate the generosity of everyone who has given us his or her support.

We, as editors, are very grateful to the publishers and editors of Palgrave Macmillan, who have kindly provided us with guidance and support to get this work published at the very high standard. Special thanks go to Farideh Koohi-Kamali, Brigitte Shull, Sara Lawrence and Vishal Daryanomel for their excellent support.

To those who have helped during the earlier phases of this project, who we did not mention, we apologise but gratefully acknowledge your assistance and kindness. We hope that this work will be an inspiration to all the authors and contributors and useful to all stakeholders, particularly decision makers, professionals, academics, postgraduate and undergraduate students, particularly in the GCC countries.

Contents

1 Introduction to Economic Diversification in the
   GCC Region   1
   Asharf Mishrif

2 Private Sector and Economic Diversification in Kuwait   27
   Anastasia Nosova

3 A Systemic Approach to Integrate SOEs and SMEs in
   Business Ecosystem   49
   Alfadhal Al-Hinai, Angela Espinosa, and Richard Vidgen

4 Implications of Public-Private Partnerships in
   Infrastructure Development for Economic Diversification   77
   Michiko Iwanami

5 Quality of Education and Labour Market in Saudi Arabia   97
   Ashraf Mishrif and Amal Alabduljabbar

6 Policy and Regulatory Frameworks for Foreign Direct
   Investment in Saudi Arabia   117
   Ahmad Al Daffaa

7 Organisational Effectiveness of Private Enterprises
   and Diversification in the Gulf Countries   137
   Shazia Farooq Fazli and Ayesha Farooq

8 Diversification Strategies in the Gulf Agriculture Sectors   163
   Salma Bani

9 Destination Place Identity, Touristic Diversity
   and Diversification in the Arabia Gulf   183
   Magdalena Karolak

10 Regional Integration, the Private Sector and
   Diversification in the GCC Countries   209
   Ashraf Mishrif and Salma Al-Naamani

Index   235

About the Editors

Ashraf Mishrif is Senior Lecturer in Political Economy of the Middle East at King's College London. He was also Senior Lecturer in International Business and Finance at Anglia Ruskin University and the University of Greenwich, UK. Mishrif has held a range of executive and advisory posts, including cultural advisor for the Egyptian Embassy Cultural Bureau in London and a member of the Academic Board of Directors at the Boston Business Management School, Singapore. He provides advisory services to companies, government departments, and international organisations, including United Nations Conference on Trade and Development (UNCTAD). His research interests include political economy of the Middle East, foreign direct investment, international trade, and economic transitions in the Gulf and the wider Middle East and North Africa (MENA) region. He authored a number of books, book chapters, and peer-reviewed papers, including *Investing in the Middle East: The Political Economy of European Direct Investment in Egypt* (2010), and the *Political Economy of Islamic Banking and Finance in the GCC Countries* (2015).

Yousuf H. Al Balushi is an experienced economist with over 20 years of professional experience at the Central Bank of Oman and the Supreme Council for National Development and Planning of Oman. He obtained his PhD from King's College London. His research interests cover monetary and fiscal policy, foreign trade, foreign direct investment, and private sector development.

NOTES ON CONTRIBUTORS

Ahmad Mohammad Al Daffaa is a PhD student at Hull University, where he examines the policy and regulatory frameworks for foreign direct investment in Saudi Arabia. He has an MBA in executive employee and MSc in marketing management, with a 20-year professional experience in marketing and sales in SABIC, Saudi Arabia.

Alfadhal Al-Hinai is a results-orientated and entrepreneurial-minded Leader with 18 years of professional experience in the Omani telecom industry. He studies PhD at Hull University, examining systemic approaches to understanding complex problems in organisations. His key interest is exploring issues generated by the growth and complexity of commercial, economic, technical, social and political environments that threaten organisational survival.

Salma Al-Naamani is a PhD student at King's College London. Salma is a lecturer of management at Ibra College of Technology in Oman, a graduate of University of Stirling with a master's degree in management.

Amal Alabduljabbar is a PhD researcher at the Institute of Middle Eastern Studies, King's College London and a Research Fellow at the Centre of Innovative Governance, Riyadh. Saudi Arabia. Her research interests focus mainly on education development and policy analysis in Saudi Arabia.

Salma Bani is a senior executive strategic programme planner in the Ministry of Municipality and Urban Planning Kingdom of Bahrain and a Ph.D. researcher at Institute of Arab Research and Studies (IARS), Cairo

Egypt. Her focus is mainly on food policy analysis. She has contributed and added value to the body of knowledge in the field of food policy in Bahrain.

Angela Espinosa is a Reader at the Centre of Systems Studies in Hull Business School and an Adjunct Professor at Los Andes Business School. She was the Director of the Secretariat of Information and Systems at the Colombian President's Office in the early 1990s. Her research interests focus on complex systems approaches to management, more specifically in methodologies to promote self-transformation and self-governance in organisations.

Ayesha Farooq is Professor of Management in the Department of Business Administration, Aligarh Muslim University, Aligarh, India. She has been awarded fellowship under the Netherlands Fellowship Programme for 'Strategic Management'. As an expert in the area of strategic management, she has publications in international and national journals of academic repute.

Shazia Farooq Fazli is Assistant Professor in the Department of Sociology, Maulana Azad National Urdu University, Hyderabad, India. She was associated with different NGOs, particularly Bill & Melinda Gates Foundation and Udaan society at Aligarh (India) working on women-related issues and AIDS. Dr Shazia is a focus group interview expert and a counsellor par excellence.

Michiko Iwanami (Ms.) is an analyst at Sojitz Research Institute where she carries out research for business support and development of Sojitz's (a Japanese trading firm) business areas focusing on the areas of the Americas. She also has worldwide experience mainly in Asia Pacific countries in infrastructure sectors.

Magdalena Karolak (Ph.D. in Linguistics, University of Silesia, Poland) is Associate Professor of Humanities and Social Sciences at Zayed University, UAE. Her research interests include transformations of societies in the Arabian Gulf and comparative linguistics. Dr. Karolak has published two monographs and over 30 journal articles and book chapters on the shifting gender relations, social media, culture and identity and political system transformations.

Ashraf Mishrif is Senior Lecturer in Political Economy of the Middle East at King's College London, where he was also Senior Research Fellow in the Middle East and Mediterranean Studies Programme. Prior to that, he was Senior Lecturer in International Business and Finance at Anglia Ruskin University (Cambridge) and the University of Greenwich (London), UK. He has authored a number of books, book chapters and scholarly papers, including the *Political Economy of Islamic Banking and Finance in the GCC* (Gerlach Press, 2015) and *Investing in the Middle East: the Political Economy of European Direct Investment in Egypt* (I.B. Tauris, 2010).

Anastasia Nosova did a PhD in Political Science in London School of Economics (LSE), Department of Government. Her research was dedicated to the dynamics of political participation of the business sector in Kuwait. She currently works in the field of business intelligence and corporate investigation.

Richard Vidgen is a Professor of Business Analytics at University of New South Wales. He has a track record of work in the IT industry and Information Systems. He uses a combination of IT and statistics (typically using the R language) to explore Big Data and data science, as well as studying the potential of business analytics for value creation (and destruction) on organisations and society.

List of Figures

Fig. 3.1	The potential integration between NSPs, SOEs and SMEs	57
Fig. 3.2	Cyclical Process Model. Source: adapted from Davison et al. (2004)	62
Fig. 3.3	OBC's Business Model	64
Fig. 3.4	The three layers of recursions in the OBC case	65
Fig. 3.5	(a) VSM of the OBC at the corporate level. (b) Generic VSM of fibre, towers and satellite	66
Fig. 3.6	OBC as a value integrator	68
Fig. 3.7	Meta-systemic functions addressed in the wider system	70
Fig. 4.1	GDP of GCC countries during 1990–2013. Source: WB 2015	87
Fig. 4.2	Oil rents (per cent of GDP) and oil prices of GCC countries during 1990–2012. Source: IMF (International Monetary Fund) Primary Commodity Prices 2015 and WB 2015	87
Fig. 4.3	Natural gas rents (per cent of GDP) of GCC countries during 1990–2012. Source: IMF Primary Commodity Prices 2015 and WB 2015	88
Fig. 4.4	Exports of goods and services (per cent of GDP) from GCC countries during 1990–2011. Source: WB 2015	89
Fig. 4.5	Fuel exports (per cent of goods exports) from GCC countries during 1990–2013. Source: WB 2015	89
Fig. 4.6	Average percentile of all six WDIs of GCC countries during 1996–2013. Source: WB and Brookings Institution 2015	92

Fig. 7.1	Conceptual model: McKinsey's 7S Framework (adapted by the authors)	147
Exhibit 7.1	Industry-wise distribution of Manappat Group of Companies	154
Exhibit 7.2	Corporate structure	156
Fig. 8.1	Food system. Source: Bani 2014	169
Fig. 9.1	Destination and competitiveness model. Source: Ritchie and Crouch 2003	191

List of Tables

Table 1.1	Sovereign wealth funds of the GCC countries (US$ billion), June 2016	8
Table 1.2	Oil as percentage of export and government revenues and GDP, 2011	12
Table 3.1	Three traditions of systems	58
Table 4.1	Comparison of PPP arrangements	80
Table 4.2	Comparison of infrastructure performances of GCC countries as of 2013	86
Table 4.3	Government performances of GCC countries as of 2013	92
Table 8.1	The economic importance of agriculture in the GCC countries, 1997–2006	167
Table 9.1	Tourism receipts by country	188
Table 9.2	International tourist arrivals (in millions)	188
Table 9.3	Hotel room supply in the GCC	194
Table 9.4	Frames analysis	202
Table 10.1	GCC interregional non-oil trade, 2000 and 2013 (US$ million)	215
Table 10.2	The relative importance of non-oil sectors in GDP of the GCC countries (percentage)	220
Table 10.3	The relative importance of oil in GCC countries, 2011 (percentage)	221
Table 10.4	GCC economic ranking in the MENA context, 2015	224

CHAPTER 1

Introduction to Economic Diversification in the GCC Region

Asharf Mishrif

INTRODUCTION

Over the past 50 years, Arab Gulf states have appreciated the wealth generated by the production and export of oil and natural gas. The rise of international oil prices, which reached more than US$100 per barrel between 2009 and 2014, is the main contributor of this wealth. By October 2016, the Gulf Cooperation Council (GCC) countries—Bahrain, Kuwait, Oman, Qatar, Saudi Arabia and UAE—have accumulated assets and capital worth over US$2.99 trillion, mostly managed by their sovereign wealth funds (SWFs) in the global markets. Substantial investments have also been made in infrastructure, education, healthcare, roads, ports, power stations and water desalination. Socio-economic conditions and social welfare have improved substantially, with gross domestic product (GDP) per capita of Qatar and UAE exceeding US$100,000 and US$66,000 per annum, respectively, making them among the highest per capita income rate countries in the world.

A. Mishrif (✉)
King's College London, London, UK

© Gulf Research Centre Cambridge 2018
A. Mishrif, Y. Al Balushi (eds.), *Economic Diversification in the Gulf Region, Volume I*, The Political Economy of the Middle East, https://doi.org/10.1007/978-981-10-5783-0_1

Unfortunately, the generation of such wealth is not sustainable due to frequent changes in international oil prices. Changes in oil prices can go either way in terms of capital surplus and capital accumulation. For example, in 2010, high oil prices helped GCC countries to have a combined fiscal surplus of some US$600 billion. However, the sharp decline in oil prices by almost 70 per cent, from more than US$100 per barrel in January 2014 to less than US$30 per barrel in January 2016, has raised serious concerns about the financial sustainability of the Gulf countries. International Monetary Fund (IMF) warned that sustained low oil prices would lead to an accumulated combined fiscal deficit of US$700 billion by 2020. This forecast is a strong warning to GCC countries of their need to build vibrant, diversified economies that can withstand the effects of oil price shocks.

An assessment of the current national visions and development strategies in GCC countries indicates that little has been achieved in economic diversification because local economic cycles remained dependent on oil and gas revenues. The fragility of the national economic cycle is evident in the negative impact of oil price fluctuations on export revenues and government income, as well as the import of goods, services and workers to meet domestic needs. Such impact affects growth levels in gross domestic product (GDP) negatively. To eliminate such effects, there is a need to transform Gulf economies from a traditional allocation state model that is dependent on the government to a modern economic growth model that is led by the private sector. Strategic transformation often entails radical changes in the style of management and addresses private sector challenges that hinder the development process.

In fact, effective transformation can help GCC countries to mobilise efficiently their national resources in long-term sustainable development. GCC countries have long realised the infinite nature of oil and gas, but the options to diversify their economies are limited. The first phase of diversification began in the 1970s by expanding the oil sector in the upstream and downstream industries, as well as the creation of oil-related industries such as petrochemicals and aluminium. It shifted substantial proportions of investment from the extractive industries to capital-intensive and energy-intensive industries such as petrochemicals, fertilisers, steel and aluminium that utilise their comparative advantage in the energy sector, as well as expanding in industries that could benefit from low-cost energy such as cement, construction and building materials. Despite having comparative advantages in these industries globally, this phase has not changed the structure of the Gulf economies. As percentage of GDP and revenues of export and government in GCC countries, oil contributed to 39.7 per cent of GDP, 78.2 per cent in export revenues and 83 per cent in government revenues in 2011. This shows that sustained growth in oil revenues, which coincides with overall economic growth and high living standards, is no longer guaranteed because of frequent disturbances in the global energy market and fluctuations in international oil prices.

More recently, a new phase of diversification has taken the form of investment in physical and human capital development, particularly in areas relating to infrastructure, schooling and health services. Diversification has gone beyond the energy sector and its related industries, with the intention of working towards the creation of knowledge-based economy. Economic visions and national development strategies are currently concentrating on export diversification and development of service industries, including finance, tourism, aviation, media, education, healthcare housing and real estates. National visions focus on key pillars such as human development, social development, economic development and environmental development—all of them contribute to sustainable development. Of course, there are numerous challenges to create knowledge economy in GCC countries, given the current condition of their education systems, low investment in research and development (R&D) that is less than 1 per cent of their GDP compared to global average of 3 per cent, and restricted civil liberty and political freedom that hinder private sector development. However, given the availability of capital and scarcity of non-energy resources, the move towards the creation of knowledge-based economy is probably the most sensible policy option for GCC countries to help create a viable economy that sustains the livelihood of society in the aftermath of the oil era.

This chapter aims to shed some light on the diversification strategies in the GCC countries. It begins first by exploring the definitions and key drivers of diversification. The next section explains why GCC needs to diversify their economies. The third section critically examines economic diversification strategies and policies as spelled out in the national visions and national development strategies. The fourth section explores various aspects supporting the private sector and increasing its role in economic diversification. Analysis underscores the aptitude of the private sector to manipulate the political settings by support reform programmes when they suit it and opposing reforms when they do not secure preferential treatment and concessions, as is the case of Kuwait. It stresses the capacity of the private sector to participate effectively with the public sector in major infrastructure projects through various schemes including public-private partnerships (PPPs). In some cases, private enterprises have taken advantage of the incentives provided by GCC common market to expand their activities in non-oil sectors in the regional market.

DEFINITIONS OF ECONOMIC DIVERSIFICATION

Economic diversification implies the development of policies that reduce the dependence on a single industry or sector such as oil in terms of its contribution to GDP, export earnings and government revenues. Decreasing dependence on oil occurs by developing non-hydrocarbon economic sectors such as services, manufacturing, tourism and agriculture in order to become new sources of government revenues. Diversification is a complex and lengthy process that requires serious structural changes in the economy. It may occur within the same sector such as energy by shifting resources and investment from the upstream to downstream industries in oil and gas or providing new opportunities for new non-fossil fuel products such as renewable or alternative energy. Diversification also occurs by opening up new non-hydrocarbon economic sectors for development such as services, finance, tourism and media or by shifting investment from one sector to another, often from the primary to the secondary and tertiary sectors to increase the value-added of national products. Hvidt (2013) argues that diversification entails a broad societal process, which transfers a country from a single source of income (oil and gas) to a society where multiple sources of income are generated across the primary, secondary and tertiary, and where large sections of population, including public and private enterprises, participate in the development process.

The motivation of diversification is to reduce or minimise economic and financial risks that are often associated with demand and price fluctuation. In such unstable and unpredictable markets as energy, diversification strategies provide comfort and practical solutions to compensate for the decline in international oil prices and hence their reduced oil export revenues. Although the risk factor is probably the most compelling force of diversification in the GCC countries, there are other reasons why these countries should diversify their economies. El Kharouf et al. (2010) spelled out some of these factors, which include low rate of sustainable economic growth, lack of public and private incentives to accumulate human capital, lack of competitiveness in the leading sectors, the likelihood of economic shocks, and sharp decline in commodity prices and their negative spillover effects in the economy. The latter factor has made it imperative for the GCC countries to consider accelerating diversification after the fall in oil prices in 2014.

In the GCC context, successful economic diversification depends on the ability of the state to implement wide-ranging structural change that addresses the imbalance between the public sector and the private sector in the development process. Hvidt (2013) argues that policies aiming at achieving diversification tend to favour greater participation of the private sector in economic development. This is not the case in GCC, where oil and gas are capital-intensive state-run industries. Hence, diversification in the energy sector sustains the leading role of the public sector in development, as long as major industries such as petrochemicals, aluminium and steel are oil-based, energy-intensive and heavily subsidised by the state. Investment in these oil-related industries is unlikely to reduce the dependence of the state on the hydrocarbon sector because their production depends largely on the availability of low-cost energy. Similarly, investments in renewable energy may provide a new opportunity for diversification from fossil fuel to non-fossil fuel energy, but shifting capital from fossil to non-fossil fuel is unlikely to reduce the role of the public sector in the economy because renewable energy is capital-intensive and run by large state-owned enterprises (SOEs). This concludes that diversification in energy cannot reduce the role of the public sector in the economy nor the dependence of the state on the hydrocarbon sector.

Thus, diversification should take place in non-hydrocarbon sectors that are largely underdeveloped. Beblawi (2011) identifies import substitution industries for diversification because this type of industries provide a diverse set of activities, most commonly manufacturing of building materials and food processing. He argues that these industries often attract small- and medium-sized enterprises (SMEs) that are labour-intensive and contribute to development outside the energy sector. The development of import substitution industries could offer the private sector greater opportunities for investment in manufacturing, tourism, finance, banking, insurance, financial services, construction and real estates. These industries do not only facilitate the expansion and growth of the private sector, but they also enable the government to spread the risk of possible economic shocks and fluctuation in oil prices, while creating a variety of income revenues.

Morakabati et al. (2014) stress the importance of export diversification and underline the association between the diversification of exports and economic development. Their analysis raises the question of whether export diversification is a natural outcome of the growth process or whether the growth process leads to diversification. They argue that export diversification is a growing trend in most developing countries; 80 per cent of these countries were exporting primary goods some 50 years ago, while now 80 per cent of them export manufactured goods. They highlight the tendency among these countries towards developing capabilities in the export of services, particularly after the introduction and implementation of General Agreement on Trade in Services in 1995. Apparently, dependence on a narrow range of exports makes the country susceptible to the negative effects of price shocks, which, in turn, destabilise the economy and discourage investment by the private sector (Shuai 2013; Ghosh and Ostry 1994). For Cypher and Dietz (2009) economic development is not just about growth in GDP, but it is about developing skilled labour workforce, creating knowledge and technological advancements, enhancing well-being of citizens and improving the quality of their life. In most GCC countries, tourism is an activity that can increase foreign direct investment (FDI), increase GDP and reduce the level of dependence on a narrow primary product range of goods.

Key Drivers of Economic Diversification in GCC Countries

In the GCC region, one can identify three key drivers of diversification. The first and foremost driver is the public sector. Hertog (2012) argues that unlike most Middle East and North Africa (MENA) countries, GCC countries have managed to create a new breed of dynamic, profitable and rapidly growing state-owned enterprises that are successful in manufacturing and services sectors and stand in contrast to the politicised and inefficient SOEs in other oil-producing countries such as Venezuela, Iran and Russia. The success of the SOEs in the Gulf countries does not necessarily mean that these countries should not develop their private sector enterprises. SOEs have the capacity to focus on major operations in the production process, while leaving enormous supporting services to be provided by private enterprises, particularly SMEs. Chapter 3 provides a clear example of the capacity of an Omani public telecom company that successfully facilitated the participation of many SMEs in the operation of the network through outsourcing and subcontracting.

The second driver of diversification is the private sector. This sector is in a much weaker position than the public sector when it comes to economic activities, because of the nature of the current allocation state model, in which a relatively small part of the population is involved in economic activities. The preference of most citizens to work for the government and the public sector undermined the base of skilful and qualified workforce; hence, most private enterprises depend on expatriates, who come to the Gulf countries on temporary basis. The private sector has the potential to become the driving force of diversification, largely because the oil sector does not provide many jobs, while the public sector is excessively overcrowded and can no longer absorb many new entrants. Although the allocation states do not need to focus on creating productive base and therefore cause systemic underdevelopment of the productive sectors, there is an emerging trend across the Gulf region to develop private sector enterprises as vehicles for employment and engines of growth. GCC countries are also looking upon FDI as means of employment and transfer of the much-needed technology, knowledge, capital and management attributes; all of them are required to support GCC countries in creating knowledge-based economy.

The third driving force of diversification is sovereign wealth funds (SWFs). Mishrif and Akkas (2016) attribute the importance of SWFs to their investment in key economic sectors such as infrastructure, finance, banking, Islamic finance, technology, transportation, telecommunications, education, construction and real estates. These financial tools have invested considerably in major infrastructure projects at their home countries, while having the capacity to make inter-GCC and international capital mobility in order to diversify their economies at the national, regional and global levels. Data shows that investments by the GCC SWFs in real estates increased substantially from US$1.1 billion in 2005 to US$12 billion in 2014, with two peaks of US$9.3 billion and US$9.6 billion in 2008 and 2013, respectively. The decline in oil prices in late 2014 affected the real estate sector, which experienced significant reduction in SWFs' investments by almost half to US$6.6 billion in 2015. GCC SWFs have also made huge investments in infrastructure, with US$14.6 billion, US$5.5 billion and US$3.5 billion made in 2009, 2014 and 2015, respectively. They invested US$17.7 billion in the industrial sector in 2009. The financial sector attracted most funds, with US$9.2 billion, US$20.2 billion, US$2.9 billion, US$16 billion and US$5.8 billion invested, respectively, in 2007, 2008, 2009, 2010 and 2011. SWFs have also invested huge funds, though to lesser degrees, in energy, healthcare and information technology. Table 1.1 shows a great potential of further investments by GCC SWFs, which possessed just under US$3 trillion, accounting for 40 per cent of total global SWFs in June 2016.

Why Diversification Matters?

In the current economic conditions, diversification has become a necessity, not a policy option in the GCC countries. The economic structure is unsustainable, and all GCC countries have suffered from the negative effects of the fluctuation in international oil prices and increasingly declining demand on fossil fuel from oil and gas in light of technological advancement in renewable energy and growing concerns over the environment, more specifically climate change. Date shows that GCC countries share specific structural economic features. They depend heavily on the hydrocarbon sector, which accounted for high government revenues at 83 per cent and approximately 78.2 per cent of total GCC exports in 2011. This type of structural weakness in Gulf economies poses a serious threat

Table 1.1 Sovereign wealth funds of the GCC countries (US$ billion), June 2016

Country	Holding funds		Total funds
UAE	Abu Dhabi Investment Authority	US$792 bn	US$1246.8 bn
	Investment Corporation of Dubai	US$196 bn	
	Abu Dhabi Investment Council	US$110 bn	
	Mubadala Development Company	US$66.3 bn	
	Int. Petroleum Investment Company	US$66.3 bn	
	Emirates Investment Authority	US$15 bn	
	Ras Al-Khaimah Investment Authority	US$1.2 bn	
Saudi Arabia	SAMA Foreign Holdings	US$598.4 bn	US$758.4 bn
	Public Investment Fund	US$160 bn	
Kuwait	Kuwait Investment Authority	US$592 bn	US$592 bn
Qatar	Qatar Investment Authority	US$335 bn	US$335 bn
Oman	State General Reserve Fund	US$34 bn	US$40 bn
	Oman Investment Fund	US$6 bn	
Bahrain	Mumtakat Holding Company	US$10.6 bn	US$10.6 bn
	Total funds		US$2984.8 bn

Sources: SWFs Institute, October 2016

to medium- and long-term sustainable development in the wake of the depleted nature of their oil and gas and fluctuation in oil prices. Since 2014, almost all GCC countries have had to rely on their foreign exchange reserves and impose significant cuts in their public expenditures to address budget deficits. The modest recovery in the oil prices from less than US$30 per barrel in January 2016 to around US$50 per barrel in October of 2016 falls short of filling budgetary gaps in GCC countries. According to the IMF's Middle East Regional Director, oil was expected to stabilise at around US$60 per barrel in the medium term, a rate lower than the budgetary breakeven point for Saudi Arabia, Qatar and the United Arab Emirates at US$79.7, US$62.1 and US$58.6, respectively (Ahmed 2016). The level drops to US$47.8 per barrel in the case of Kuwait, but it shoots up to US$77.5 and US$93.8 in the case of Oman and Bahrain, respectively. In order for the GCC countries to balance their budgets, they had to cut back their pending in the next five years and find ways to raising non-oil revenues.

The impact of budgetary gaps has had negative effects on the overall growth in the GCC region as a whole, with regional GCC expected to be at just under 2 per cent in 2016. The Saudi GDP has declined from 3.5 per cent in 2015 to 1.2 per cent in 2016, while the economies of UAE, Kuwait and Qatar have expanded by around 2.3 per cent, 2.5 per cent and 2.6 per cent, respectively. The rapid economic growth fuelled by high oil prices in the past ten years has ended. In September 2016, Saudi Arabia introduced drastic austerity measures, cutting salaries of cabinet ministers by 20 per cent, slashing benefits for the 160 members of the consultative council and limiting overtime pay and allowances for civil servants. The fall in oil revenues forced some GCC governments to cut energy subsidies and shelve many of their infrastructure projects. Further measures to balance their budgets and diversify revenues are evident in the commitment of GCC government to levy a value-added tax of around 5 per cent in 2018. More socially sensitive measures such as reviewing and cutting public sector wage bills, where GCC countries spend twice as much as public wage bills than other emerging markets, could be seen as a way to encourage Gulf citizens to seek employment in the private sector that is currently run by expatriates (Kerr 2016).

Indeed, the urgency to diversify Gulf economies does not arise just from the above fiscal and financial factors. GCC countries are increasingly facing huge political, economic, demographic, social and environmental challenges, which affect directly and indirectly their sustainable economic development. Economically, non-hydrocarbon sectors remain weak and continue to be dependent on oil revenues and, in turn, on the price of oil. For example, private enterprises are heavily dependent on the public sector and government expenditures. This is evident in the reliance of industries such as manufacturing, petrochemicals, water desalination and aviation on low energy costs and effective government subsidies to maintain global competitiveness. The banking and financial services are dependent on the flow of money determined by oil revenues. Any change in oil-enabled government spending policies will have huge impacts on all sectors of the GCC economies. The association between these economies and government development expenditures and international oil prices has become clear with the current drop in oil prices that led GCC countries to take exceptional measures by either drawing on foreign reserves or issuing public bonds to close budget deficits.

Politically, the changes in the energy markets may create frequent shocks to the GCC countries, as these countries still rely on oil revenues to secure their own political legitimacy. The effects of energy market fluctuations are likely to be painful on the more populous and less wealthy countries such as Bahrain, Oman and Saudi Arabia, which are less prepared than Qatar, UAE and Kuwait, in weathering the negative effects of declining oil revenues. Since 2011, the former three countries have faced difficulties in dealing with popular uprisings and disturbances and responded by balancing reduced budgets with the need to bolster their political legitimacy through economic largesse for their population. For example, in 2011, Saudi government provided one of its largest subsidy programmes, with US$136 billion to support housing and employment, particularly for young generation. With this unfound and unexpected uncertainty over political legitimacy, the need for new modes of economic development based on increased productivity and an end to long-standing rentierism becomes more pressing. Malik (2015) goes further to argue that economic diversification carries deep power implications for ruing elites. He thinks that good economic policies rarely constitute good politics, because structural changes demanded by economic diversification promise to empower business constituencies that could potentially challenge the ruling elite, particularly in a relatively liberal system such as Kuwait and UAE. He believes that for diversification to succeed, its political costs for ruling elites must be offset and resource-dependent elites must be compensated for the losses they will risk.

Environmentally, there is a growing international environmental consciousness, which is driving demand for machinery with increased efficiency, leading to the subsequent drop in demand for energy as well as increased potential of renewable energy sources. This comes amid concerns about climate change, hence calling for a reduction in carbon emissions from fossil fuel and the signing of the Paris Agreement in December 2015. In contrast to the economising of fossil fuel use in the developed countries, domestic energy use in the GCC countries continue to grow. Indeed, this massive reduction in oil revenues, together with the declining overall demand for fossil fuels owned to advanced technology in renewable energies and rise in the production of non-conventional fossil fuels such as shale gas, which is currently produced in large quantities in the US, Canada and China, has already placed huge strains on Gulf economies.

GCC Diversification Strategies and Policies

The Gulf countries have underlined their awareness of the depleted nature of oil and gas in economic planning. National visions and development plans have stressed the need for economic diversification since the mid-1990s. These visions and plans highlight the aims and aspirations of the GCC governments in relation to economic and social development. Four key elements have broadly featured in the national visions: human, social, economic and environmental development. They focus on broader concepts such as sustainable development and inclusive growth, which are difficult to attain and measure given the nature, size and structure of Gulf economies. However, economic diversification has been a permanent feature in all Gulf national visions and economic plans. Some of these visions such as the Bahraini Vision 2030 have looked upon the private sector as a driving force for economic development, while others such as the UAE Vision 2021 stressed the important role played by the public sector in the development process.

Oman Diversification Strategy

Oman Vision 2020 that was designed and announced in 1995 and covered the period 1996–2020 underscores the limited oil and gas reserves and therefore unreliability as main sources of income in the long run. Omani diversification strategy aimed at achieving structural changes in the economy by diversifying the production base, increasing the role of the private sector in the economy and developing human resources capabilities. This means that the country has had to embark on the liberalisation and expansion of non-oil sectors and enable new industries to grow and lead in the development process. The strategy aimed to expand key industries such as services, tourism, mining, agriculture and fisheries in order to reduce the share of the oil sector to only 9 per cent of GDP by 2020. Details of how this could be achieved are spelled out in three five-year economic plans: the Seventh Five-Year Plan (1996–2011), the Eighth Five-Year Plan (2011–2016) and the Ninth Five-Year Plan (2017–2021). Both the vision and three plans have focused on three main areas for development. The first area is the development of infrastructure by investing more than half of the Eighth Five-Year Plan in the construction of airports and roads and another 26 per cent in seaports, water and housing. The second area is supporting private sector development, particularly SMEs. It is believed that the private sector is more capable of attracting international investment and generating jobs, as well as enhancing the quality and competitiveness of the Omani workforce. The third area is the improvement in the economic environment. Oman has introduced extensive economic reform programmes, most notably the liberalisation of investment environment including investment and competition laws. Despite its pioneering position and ranking as the second most diversified economy among GCC countries, Oman is heavily dependent on the hydrocarbon sector as oil accounted for 41 per cent of GDP, 77 per cent of government income and 65 per cent of export revenues in 2011, as shown in Table 1.2. The Vision 2040 that is currently being developed by the Supreme Council of Development may have concerted plans to overcome the challenges of economic diversification.

Table 1.2 Oil as percentage of export and government revenues and GDP, 2011

Country	% of export revenues	% of government revenues	% of GDP
Bahrain	69	86	24
Kuwait	90	93	45
Oman	65	77	41
Qatar	91	80	46
Saudi Arabia	85	85	50
UAE	69	77	32

Sources: Martin Hvidt 2013

Bahrain Diversification Strategy

Bahrain is in a similar position as Oman when it comes to dependence on oil in economic development. As Table 1.2 shows, oil accounted for 86 per cent of government income, 69 per cent of export revenues and only 24 per cent of Bahrain's GDP in 2011. The country introduced its Vision 2030 in 2008, which followed by a more detailed National Economic Strategy in the following year. The vision aimed to shift the economy from dependence on oil to creating "a productive, globally competitive economy, shaped by the government and driven by a pioneering private sector" (Bahrain Economic Development Board 2008). It also aimed at creating enough new jobs for its growing population and doubling the income per capita of its household by 2030. The strategy is an ambitious one, as the country puts the development of its human capital at the heart of its development plans. This is expected to happen through the attraction of foreign investment that could provide jobs with high-level knowledge competences and as a result high wages. Lack of foreign investment after 2011 uprisings undermined the capacity of the state to attain such objectives, hence offering nationals jobs in the overcrowded public sector and gaining legitimacy through redistributing oil revenues.

Diversification strategy focuses on three main areas for development. The first area is the development of the private sector through the promotion of entrepreneurship and supporting innovation and the creation of national innovation systems across the country. Also, there is a tendency in the government towards supporting creative industries and creating knowledge-based and high-value-adding companies, particularly in the high-tech sector. The second area for development is turning the country into a global financial hub. Financial services is the leading sector in the diversification strategy, with significant numbers of national and international banks and financial services companies operating in the country since the 1970s. Up to 2011, Manama was considered one of the key global financial cities, and its proximity to the emerging markets in Asia and the Gulf and its connections with European and US markets have turned the city into a regional financial centre for both conventional and Islamic finance, as well as financial services. Other key economic sectors for development have been tourism, services, logistics and manufacturing, particularly its aluminium industry (e.g. ALBA aluminium smelter). This adds to the already diversified Bahraini economy, where services and industry accounted for around 50 per cent of GDP in the 2000s (Koren and Tenreyro 2010). The third area is human resources development, where education plays a prominent role in building a knowledge-based society. Investments in primary, secondary and higher education, with particular attention paid to transferable skills and training, are essential for improving the quality of national workforce and increasing its employability in the private sector.

Qatar Diversification Strategy

Qatar also announced its national Vision 2030 in 2008, followed by Qatar National Development Strategy 2011–2016 that provided a detailed account of the expenditure and implementation of the economic plans. The pace of economic planning and implementation is much faster than any other GCC member state because of the country's commitment to hosting the Fédération Internationale de Football Association (FIFA) World Cup in 2022. Unlike Oman and Bahrain, Qatar is less enthusiastic about economic diversification because of its huge oil and gas reserves. It is estimated that the country has the largest gas reserves in the world and sufficient reserves to keep oil production going for the next 45 years (Hvidt 2013). This makes the utilisation of hydrocarbon resources key to future economic development and diversification. However, the vision is an ambitious one that aimed at transforming Qatar into an advanced country by 2030, capable of sustaining its own development and providing a high standard of living for its population for generations to come. It also aims at creating a knowledge economy in a way that makes the country a regional hub for knowledge and high-value industrial and economic activities. One of its key methods of achieving this end is economic diversification by supporting private enterprises, promoting entrepreneurship, improving the business climate, reforming labour market and strengthening regional integration. Progress on these fronts has been slow, despite the fact that Qatar spent around 5 per cent of its GDP on education in the past 5 years, and built the Education City, with a large number of foreign colleges and universities facilitating skills and knowledge transfer to young population. Hvidt (2013) highlighted a number of factors that could also explain the slow pace of diversification. The chief among these factors are the small size of the economy and its consumer base, as well as the low wage in the private sector vis-à-vis the public sector, which discourage citizens from seeking employment in the private sector. Data confirms that only 0.3 per cent of citizens work in the private sector, while the percentage of all Qataris in the workforce does not exceed 6 per cent (General Secretariat for Development Planning 2011). This makes the prospect of developing a national workforce that is competent to lead on bolstering the private sector and increase its role in economic development and diversification limited.

Kuwait Diversification Strategy

Kuwait is the most dependent GCC country on oil, which accounted for 90 per cent of export revenues, 93 per cent of government income and 45 per cent of GDP in 2011. The Kuwait Vision 2035, announced in 2010, aimed to turn the country into a regional trading and financial hub through economic diversification and development. This announcement of the vision was followed by the approval of the first Five-year Development Plan (2010–2014) since 1986, in which the government pledged to spend US$125 billion on the implementation of the plan. Significant investments have been made in major infrastructure projects such as the Silk City in Subiyah, the deep-sea container port in Shatt Al-Arab, and new railway and metro systems, as well as schools and hospitals. The vision expected a greater role by the private sector in these projects by contributing almost half of their total costs. It also hoped that the creation of a well-developed infrastructure could attract both domestic and foreign investment into the country. Previous studies argue that Kuwait is the least diversified economy in the GCC region, largely because of its positive fiscal balance and constant dispute between the legislative authority (parliament) and the executive power (government) that paralyse the decision-making process for many years (Hvidt 2013). There may be a lack of political consensus on the direction of development, but what really affects the development process is the psychological effects and physical destruction of the First Gulf War (1980–1988) and Second Gulf War (1990–1991) and how this influences the perception of decision makers, who are still haunted by the high levels of insecurity in the region. High political and security risks are the most discouraging private and foreign investments in Kuwait. However, Kuwait is currently focusing on developing intangible infrastructure such as governance, rule of law, transparency and accountability in the public sector, with emphasis on the development of human and administrative capabilities.

UAE Diversification Strategy

UAE announced its Vision 2021 in 2010. The vision provided the general objectives and aspirations of the UAE government, while the UAE Government Strategy 2011–2013 spelled out details of specific objectives and programmes. The vision 2021 aimed that the UAE is to "sustain its drive towards economic diversification, as this is the nation's surest path to sustainable development in a future that is less reliant on oil. This means expanding new strategic sectors to channel our energies into industries and services where we can build a long term competitive advantage". The shift from oil-based to non-oil-based economic development focused on fostering new high-growth sectors and industries that are internationally competitive. This means that growth in the UAE economy would be driven by knowledge and innovation; fuelled by investment in education, R&D and vocational training; supported by strengthening the regulatory and legal systems; and encouraged by the creation of high-value-added sectors in order to enhance the country's competitiveness. The means of diversification has taken several streams, most notably the concentration on the development of the SMEs sector and traditional manufacturing industries, including petrochemicals, fertilisers, plastics and metals. Significant investments have also been made in high-tech industries such as renewable energies and aviation. Other sectors of successful diversification are services, real estates, cultural tourism, healthcare, construction and logistics.

Several factors facilitated economic diversification in UAE. The chief among these factors are the political and economic setting, the business-friendly environment, openness to international trade and investment, political support to entrepreneurial and economic activities, and attractiveness of the country to foreign direct investment outside the hydrocarbon sector. These factors complement the developmental state model that is still visible in UAE in the form of state entrepreneurship and state-led economic development. As explained by Mishrif and Kapetanovic in Volume II, these factors have been instrumental and effective in setting Dubai as a model for economic diversification, with oil accounting for only 1.4 per cent of GDP in 2013. The success story of Dubai is looked upon for emulation not only in Abu Dhabi, Doha, Manama, Muscat and Kuwait but also in non-oil-producing countries such as Egypt, Jordan, Tunisia and Morocco. Surprisingly, the Vision 2021 illustrates a striking contrast between allocating a limited role for the private sector in economic development and supremacy of the state as the principal actor and driving force in economic planning and development at the time when the country claims to be operating in a globalised market economy. Hvidt (2013) labelled this special economic model "diversification without privatisation", a model that is market driven and based on public ownership. The efficiency and success of public sector companies such as the Mubadala Development Corporation, which create or buy enterprises and operate them on market terms, elevated them to a level where they become entrusted to lead in developing the Emirate society.

Saudi Diversification Strategy

Saudi Arabia began its diversification strategy over a decade ago. The Long-Term Strategy (2004–2024) indicated, among its many aims, that the Kingdom increases the role of non-oil production in the economy and reduces the share of oil and gas in total exports from 72 per cent to 37 per cent by 2024. By 2011, the share of oil in export revenues increased to 85 per cent, while accounting for 85 per cent of government income and 50 per cent in GDP. This unsuccessful phase of diversification was hindered by the growing rate of youth unemployment, low living standards and considerable rise in poverty among Saudis mainly caused by decline in economic growth to an average of 4 per cent that was translated to financial constraints and budget deficits during that period (Saudi Ministry of Economy and Planning 2010). There was also lack of direction on which role the private sector would take in economic development, despite the repeated calls for a greater role of private enterprises in the economy and liberalisation of the economy after the accession to the World Trade Organisation in 2005.

In 2016, Saudi Arabia launched its national Vision 2030. The vision aimed to turn Saudi Arabia into a global investment powerhouse. The second pillar of the vision that relates to the economy states: "our nation holds strong investment capabilities, which we will harness to stimulate our economy and diversify our revenues. We are determined to reinforce and diversify the capabilities of our economy, turning our key strengths into enabling tools for a fully diversified future". The vision identifies a number of measures to achieve economic diversification.

1. The transformation of Aramco from an oil-producing company into a global industrial conglomerate, expanding its activities beyond the oil and gas sector.

2. The transformation of the Public Investment Fund into the world's largest sovereign wealth fund, by increasing its assets from SAR 600 billion to over SAR 7 trillion.
3. Encouraging Saudi companies to become multinational corporations by expanding across borders and operating in global markets.
4. Development of the manufacturing sector, particularly in armament and manufacturing of military equipment, machinery and software.
5. Upgrading the administrative system by expanding the variety of digital services to reduce delays and cut tedious bureaucracy.
6. Improving the business environment, reforming the regulatory system and adopting wide-ranging transparency and accountability reforms and, through the body set up to measure the performance of government agencies, hold them accountable for any shortcomings.

When it comes to the key drivers of economic development and diversification, the Saudi vision balances between strengthening public sector governance by restructuring government agencies continuously and expanding the private sector through a comprehensive privatisation programme. The vision seeks to shift the role of the government from providing services to one that focuses on regulating and monitoring them. Meanwhile, it seeks to increase the contribution of the private sector, which is currently less than 40 per cent of GDP, in the economy by privatising some government services and opening new economic sectors such as healthcare, education, energy, housing, and some municipal services for private and foreign investment. The vision highlights the commitment of the Kingdom to provide better opportunities for partnerships with the private sector through the three pillars: our position as the heart of the Arab and Islamic worlds, our leading investment capabilities and our strategic geographical position (Council of Economic and Development Affairs 2016).

SHORTFALLS IN GULF DIVERSIFICATION STRATEGIES

Previous studies on economic diversification in GCC countries conclude that diversification has lacked both the pace and depth in policy implementation (Callen et al. 2014; Hvidt 2013; Seznec 2011; Beblawi 2011; ESCWA 2001). These studies argue that there seem to be no compelling reasons to unsettle the current economic structure of these countries. Industrialisation has been confined only to the hydrocarbon sector, expanding in both the upstream (exploration) and downstream (refinery and distribution), as well as oil-related industries, mainly petrochemicals, aluminium, steel and fertilisers, which gained its competitive advantage from low energy cost and state subsidies. Although the expansion in non-oil industries such as services, banking and tourism has been the greatest achievement in this domain, the contribution of these industries to the export and government revenues remained small. Beblawi (2011) attributes this to the heavy dependence on oil and argues that the expansion in oil-based industries and even import substitution industries is unlikely to survive in the post-oil era. This argument might reflect the heavy subsidies provided by the state to these industries, which made them uncompetitive and the protective environment in which these industries operate.

Beblawi's argument complements that of Looney (1994), who both underline the lack of overall industrialisation strategies due to problems related to the bureaucratic and administrative system, the nature of the labour forces in the industrial sector that is exclusively dependent on expatriates, and insufficient incentives at the production and export levels. At the regional level, the GCC countries have yet failed to take advantage of the dynamics of regional integration by coordinating their industrial policies and allocating industrial activities among member states. The establishment of the 2003 customs union and 2008 common market, which created a single external tariff and enabled free movement of factors of production such as goods, services, capital and labour, have yet had limited impact on the industrial and wide-ranging economic development of the GCC member states.

Despite the huge financial surplus and heavy investment in infrastructure, outcomes of GCC government policies have fallen short of targets set out in their national visions, while the challenges of economic diversification persist. The pace of change in the structure of GCC economies is very limited because of their heavy dependence on the hydrocarbon sector to date. National visions stressed the vital role of the state as both regulator and operator in the management of the economy, while calling for the need to consolidate the public sector, which contributes over 60 per cent of GDP. The continuity of the allocation state model is also a major challenge of diversifying GCC economies. Theoretically, diversification could be a remedy of the problems resulting from the allocation state model by decreasing volatility and increasing sustainable high-income levels, but current strategies have neither well-defined mechanisms nor clear milestones for a gradual shift towards a more production-based model, where most economic forces, including the private sector, engage actively in the development process.

Role of the Private Sector in GCC Diversification: The Way Forward

Functioning as a fully flagged market economy seems a far distance, particularly when GCC governments favour the public sector as the main source of job creation and the engine of growth. The limited role of the private sector is visible in restricting its investments in areas where the government does not want to invest in, while most private sector companies are heavily dependent on subcontracting and outsourcing from state-owned enterprises. However, the move towards a more production-based model that fosters the growth of the private sector is gradually emerging. The Saudi Vision 2030 offers new lights in its call for privatisation and greater role of the private sector in economic development. The partial privatisation of Aramco signifies a new trend, in which the state, the private sector and citizens are engaged in production, and government relies on proceeds from production to finance social and economic development programmes.

Although the public sector is still a major force in GCC economies, the private sector has already made its marks in diversifying Gulf economies. The private sector has been actively supporting the government in its economic reform programmes, particularly widening the scope of sectors and activities available to private enterprises. This is true in the case of Bahrain, Oman, UAE and, to a lesser extent, Kuwait, where the attitude of the private sector towards economic liberalisation is formed in accordance with its rent-seeking interests. The case of the Kuwait private sector underlines the conservative position of this sector towards economic liberalisation, as many of private enterprises prefer to operate in a protective environment (Nosova, Chap. 2). Nosova's analysis underlines the desire of the private sector to maintain its monopolistic and elitist position with reserved preferential treatment from authorities, while fearing of opening up the market for competition, which could expose their inability to compete with foreign companies.

In line with the position of the Kuwaiti private sector, Omani, Saudi and Emirati private sectors have been seeking new means to overcome their limited resources and fear of withstanding competition in the Gulf markets. Chief among these methods is the creation of a systemic approach to integrate public and private enterprises in national strategic projects. Al-Hinai, Espinosa and Vidgen (Chap. 3) provide a holistic model for designing a new state-owned enterprise in order to play a greater role in governmental initiatives towards economic diversification and to create a platform for a value co-creation and experience sharing. While this model supports other governmental initiatives towards diversification, such as generating jobs, employing local workforce and building national knowledge, it could enhance collaboration and promote alliances particularly with SMEs and connect state-owned enterprises with numerous potential private companies. Public-private partnerships (PPPs) provide another avenue for private enterprises to engage with the public sector in large-scale infrastructure projects. The significance of PPPs lies in the fact that infrastructure is one of the key sectors for economic diversification in GCC countries. As explained in Chap. 4, Iwanami argues that GCC countries have the potential to benefit from PPPs in infrastructure development through substantial improvement in such services as water supply, sanitation, power generations, electricity, roads, ports and telecommunications, which, in turn, achieves economic diversification via increased competition. The importance of regulation for the successful implementation of PPPs provides an opportunity for private sector companies to share their concerns over voice and accountability since preparation and implementation of PPPs often corresponds to the interests and needs of the business community and society. Practically, PPPs provide an excellent opportunity to the private sector to be consulted on government regulations; to benefit from the large pools of financial, technological, managerial and operational capabilities created by the government and the public sector; and to contribute effectively to the delivery of infrastructure services.

An improvement in the regulatory environment can significantly strengthen the role of the private sector in economic development. On the one hand, the performance of private sector companies is largely affected by the quality of education system and labour market. Mishrif and Alabduljabbar (Chap. 5) argue that the failure of the Saudi education system to provide good quality education is a major contributing factor to the high levels of unemployment among young Saudis and their inability to secure jobs in the private sector. They attribute the deficiencies in the education system to lack of a clear vision set by the Ministry of Education, the absence of a unified educational strategy and the limited interference of different factions, mainly religious leaders, in setting the curricula and broader education strategies. They also highlight the poor organisational structures and the centralisation of the ministerial functions at structural level, while stressing the outdated teaching and learning methods, lack of transferable and analytical skills, and limited access to information technology and its utilisation in the learning process. Such deficiencies hinder the prospect of Saudi citizens in participating in the increasingly globalised marketplace.

On the other hand, the regulatory environment can positively affect the quality and performance of the private sector in GCC countries. Domestic and foreign companies are not only governed by various laws that determine their incorporation, legal structure and business activities, but they are also affected by the level of efficiency and transparency in the legal and regulatory systems as well as the administrative system, where corruption, red tape and lack of information have negative effects on their operation. In the GCC context, Al-Daffaa argues that the creation of the Saudi Arabian General Investment Authority (SAGIA) has significantly improved the Saudi regulatory environment through regulating, managing and controlling foreign investment (Chap. 6). Such improvement in the regulatory framework has contributed to significant increase in the levels of FDI growth, which reached US$36.4 billion in 2009 (World Investment Report 2015). With the country now entering an era of (limited) privatisation, the success of this process depends on the ability of the country to develop its regulatory system. The privatisation of state-owned enterprises will increase the number of private and foreign companies, which, in turn, expands economic activities in new industries other than the hydrocarbon sector.

Shazia Farooq Fazli and Ayesha Farooq (Chap. 7) take a different stand to examine the organisational effectiveness of private enterprises and diversification in the Gulf countries. They use the conceptual model that incorporates McKinsey's 7S Framework to assess the extent to which specific management practices contribute to the effectiveness and productivity of the organisations and provide competitive advantage. They argue that the GCC development strategies rely, to some extent, on the local private sector for diversification, job creation and the building of a more productive and less oil-dependent knowledge economy. This is why private enterprises should redefine their boundaries and play their role effectively in economic development, at the time when GCC countries are undergoing an extraordinary economic and social transformation, a transformation that provides huge investment opportunities for the private sector in non-oil industries.

GCC private enterprises can benefit from easy access to capital and highly skilled foreign labour in their home markets and in sectors that are not attractive to the public sector such as agriculture and tourism. Although agriculture contributes less than 1 per cent to GDP in all GCC countries due to arid climate and shortage of fresh water, this sector has huge potential for private sector companies because GCC countries import between 80 per cent and 90 per cent of their food consumption. Bani (Chap. 8) argues that with demand in the GCC expected to rise significantly, food imports to the region will increase by as much as 100 per cent; such rise in demand will require significant investment in agriculture, a sector that is exclusively dominated by the private sector. Although GCC countries do not have a comparative advantage in field crop production, they have provided the opportunity to private sector companies to import most basic commodities and other food, as well as operating in retails and manufacturing of foodstuffs and beverages. Bani also argues the agricultural sector in GCC needs to boost agricultural output through productivity increases and promote economic diversification that leads to sustainable aquaculture, horticulture and poultry. Gulf private investments in agriculture have been expanded nationally and internationally, with many Gulf companies investing heavily in the acquisition and cultivation of hundreds of thousands of acres in countries such as Egypt, Sudan and Ethiopia. Tourism is another promising sector for the private sector. Karolak (Chap. 9) compares tourism models of Bahrain, Kuwait, Qatar, Oman and UAE to assess the extent to which each of these countries has managed to create a distinctive place identity and whether these identities are competitive enough to secure a flow of international tourists in the future. Using the method of content analysis and critical discourse analysis, her research brings new evidence to the study of semiotics in tourism in general and identifies some tourism strategy gaps for improvement in the respected countries and for the GCC region.

Finally, one cannot underestimate the impact of regional integration on private sector development and diversification in the GCC countries. Mishrif and Al-Naamani (Chap. 10) underscore the importance of this dimension by examining the effects of the 2003 customs union and the 2008 common market on economic diversification strategies in GCC countries. They argue that economic integration arrangements have facilitated the internationalisation of SMEs in the GCC region market, by taking advantage of the free movement of factors of production and elimination of all barriers to trade in goods and services. They conclude that regional integration arrangements have also played an essential role in facilitating economic diversification in specific sectors such as services and retails, while more efforts are needed to diversify their manufacturing, so they can compete internationally.

Conclusion

This chapter provides an overview on economic diversification in the GCC countries. While defining the concept of diversification, it identified the public sector, the private sector and sovereign wealth funds as the main drivers that can accelerate the pace and scope of diversification. The sharp drop in oil prices by more than 70 per cent since 2014, together with the political, social and demographic changes that have taken place in the Gulf region, has made economic diversification a top policy priority in all GCC countries. This is clearly underlined in the spirit and text of the national visions and strategic development plans of six GCC countries. Analysis of these visions and their implementation shows that the countries that have low proved oil reserves are more enthusiastic to diversify their economy than those with high levels of proven oil and gas reserves. The chapter concludes that the private sector has the capacity, enthusiasm and motivation to participate in economic diversification, particularly in the non-oil sectors that are not attractive to or left out by the public sector.

References

Ahmed, M. (2016). Spending cuts a must in Gulf despite oil recovery, Interview with AFP, Dubai, 19 October 2016.

Beblawi, H. (2011). Gulf industrialization in perspective. In J.-F. Seznec & M. Kirk (Eds.), *Industrialization in the Gulf: A socioeconomic revolution* (pp. 185–197). London: Center for Contemporary Arab Studies, Routledge.

Callen, T., Cherif, R., Hasanov, F., Hegazy, A., & Khandelwal, P. (2014). Economic diversification in the GULF COOPERATION COUNCIL (GCC) COUNTRIES: Past, present and future, IMF Staff Discussion Note, December 2014, SDN14/12.

Council of Economic and Development Affairs. (2016). Saudi Vision 2030, National Transformation Program 2020, Riyadh, Saudi Arabia.

Cypher, J., & Dietz, J. L. (2009). *The process of economic development* (3rd ed.). London: Routledge.

Economic and Social Commission for Western Asia. (2001). *Economic diversification in the oil-producing countries: The case of the Gulf Cooperation Council Economies*. New York: United Nations.

Economic Development Board. (2008). *Our Vision: The Economic Vision 2030 for Bahrain*, Manama, Bahrain.

El Kharouf, F., Al-Qudsi, S., & Obeid, S. (2010). The Gulf Cooperation Council sovereign wealth funds: Are they instruments for economic diversification or political tools? *Asian Economic Paper*, 9(1), 124–151.

General Secretariat for Development Planning. (2011). *Qatar national development strategy 2011–2016*, Doha, Qatar.

Ghosh, A., & Ostry, O. (1994). Export instability and external balance in developing countries. *IMF Staff Papers*, 41, 214–235.

Hertog, S. (2012). How the GCC did it: Formal and informal governance of successful public enterprise in the Gulf Co-operation Council countries. In A. Amico (Ed.), *Towards new arrangements for state ownership in the Middle East and North Africa* (pp. 71–92). London: OECD.

Hvidt, M. (2013). Economic diversification in Gulf Cooperation Council (GCC) countries: Past record and future trends, Kuwait programme on Development, Governance and Globalisation in the Gulf States, London School of Economics and Political Science, Issue No. 27, pp. 1–49.

Kerr, S. (2016). IMF cuts Gulf states' GDP growth forecast to 1.8%. *Financial Times*, 25 April 2016.

Koren, M., & Tenreyro, S. (2010). Volatility, diversification and development in the Gulf Cooperation Council countries, Kuwait programme on Development, Governance and Globalisation in the Gulf States, London School of Economics, Research Paper No. 9.

Looney, R. (1994). *Industrial development and diversification in the Arabian Gulf economies*. Greenwich, CT: JAI Press.

Malik, A. (2015). The Gulf economies' coming meltdown? How to prevent it? *Foreign Affairs*, November 5.

Ministry of Economy and Planning. (2010). *Brief report on the ninth development plan 2010–2014*. Riyadh: Ministry of Economy and Planning, Saudi Arabia.

Mishrif, A., & Akkas, E. (2016). *Gulf sovereign wealth funds and their impact on the development of Islamic finance and banking*. Paper presented at the 2016 Gulf Research Meeting, University of Cambridge, UK, 16–19 August 2016.

Morakabati, Y., Beavis, J., & Fletcher, J. (2014). Planning for a Qatar without oil: Tourism and economic diversification, a battle of perceptions. *Tourism Planning and Development*, 11(4), 415–434.

Seznec, J. (2011). Financing industrialisation in the Arab Persian Gulf. In J. F. Seznec & M. Kirk (Eds.), *Industrialization in the Gulf: A socioeconomic revolution* (pp. 30–43). London: Center for Contemporary Arab Studies, Georgetown University/Routledge.

Shuai, X. (2013). Will specialisation continue forever? A case study of interaction between industry specialisation and diversity. *Annals of Regional Science*, 50, 1–24.

United Arab Emirates Cabinet. (2010). *UAE Vision 2021: United in ambition and determination*. Abu Dhabi: Government of UAE.

United Nations Conference on Trade and Development. (2015). *World Investment Report 2015: Reforming international investment governance*. Geneva: UNCTAD Publications.

CHAPTER 2

Private Sector and Economic Diversification in Kuwait

Anastasia Nosova

INTRODUCTION

Due to a similar historical path, which led the Arab states of the Gulf to evolve from vague political entities under British protectorate rule into influential political players and major oil exporters in the world over a span of less than a century, the six member states of the Gulf Cooperation Council (GCC) share many common features in their political, economic and social development. For the same reason, they also face similar problems and challenges, which stem from the very nature of their rentier economic systems, political rule and social composition. Oil rents have enabled the Gulf states to establish lucrative welfare systems to distribute wealth to their national population in exchange for political obedience. However, the Gulf rentier states' economies have long been proclaimed unsustainable in the long term. Multiple recommendations from various international organisations and consultancies have been continuously issued stating the necessity for the Gulf countries to diversify their sources of income and reduce the growing budget spending, which has become a

A. Nosova (✉)
London School of Economics, London, UK

© Gulf Research Centre Cambridge 2018
A. Mishrif, Y. Al Balushi (eds.), *Economic Diversification in the Gulf Region, Volume I*, The Political Economy of the Middle East,
https://doi.org/10.1007/978-981-10-5783-0_2

serious economic burden expected to result in budget deficit and fiscal crisis in the not-so-distant future even in the wealthiest of those states. In essence, all these policies are based around the idea of reducing the role of state in economy and empowering the private sector as, potentially, the main employer and economy diversifier.

With regard to such economic diversification attempts, Kuwait represents an interesting case for analysis. The country has large amounts of proven oil reserves and relatively small national population, which places it in a better position compared to other GCC states, such as Bahrain, Oman and Dubai (which have less resources available) and Saudi Arabia (which has a much larger population to accommodate within its welfare system). Nevertheless, the vulnerability of oil dependency has long been acknowledged and heatedly debated in Kuwait, and the notion of diversification and reduction of budget spending has been migrating from one development plan to another. The necessity to take concrete policy steps has been recently reiterated by the International Monetary Fund (IMF) report revealing the gloomy prospect of the country facing a real budget deficit by as early as 2017, despite the continuing budget surpluses since 1995 (Dokoupil 2014; Kuwait Times 2013a; The Economist 2014). However, Kuwait has been significantly lagging behind its Gulf peers in terms of its non-oil sector development. Certain policies have been introduced so far, but their implementation has been largely problematic, and success—limited. The country is still notorious for its business environment and attracts a relatively low amount of foreign direct investment (FDI) compared to the rest of the Gulf.

The responsibility for the slow pace of those restructuring policies has been largely put on the government for being too reluctant to enforce them and opting for populist policies for the sake of regime security. At the same time, although Kuwait is the only Gulf state with more or less consistent history of parliamentary politics, the parliament itself and its protective stance on public benefits is also very often cited as the major obstacle for economic restructuring and speeding up development (Herb 2009; Hertog 2013b).

The main critique that the present work is offering is that the discourse on economic diversification reform policies seems to pay disproportionately little attention to the analysis of the existing private sector in Kuwait and its role and capacity in promoting or opposing those government initiatives. Most of policy recommendation and analytical papers address the private sector as a mere (and often very vaguely defined) object of those state policies, disregarding the form and shape in which it currently exists, and as a result, dismissing the factors its existence is introducing to the process of policies' implementation.

Despite the above-mentioned reputation of Kuwait as a supposedly hard environment to do business, the country is in fact home to quite a few globally successful companies: 11 out of top 100 Arab companies are of Kuwaiti origin (Forbes 2015). It is also known for its historically prominent merchant elite. Since the time prior to the discovery of oil, Kuwait has been a clearly stratified society, with a merchant elite being the major economic power and having a strong leverage in the country's political affairs. This historically formidable position of merchants vis-à-vis the ruling powers enabled them to get a significant share of oil-generated wealth. Most importantly, their substantial economic benefits were secured by protectionist legislation, which effectively created immense opportunities for local business actors and protected them from foreign competition. Therefore, despite all the structural changes that the country has been going through after the discovery of oil, its business community has largely retained its pre-oil elitist oligarchic composition. The pattern of distribution of wealth and protection to private sector ensured that the business opportunities and financial support were channelled to a relatively small merchant elite group.[1] Its core consists of those who were prominent since the pre-oil times.

Thus, does the private sector itself, that is, Kuwait's established business community, support those policies and measures, which the economic diversification proponents consider crucial for the country's further development? Can the government rely on the private sector if it chooses to address the process of economic restructuring on a larger scale, and what kind of state-business interaction should we expect in this case?

The existing literature on Kuwait's business, and GCC private sector in general, proposes two opposite answers to these questions. Some authors, for example, Pete Moore (2002, 2004) and Giacomo Luciani in his earlier works (2005, 2007), suggest that business in the Gulf is capable of positive and productive cooperation with the government and can become a vanguard of economic reformation. In case of Kuwait in particular, Moore explains such capability through the analysis of the historical role that the business elite has been playing in the country's reform movements at various points of time, suggesting that its reform potential can be mobilised especially in times of political and fiscal crises.

However, more recent works on the topic, by such authors as Steffen Hertog (2013a, 2013b) and Rivka Azoulay (2013), actually point on the passivity of the Gulf capitalist class, which stems from its complete state dependency, its general preference of the status quo and incapacity of any significant political action. Therefore, it is argued that the contribution of the private sector in the Gulf to the reforming process is no more than "modest" (Hertog 2013b: 2). Such perception, to a large extent, follows Jill Crystal's approach to Kuwait's business community as a group, which was bought off by the ruling powers with oil income, and since then, its political powers have been substantially curbed (Crystal 1995).

In the present work, we suggest that although according to the conventional perception, domestic capital should be supportive of the economic reforms and liberalisation prescribed by international organisations and ultimately aimed at economic diversification and sustainability, the case of Kuwait illustrates that the attitude of the local capitalist class can be much more nuanced and proves that there is a variation in response to those universal recommendations. We argue that the private sector in Kuwait, in its current state, that is, in its monopolistic, elitist form with reserved preferential treatment from authorities, forms its attitudes towards various reform policies in accordance with its rent-seeking interests and its general desire to maintain privileged positions. Therefore, it is benefitting from some of those reform policies when possible and resisting others when necessary. This means that the established business community is supportive of the initiatives that are aimed at the expansion of the scope of the private sector's activity. However, policies that are intending to broaden the scope of actual private sector players through encouraging new and foreign businesses to operate in Kuwait do not fall in line with the interests of the established business actors. In this case, they are not only incapable and unwilling to contribute to the promotion of any of those restructuring policies but in fact constitute an active force opposing those policies and one of the major stumbling blocks for their implementation.

In order to develop the argument, we will analyse the major streams of economic diversification policies that are pursued in Kuwait and address the policies that are potentially beneficial for the existing private sector, for example, privatisation of government entities and stocks, larger involvement of private sector in government's project through Build-Operate-Transfer scheme and those which do not fall in line with the interests of the established business actors—that is, labour nationalisation, attempts to open up the economy for foreign business and FDI, and amend the private sector regulation as per international standards through the establishment of market regulation bodies. We will analyse the attitude and reaction of Kuwait's business community towards these various initiatives and examine the ways in which such reaction impacts the success or failure of economic diversification policies.

Economic Diversification Policies in Kuwait: Reducing the Budget Spending

There are several major streams of reform policies that have been pursued by Kuwaiti authorities as steps towards economic restructuring and rationalisation. Namely, there are measures, which are aimed at cutting down the current budget spending, such as the reduction of subsidies on commodities and services and restructuring of employment patterns to reduce state's spending on wages. Another set of policies are targeting the expansion of the private sector's role in the economy, which is meant to diversify the sources of income away from state-dominated oil sector, as well as to boost national employment. The present part of the chapter will begin with addressing some of the major reform initiatives of the first type, that is, labour nationalisation and subsidies reduction, while the next part will talk in more detail about a range of policies, which are directly targeting the empowerment of private sector in Kuwait.

Labour Policies

Kuwait's Labour Law stipulates that every citizen has the right to a job in the public sector (Abdalla and Al-Homoud 2012: 5). From the very beginning of the welfare state in Kuwait, government employment has been one of the important means of wealth distribution, as it is coming with significant financial incentives, and is in general less demanding compared to the private sector. This policy has led to the bulging of the government sector and the subsequent fast increase of budget spending on wages. According to the official statistics, as of 2013, 245,666 Kuwaitis worked in the public sector, as opposed to around 56,829 in the private sector (Central Statistical Bureau 2015), while public sector salaries and subsidies increased by 540 per cent within 2001–2011 period (Al-Zumai 2013: 9). In 2013, total national population of Kuwait was estimated to be 1,159,787 (33.6 per cent), while the amount of non-Kuwaitis reached 2,288,352 (66.4 per cent). The number of non-

Kuwaitis working in private sector is 1,249,033, which means that Kuwaitis (56,829) constitute only 4.4 per cent of private sector labour force. The important factor that contributes to the aggravation of situation is the rapid rise of the population. It is estimated that 51 per cent of the population is currently under 21 years old (Oxford Business Group 2014), which means that the number of new labour market entrants will be ever growing in the coming years, while the oversaturated public sector already has little capacity to accommodate them.

Shifting the part of the burden of employment to private sector is generally seen as a solution recipe, which has been continuously prescribed to the GCC governments by various international organisations and consultancies. The patterns of fulfilling those prescriptions have been more or less uniform in all GCC states and have been based around labour nationalisation, supporting entrepreneurship and widening the scope of private sector operation. Labour nationalisation policies, on the one hand, aim to decrease the demand and supply of immigrant workers and, on the other hand, to increase the demand of national workers. Naturally, in none of the six Gulf states these attempts have been welcomed by the private sector, which perceives it as "tax on business", because of higher cost and lower productivity of local employees (Hertog 2013b: 16).

Kuwait was among the first GCC states to approach this issue seriously and to introduce quotas of private sector jobs for nationals, with incentives for companies, which comply with the regulation, and penalties for those, which do not. In 1993, a bill was passed proposing a quota of 30 per cent private sector jobs for nationals. The quota was later reviewed and adjusted for each sector. Companies in some sectors, mainly labour-oriented, were almost exempted from labour nationalisation requirements, as with the quota, they would simply operate at significant financial loss. For example, agriculture and manufacturing sectors have only a 3 per cent national employee quota. Other sectors, such as banking, financial services and communications, were assigned much higher quotas ranging from 15 to 66 per cent, as they are less qualitatively affected by labour nationalisation and can afford to pay higher salaries. Penalties for not meeting the labour requirement quotas are serious and include bans on importing foreign workers, barring from government contracts and government land (Markaz 2012: 17).

In 1997, the government also established a specialised entity, the Manpower and Government Restructuring Program (MGRP), aimed at the development of policies to encourage the transfer of national labour from public to private sector. In 2000, the MGRP was authorised to pay salary subsidies to national private sector employees (as per Law 19/2000). Kuwait is the only GCC state providing these salary subsidies on a consistent basis (Hertog 2014). This is arguably the most important factor responsible for the relative success of labour nationalisation policies in the country.

It is clear that apart from subsidies and the prospect of penalties, there is little incentive for the private sector actors in Kuwait to substitute foreign workers with national labour force. Although the owners of large family corporations and members of established business elite claim that they wholeheartedly support labour nationalisation, which they see as a social obligation, and even if their companies meet the quota or even exceed it, this does not necessarily mean developing the national workforce or integrating it in business operation (personal interview with a member of an old merchant family; Kuwait, November 2014). In reality, there are multiple ways that the private companies utilise to avoid meaningful fulfilment of quota requirements, such as fake or shadow employment.

Subsidies Policies

Separate set of measures aimed to ease the budget burden of current spending is related to the reduction of subsidies on various services, commodities and products that Kuwait's residents have been enjoying since the onset of the welfare state. According to the IMF, Kuwait's subsidies were worth US$287bn in 2011, which constituted about 12 per cent of the total GDP of all Arab countries, and about 32 per cent of the government's revenues (Kuwait Times 2015b). Thus, international organisations and consultancies have long been urging Kuwaiti authorities to reform the subsidies policies, especially in the light of the falling oil prices and shrinking revenues.

So far, the government has been putting a lot of effort in trying to resolve the issue of subsidised commodities, particularly after the call by the Amir in October 2015 to cut the state spending in response to decreasing oil revenues (Kuwait Times 2015c). The cabinet has recently announced that it is planning to lift fuel subsidies and introduce new water and electricity consumption prices (Kuwait Times 2015e). However, the issue is highly contentious, and the parliament has been largely opposing indiscriminate subsidies lift. For this reason, the latest plan to remove water and electricity subsidies, for instance, targets only expatriates and commercial and industrial enterprises, while citizens are not affected.

It is important to note here that, as elsewhere in the GCC, the private sector in Kuwait is also heavily dependent on state-subsidised utilities, such as water and electricity, and therefore it will be the first to be affected if the subsidies are removed. This became obvious after the government's recent attempt to increase the price of subsidised diesel and kerosene. On 1 January 2015, the government increased the price of diesel for consumers from 0.055 KD to 0.170 KD per litre [1 Kuwaiti Dinar equals US$3.3] (Arabian Business 2015). Certain sectors of business activity, such as transport, food production, catering and construction materials manufacturing, were immediately affected. As a result, the government's measure was followed by price hikes and strikes, and the cabinet was attacked by a large number of MPs demanding the abolishment of the subsidies lift (Kuwait Times 2015a). This development made the government halt its plans to deal with other subsidised commodities for almost a year. At the same time, exemptions from diesel price hike for various businesses were agreed upon with the government, thus the effect of the subsidy lift was ultimately minimal (Kuwait Times 2015a). In further discussions of subsidies reduction, the Minister of Commerce promised that electricity and fuel subsidies for key economic and industrial sectors would be preserved, because of the government's "desire to encourage them for the sake of enhancing their contributions to the economy and diversifying it" (Kuwait Times 2015c).

However, not all policies targeting the removal of subsidies are harmful to merchants' interests. There have also been proposals and reform attempts in the sphere of other state distribution patterns and subsidies on services. One of such initiatives, namely, the reform of housing allowance, illustrates the business opportunities that the subsidies lift can open for certain private sector actors.

Thus, the government has recently decided to substitute cash handouts of house-building allowance with subsidised building materials of equal value. A total of 25 per cent of the price will be subsidised by government, and 75 per cent paid by customer. The government will choose the company to supply those materials, through government tenders. The priority will be given to Kuwait industrial companies, followed by the Gulf producers and then foreign companies (personal interview with a member of the parliament's committee for financial and economic affairs; Kuwait,

April 2014). Therefore, such measures will most likely benefit some of the local building materials' suppliers.

Thus, the private sector in Kuwait is as dependent on the government for state spending, subsidised commodities and provision of cheap foreign labour as the population at large. The analysis of the government initiatives, which are aimed at reducing the budget spending, such as employment nationalisation and subsidies reduction, shows that they largely do not fall within the interest of the business community in Kuwait, and it utilises various means to avoid their meaningful implementation, negotiate exemptions or even, in some cases, utilise the business opportunities that emerge from those state initiatives.

ECONOMIC DIVERSIFICATION POLICIES IN KUWAIT: EXPANDING THE PRIVATE SECTOR

Another group of reform policies is meant to expand the role of private sector in the economy and broaden the scope of private sector actors in Kuwait. This, on the one hand, means providing more space for private sector operation through reducing the role of state in the economy. On the other hand, it also means opening up the economy and attracting foreign direct investments through improving the business environment, loosening legislative restrictions and enhancing regulation in accordance with international standards.

Privatisation

Since the beginning of the steady flow of oil export revenues, Kuwait's economy has been dominated by the government through state control of the oil industry. Furthermore, many of the large enterprises established after the independence were created jointly by private sector and the government and were substantially supported by state capital. By the early 1990s, the government owned shares of various amounts in 61 biggest companies, which accounted for 70 per cent of total market capitalisation (Sartawi 2012: 98). Although the rate of state ownership has been changing throughout time, the government still retains significant amount of shares in the top companies. The government invests mainly through Kuwait Investment Authority (KIA), Public Institution for Social Security, Public Authority for Minors Affairs, as well as Kuwait Awqaf Public Foundation, Zakat House, and such investments have been one of the means to keep the stock floating, and to distribute wealth and support to the private sector (personal interview with a teaching member of staff in Economics Department, KU; Kuwait, May 2014). Enterprises with state ownership have been also granted land concessions and customs exemptions (Sartawi 2012: 96).

The attitude of the private sector towards it is in a way ambiguous—on the one hand, the state ownership is treated as a way to support and back up the business sector particularly in times of crises; on the other hand, the private sector also sees it as government's means to dominate and overtake businesses. Therefore, business actors generally criticise the government for not providing more space and opportunities to private sector and push for privatisation.

In the government's view, the privatisation is seen as means to reduce state spending and to improve services, which the government already finds difficult to cope with. That is why the privatisation programme was first launched during the 1990s to ease the budgetary strains after the Iraqi invasion. It is worth noting that Kuwait was the first GCC state to embark on privatisation policy. Part of state shares were disposed of, so the government ownership in some of the companies was substantially reduced, while others were privatised completely. KIA's ownership in the Kuwait Stock Exchange (KSE) declined from 61 companies in 1993 to 14 companies in 2011. Furthermore, in May 2010, a new privatisation law was adopted by the parliament.

However, despite all these seemingly active efforts to promote privatisation, there are still serious restrictions that the private sector is facing in the process. First of all, the law does not allow privatisation of entities related to downstream oil and gas industry, as well as entities in the sphere of health and education services. An investor is also not allowed to bid for a privatised entity, if they both operate in the same field, in order to avoid the conflict of interest. The privatisation process itself is carried out through the creation of a shareholding company, in which the government retains a golden share and which is subject to regulatory scrutiny and price control. Finally, the law comprises several provisions that protect the rights and benefits of national employees working in a privatised entity—a private owner would not be able to lay them off or to reduce their salaries or benefits during a fixed number of years (DLA Piper 2010). All these legislative restrictions make the privatisation less attractive for the private sector investors, and the business community has been continuously voicing its dissatisfaction with the law and pushing the government to open up such fields as oil industry and services for privatisation and larger private involvement. As a result, the government has recently called for an amendment of the privatisation law. There have also been attempts to pursue a broader-scale privatisation in the past several years, with such entities in line for being privatised as postal service, Kuwait Stock Exchange, Cooperative Societies, sports clubs, certain sectors of the Ministry of Electricity and Water, and some private clinics affiliated to the Ministry of Health.

Build-Operate-Transfer

Build-Operate-Transfer (BOT) is another scheme that is also aimed at expanding the role of the private sector in the government development projects, thus reducing the burden on the state's finances. BOT is one of the types of public-private partnership, according to which the private sector entity carries out the construction and operation of a certain facility for a fixed period of time, after the end of which the facility is transferred back to the government (Kuwait Times 2013b).

In case of Kuwait, the private sector's cooperation with the government on certain projects has been ongoing since the 1980s; however, a comprehensive BOT law was lacking until 2008. Despite being highly anticipated, the 2008 BOT law was again considered too restrictive by the private sector investors, similarly to the privatisation law. The main concerns of the business community were related to the limited amount of years the private entity was allowed to operate the projects, inability to mortgage the assets within the project to ensure financial security, the absence of intellectual property protection, as well as the high probability of arbitrary project cancellations by the government (multiple personal interviews in Kuwait, 2014). For these reasons, not a single BOT project has been launched since the law was passed, and the business community has been pushing for its amendment. The parliament ultimately voted to amend the law in June 2014 making it much more in line with the private sector's interests.

If the first half of the section was addressing policies that could potentially benefit the dominant business players and therefore were actively promoted by them, the next section will analyse another batch of diversification policies—those which aim to improve the business legislative environment and regulation in order to increase transparency, compliance with international standards, and by doing so, ease the way for new and foreign businesses to emerge and operate in Kuwait. It will be shown that, although the ultimate aim of those policies is to strengthen and diversify the private sector, opening up the private sector for foreigners, boosting competition and enforcing stricter regulation do not comply with the interests of the major business players, whose prominence is to a large extent reliant on protectionist legislation, lack of regulation and monitoring and informality in doing business. The reaction of the business community to the regulation policies is the example of merchants' direct and active interference in policymaking.

Foreign Business and FDI

The government was to some extent pressured to embark on the path of opening up the economy when Kuwait joined WTO in 1995. Although Kuwait was one of the first among the GCC to join the organisation, it still falls far behind its neighbours in terms of attractiveness for foreign business and foreign investments. The Commercial Companies Law of 1960 effectively limited foreign business participation in Kuwait to partnerships with local businessmen, with the latter owning the majority of shared capital, while the ownership in shareholding companies was allowed to Kuwaiti nationals only. However, the FDI and expansion of foreign business in Kuwait were deemed necessary first and foremost as a way to import technology know-how, and boost national employment (and much less so as capital injection); therefore, from the early 2000s, the government started to take certain legislative steps to ease the situation for foreign business (personal interview with an analyst in one of the largest financial and investment companies in Kuwait; Kuwait, May 2014). The Law No. 20 of 2000 permitted foreign ownership of shares in shareholding companies listed in Kuwait Stock Exchange, as well as foreign participation in the establishment of those companies. In 2008, a resolution was passed extending the permission of foreign ownership to non-listed shareholding companies, while the recent Companies Law No. 97 of 2013 has eliminated foreign ownership restrictions in shareholding companies altogether allowing up to 100 per cent ownership but keeping the restrictions in other types of companies.

Furthermore, in 2008, a new law (Law No. 2/2008) regulating the taxation of foreign business in Kuwait introduced a flat 15 per cent tax, instead of income-dependent 5–55 per cent tax range, which was in force since 1955. Various conditions have been also stipulated, under which the tax could be reduced or exempted from altogether. Kuwait also established a Free Trade Zone (FTZ) in 1999, which was intended to offer foreign companies tax-free corporate income with no obligation to have local partners.

In 2013, the government introduced the Promotion of Foreign Direct Investment Law (Law No. 116 of 2013) and replaced the Foreign Investment Office with the new Kuwait Direct Investment Promotion Authority (KDIPA), which is aimed to supervise both foreign and domestic investments, ease the bureaucratic procedures of applying for FDI licence and also allow the operation of 100 per cent owned foreign companies in various sectors. It is hoped that the authority will improve the overall investment climate, develop competition and provide further investment opportunities for both local and foreign investors.

In one of the most recent moves (September 2014) aimed to boost FDI, Kuwait's Minister of Finance Anas Al-Saleh announced the suspension of the Offset Programme, which was established in 1992 and imposed an obligation on foreign companies, who won government contracts, to invest a 3–10 per cent portion of a contract's value in local economy. However, there were allegations that the fund did not serve its purpose anyway and was misallocated (personal interview with a Kuwaiti partner of an international auditing company; Kuwait, November 2014).

Thus, it is obvious that during the last decade and a half, certain measures have been taken by Kuwaiti government to loosen the protectionist legislation and open up the economy. This however had very little impact on the ground. According to Kuwait Economic Society report (2013: 6), during the period from 2000 to 2011, Kuwait attracted the smallest amount of FDIs in comparison with the rest of the GCC. In 2011 and 2012, Kuwait did better and actually more than doubled its FDI rate (to US$3.26bn and US$2.87bn, respectively); however, that was partly attributed to a Qatari investment that year, as Qatar Telecom increased its stake in Kuwait's telecommunication provider Wataniya from 52.5 per cent to 92.1 per cent. In 2013, the rate decreased again to US$1.84bn (compared to US$10.49bn in UAE and US$9.3bn in Saudi Arabia).

At the time of writing there were 11 non-Kuwaiti companies listed in Kuwait Stock Exchange out of total 208. Out of those 11, five were UAE cement companies, while the rest were Bahrain-based banks, investment and insurance companies and one Egypt-based Egypt Kuwait Holding Company. Non-Kuwaiti banks and financial services companies alike—all are either subsidiaries of Kuwaiti companies or have representatives of the most prominent Kuwaiti business families among their board members.

Thus, as of the present day, the largest investors in Kuwait are still fellow GCC states, which have never been as restricted legislatively as other foreign investors. All in all, KSE has minimal foreign capital so far (personal interview with a senior official at CMA; Kuwait, June 2014).

Furthermore, although Kuwait has allowed foreign banks to open branches in the country, the Industrial and Commercial Bank of China has been the only bank to use the opportunity so far. However, even these branches are opening not for retailing purposes, but for financing infrastructural projects, in which Chinese companies are involved (personal interview with a senior official at CMA; Kuwait, June 2014).

At the same time, the earlier-mentioned Free Trade Zone has hardly been serving its purpose too: in 2010, the Ministry of Commerce and Industry accused the private National Real Estate Company, which has been operating the FTZ, of renting it out for commercial purposes instead of developing it as a business hub, and tried to overtake it. The area has been subject to litigation and in general state of limbo ever since.

Therefore, the legislative amendments and initiatives introduced by the Kuwaiti government do not seem to have brought any serious qualitative change with regard to foreign direct investments and foreign business in Kuwait. The only meaningful way for foreign investments to be involved in Kuwait's economy is through government contracts. Most of the respondents, government officials and businessmen alike, stated that although the laws have been passed, the results are not achievable in the short term: "The infrastructure is there, laws are there, but the problem is how we apply this law—[it is] too slow because of bureaucracy" (personal interview with an analyst in one of the largest financial and investment companies in Kuwait; Kuwait, May 2014). Indeed, Kuwait's notorious red tape—"extra-legal practices" and "poor regulatory frameworks"—is cited as the main reason of the failure to FDI-attracting efforts (KES 2013: 7). The country's reputation in the eyes of foreign business has been recently further damaged by several cases of arbitrary cancellations and postponements of business projects and deals with international companies as a result of the allegations of corruption by the Parliament.

Although the representatives of Kuwait's private sector would formally acknowledge the necessity of foreign investments and business for the sake of "employment and capital injection" (personal interview with a member of an old politically active merchant family; Kuwait, November 2014), any meaningful progress in this direction, such as eliminating the agency law and allowing foreigners to do business freely in Kuwait, would seriously threaten their current privileged position. In more private conversations, they would show scepticism towards the whole discourse about the urgency of foreign investments and the progress that has been made in this direction (personal interview with members of two merchant families; Kuwait, February and May 2014). Some already complain about the competition with foreigners over government tenders that Kuwaiti companies struggle to win, and accuse the government of having "no knowledge [of] how to make local business grow" (personal interview with a member of parliament, who is also related to one of the old Sunni merchant families; Kuwait, March 2014). Therefore, the very slow pace with which those policies are implemented on the ground and the burden of inefficient bureaucracy, which slows them down even further, are actually beneficial for local business players.

There is no doubt that big business in Kuwait also suffers from red tape, which they see as the result of "jealousy" from a parasitic public sector. However, the social position of individuals in the business elite, and the availability of sufficient funds, enables them to overcome this red tape. "They do not wait in line" for months ... but "go [straight] to officials to cut through red tape" (personal interview with a businessman of medium rank; Kuwait, November 2014). This corrupt pattern of public-private relations creates an opportunity for mutual benefit and a shadow economy of its own hidden behind inefficient bureaucracy. It allows public sector officials to prey on business and make profit by creating obstacles, while also, creating a barrier for entrance and operation to the private sector, restricting it to a small circle of established business players. While it might be costly and time-consuming for them too, it pays off by scaring away foreign players, making it impossible to navigate the system without a powerful and well-connected local partner, preserving the established monopolies (personal interview with a member of an old politically active merchant family; Kuwait, November 2014). This symbiosis steers the wheel of corruption.

Thus, as long as their interests are protected, the major business players have little incentive to change the situation. In fact, improvement in the business environment, reduction of red tape and corruption in the public sector contradict the rent-seeking interests of the existing private sector. Therefore, its very nature and mode of interaction with public sector would obstruct any policies aimed at nourishing new business players and attracting foreign companies.

The local business might be interested in foreign investments, because there is a reserved role for them, rather than out of genuine desire to open up the economy for competition. It is indicative that the idea of eliminating the agency and partnership requirement altogether is currently totally out of government's (and Parliament's) agenda (personal interview with a member of the parliament's committee for financial and economic affairs; Kuwait, April 2014). The "sacred rule of agency" is kept completely untouched (personal interview with a Kuwaiti partner of an international auditing company; Kuwait, November 2014). Therefore, foreign business is still very restricted, despite that the conditions got better on paper. "Still the game is benefiting the old established players", and the policies, as long as they do not bring any tangible impact, do not threaten their interests (personal interview with a member of Kuwait Economic Society; Kuwait, May 2014).

Market Regulation

However, another example of a much more contentious government initiative—the establishment of the Capital Market Authority (CMA)—shows that if they do, the business community would find formal and informal means to interfere and reverse or amend the legislation.

CMA represents one of the latest and most serious efforts to improve the capital market environment in Kuwait. It is widely known that the capital markets in all GCC states generally suffer from the lack of transparency and information asymmetry (i.e. trading with the use of insider information), and poorly comply with international corporate governance standards (Al-Kuwari 2013: 26–28), which naturally repels foreign business. Not being an exception, Kuwait stock market has been known for slack rules in terms of information disclosure and manipulative trading by large shareholders (Goma and Smith 2011).

The idea of creating a regulatory body to supervise the capital market has been long discussed in political circles, and the proposal has been out since 2006. However, the Parliament discussion was delayed because of multiple proposals (from Kuwait Stock Exchange and Ministry of Commerce and Industry), and it was not until February 2010 that the CMA was finally established. Despite having the oldest stock market in the region, Kuwait was remarkably the last GCC state to set up a regulatory body.

The bylaws were published in March 2011, and the problems started to occur when the new authority vigorously embarked on implementing the regulation. Many respondents, both those who were very critical towards the authority and those who supported the initiative, pointed out that the regulation was not very well thought through and generally too strict. For this reason, the attempt to bring a previously very poorly regulated market environment to immediate compliance with the new regulation was doomed to fail.

The CMA further started to clear the market of debt-stricken companies, which were unable to meet their financial obligations and accumulated losses exceeding 75 per cent of their capital. The Authority also carried out "seasonal" suspensions, that is, suspended the trading of companies, which failed to comply with corporate regulation and did not submit financial data or did not hold a general meeting by the end of financial year (Kuwait News Agency 2014). Furthermore, it launched a heavy-handed campaign against illegal trading practices.

The risk of large fines and severe punishment, as well as the cost of implementation of CMA regulations and the desire to protest the crackdown campaign and harsh measures, have pushed some of the listed companies to withdraw their shares from trading. By February 2014, up to 20 companies were reported to have opted to delist their shares. The withdrawal caused another big slide in the stock prices, and in 2014, Kuwait was the worst-performing market in the GCC (Saleem 2014).

This increasingly conflicting situation prompted Kuwait Chamber of Commerce and Industry (KCCI) to intervene as a formal lobbying and advisory body to demand amendments and more flexibility of the corporate governance regulation, extension of the period given for its implementation and the lowering of the costs and fines (Al-Saleh 2014). At the same time, many parliament members expressed their readiness to help the private sector and put pressure on the government to amend the CMA legislation. Such pressure ultimately forced the CMA to back down with the legislation. In the face of looming interrogation by several MPs, the Minister of Commerce and Industry promised to prepare a comprehensive amendment to the CMA law very shortly (Kuwait Times 2014).

Thus, the case of the CMA illustrates that the merchants' political interference in Kuwait can be active and powerful, and there are multiple means through which their influence is channelled.

Conclusion

The present work has attempted to analyse the complex attitude of Kuwait's business sector towards the government's efforts of economic restructuring and rationalisation. The business is naturally supportive of the idea of such restructuring being based around the empowerment of private sector and expansion of its scope of operation. However, a closer look reveals that its stance on various economic diversification policies and initiatives is largely defined by its rent-seeking self-interests, which stem from the very nature of a rentier system-based private sector—highly state-dependent and oligarchic, and in case of Kuwait, with a long history of protecting and expanding its economic interests and privileges. Thus, the response of the private sector to such policies varies accordingly, where it tries to benefit from them if possible, or resist (actively or passively) if necessary.

It has been also shown that Kuwaiti merchant community retains significant means of influence, which can be utilised to reverse policies or negotiate exemptions in cases which compromise their vital interests. The latter, in their turn, are concentrated around the preservation of the elitist, monopolist nature of private sector with high entry barriers and special relations with ruling powers. The chapter has further illustrated how in some cases the business actors' attitude towards certain economic diversification policies, and their subsequent political interference, can defy and deform the whole initial idea behind those policies. Such behaviour reinforces the already strong monopolist businesses, while the attempts aimed at economic diversification and benefitting the population at large in the long term perspective are moving too slowly or face stalemate.

Acknowledgement This research was supported by the UK Economic and Social Research Council under Grant ES/J012696/1.

Notes

1. According to the views of the respondents from of the merchant background, there are approximately 50 large business groups

References

Abdalla, I., & Al-Homoud, M. (2012). Foreign faces in Kuwaiti places: The challenges of human capital utilization in Kuwait. *International Journal of Business and Management, 7*(20). Canadian Center of Science and Education.

Al-Kuwari, D. (2013). *Mission impossible? Genuine economic development in the Gulf Cooperation Council Countries*, London School of Economics Kuwait Programme Research Papers.

Al-Saleh, T. (2014). Balancing between regulatory, developmental roles of CMA. *Kuwait Times*, 30 March. Retrieved March 2015, from http://news.kuwaittimes.net/balancing-regulatory-developmental-roles-cma/

Al-Zumai, F. (2013). *Kuwait's political impasse and rent-seeking behaviour: A call for institutional reform*, London School of Economics Kuwait Programme Research Papers.

Arabian Business. (2015). Kuwait postpones plan to remove petrol, power subsidies. *Arabian Business*, 4 January. Retrieved December 2015, from http://www.arabianbusiness.com/kuwait-postpones-plan-remove-petrol-power-subsidies-577281.html

Azoulay, R. (2013). The politics of Shi'i merchants in Kuwait. In S. Hertog, G. Luciani, & M. Valeri (Eds.), *Business politics of the Middle East* (pp. 67–100). London: Hurst.

Central Statistical Bureau. (2015). Retrieved July 2015, from https://www.csb.gov.kw/Default_EN.aspx

Crystal, J. (1995). *Oil and politics in the Gulf: Rulers and merchants in Kuwait and Qatar*. Cambridge: Cambridge University Press.

DLA Piper. (2010). *New Kuwaiti privatisation law under the microscope*. Retrieved December 2015, from http://information.dla.com/information/published/Kuwait_Privatization_Law_English.PDF

Dokoupil, M. (2014). Kuwait budget surplus up in last fiscal year as spending slows. *Reuters*, 28 September. Retrieved January 2015, from http://www.reuters.com/article/2014/09/28/kuwait-budget-idUSL6N0RT09220140928

Forbes. (2015). Retrieved March 2015, from http://www.forbesmiddleeast.com/en/lists/read/2014/top-companies-in-the-arab-world/listid/177?page=1

Goma, E., & Smith, M. (2011). Confused in Kuwait: Market frets over new regulator. *Reuters*, 5 October. Retrieved January 2015, from http://www.reuters.com/article/2011/10/05/kuwait-regulator-idUSL5E7L208620111005

Herb, M. (2009). A nation of bureaucrats: Political participation and economic diversification in Kuwait and the United Arab Emirates. *International Journal of Middle East Studies, 41*(3), 375–395.

Hertog, S. (2013a). Introduction: The role of MENA business in policy-making and political transitions. In S. Hertog, G. Luciani, & M. Valeri (Eds.), *Business politics of the Middle East* (pp. 1–16). London: Hurst.

Hertog, S. (2013b). *The private sector and reform in the Gulf Cooperation Council*, London School of Economics Kuwait Programme Research Papers.

Hertog, S. (2014). The GCC's national employment challenge. *The Washington Post*, 31 July. Retrieved January 2015, from http://www.washingtonpost.com/blogs/monkey-cage/wp/2014/07/31/the-gccs-national-employment-challenge/

Kuwait Economic Society (KES). (2013). Blueprint for public sector good governance in Kuwait: Four policies for administrative reform, July 2013.

Kuwait News Agency. (2014). CMA's suspension of certain shares jeopardizes traders' financial rights. *Kuwait News Agency*, 1 April. Retrieved February 2015, from http://www.kuna.net.kw/ArticleDetails.aspx?id=2369948&language=en

Kuwait Times. (2013a). Kuwait cannot fulfill 76% of IMF recommendations. *Kuwait Times*, 2 October. Retrieved January 2015, from http://news.kuwaittimes.net/kuwait-fulfill-76-imf-recommendations/

Kuwait Times. (2013b). Politics eclipses Kuwait development hopes—BOT law amendments on hold. *Kuwait Times*, 25 December. Retrieved December 2015, from http://news.kuwaittimes.net/politics-eclipses-kuwait-development-hopes-bot-law-amendments-hold/

Kuwait Times. (2014). CMA law to be amended soon. *Kuwait Times*, 19 November. Retrieved March 2015, from http://news.kuwaittimes.net/cma-law-amended-soon/

Kuwait Times. (2015a). Govt faces heat after raising diesel prices—MPs slam price gouging, want decision reversed. *Kuwait Times*, 3 January. Retrieved December 2015, from http://news.kuwaittimes.net/govt-faces-heat-raising-diesel-prices-mps-slam-price-gouging-want-decision-reversed/

Kuwait Times (2015b). IMF urges economic reform in Kuwait to ease deficit. *Kuwait Times*, 23 September. Retrieved December 2015, from http://news.kuwaittimes.net/website/imf-urges-economic-reform-in-kuwait-to-ease-deficit-officials-advise-remedy-for-unjust-subsidies-system/

Kuwait Times. (2015c). Plans to raise corporate tax, cut subsidies. *Kuwait Times*, 8 December. Retrieved December 2015, from http://news.kuwaittimes.net/website/10715-2/

Kuwait Times. (2015d). No fuel subsidies for expats, deserving citizens to be exempted. *Kuwait Times*, 13 December. Retrieved December 2015, from http://news.kuwaittimes.net/website/no-fuel-subsidies-for-expats-deserving-citizens-to-exempted/

Kuwait Times. (2015e). Lifting fuel subsidies, rationalizing energy's waiting official announcement—MP warns minister over Jahra's 'suspicious cafés. *Kuwait Times*, 19 December. Retrieved December 2015, from http://news.kuwaittimes.net/website/lifting-fuel-subsidies-rationalizing-energys-waiting-official-announcement/

Luciani, G. (2005). From private sector to national bourgeoisie: Saudi Arabian business. In P. Aarts & G. Nonneman (Eds.), *Saudi Arabia in the balance: Political economy, society, foreign affairs* (pp. 144–184). London: Hurst & Company.

Luciani, G. (2007). Linking economic and political reform in the Middle East: The role of the bourgeoisie. In O. Schlumberger (Ed.), *Debating Arab authori-*

tarianism: Dynamics and durability in nondemocratic regimes (pp. 161–176). Stanford: Stanford University Press.

Markaz. (2012). Towards sustainable economic development: Policies towards involving Kuwaitis in the Private labour market. *Kuwait Financial Centre S.A.K. (Markaz)*, May 2012.

Moore, P. W. (2002). Rentier fiscal crisis and regime stability: Business-state relations in the Gulf. *Studies in Comparative International Development*, 37(1), 34–56.

Moore, P. W. (2004). *Doing business in the Middle East: Politics and economic crisis in Jordan and Kuwait*. Cambridge: Cambridge University Press.

Oxford Business Group. (2014). *The report: Kuwait 2014*. Retrieved January 2015, from http://www.oxfordbusinessgroup.com/analysis/encouraging-entrepreneurs-new-measures-stimulate-growth-smes

Saleem, N. (2014). Kuwait hits 6-wk low on stock suspensions; most of region retreats. *Reuters*, 2 March. Retrieved January 2015, from http://www.reuters.com/article/2014/03/02/mideast-markets-wrap-idUSL6N0LZ0G020140302

Sartawi, M. (2012). *State-owned enterprises in Kuwait: History and recent developments. OECD towards new arrangements for state ownership in the Middle East and North Africa*. OECD Publishing.

The Economist. (2014). Kuwait's spending: Tighten your belts. *The Economist*, 4 February. Retrieved January 2015, from http://www.economist.com/blogs/pomegranate/2014/02/kuwaits-spending

CHAPTER 3

A Systemic Approach to Integrate SOEs and SMEs in Business Ecosystem

Alfadhal Al-Hinai, Angela Espinosa, and Richard Vidgen

INTRODUCTION

This chapter focuses on the integration between state-owned enterprises (SOEs) and small and medium enterprises (SMEs) through national strategic projects (NSPs). It offers a holistic model for designing a new state-owned enterprise (SOE) in order to play a greater role in governmental initiatives towards economic diversification. By performing systemic analysis of the organisation and its environment, suggestions are made to enhance collaboration and promote alliances, particularly with SMEs, in a multi-stakeholder environment. It uses the Viable System Model (VSM) in addition to other systemic approaches to unfold the complexity resulting from the environment, to identify the SOEs' core operational activities, and to connect them with numerous SMEs and other private companies.

It attempts to offer a model about how an SOE can be crafted as a vehicle for driving and empowering SMEs, to work collectively with other organisations to resolve different issues facing their viability and sustainability. Through such complex network of relationships, SOEs and SMEs

---

A. Al-Hinai (✉) • A. Espinosa • R. Vidgen
University of Hull, Hull, UK

© Gulf Research Centre Cambridge 2018
A. Mishrif, Y. Al Balushi (eds.), *Economic Diversification in the Gulf Region, Volume I*, The Political Economy of the Middle East,
https://doi.org/10.1007/978-981-10-5783-0_3

could play a significant role in orchestrating the business ecosystem by providing intellectual influence, shaping the network structure and its infrastructure, and setting ethos and standards. All these participatory processes would create a platform for a value co-creation and experience-sharing which could support other governmental initiatives towards economic diversification like generating jobs, employing local workforce and building national knowledge.

Organisational Complexity

Nowadays, public and private organisations are facing high complexity in their operating environment due to several factors, such as the technological revolution, globalisation, market fragmentation, rapid economic change, increasing competition pressure, global interdependence, blurred boundaries between government and business, lack of perception of environmental risks, unsatisfactory legal processes for solving complex problems and shrinking finance for social programmes (Gulati 1995, 1998; Hoverstadt 2008; Taket and White 2000). These environmental pressures lead organisations to engage in a variety of alliances and relationships, which help partners strengthen their competitive position by enhancing market power, accessing different resources, learning new skills, entering new markets and reducing risks (Hertog 2012; Park and Ungson 1997; Prashant and Harbir 2009; Yoshino and Rangan 1995).

The large number of such alliances and relationships have formed a complicated inter-organisational system that is best viewed as part of a complex network rather than a top-down and hierarchical organisation. These networks improve many aspects in organisations, such as innovation, production, marketing, and connecting customers and investors (Palmer 2009). However, they also raise issues of network influence, cascading, contagions and interdependent risks that cannot be controlled through standard mechanisms that rely mainly on command-and-control hierarchies (Kleindorfer and Wind 2009). Furthermore, organisations have moved to a new concept of 'connect and collaborate', which lets them respond faster to changes in global demands, have less control over their own destinies and pay high attention to their networks (Iacobucci and Salter II 2009).

Consequently, due to such complex relationships, the assignment of designing new organisations requires a holistic approach to identify and reorganise those relationships that evolve from the engagement and cooperation with networks and their agents (Hoverstadt 2008). For this reason, a number of scholars have been concerned with the adaptation to complexity in the environment and have suggested new models that enable organisations to link their designs, internal regulations and structures to match this complexity in order to gain appreciation of their interdependence, pool their insights and achieve high responsiveness, efficiency and stability among themselves (Beer 1981; Espinosa et al. 2008; Espinosa and Walker 2011; Taket and White 2000).

Therefore, this chapter offers a model of linking an SOE and SMEs via a national strategic project by crafting the SOE as a vehicle for various organisations to collaborate and work together, and to deal with different types of complexity associated with their corresponding operating environment. The SOE, through such alliances and cooperation, could play a significant role in orchestrating the business ecosystem by providing intellectual influence, shaping the network structure and its infrastructure, setting ethos and standards, and managing customer interfaces. Therefore, values will be co-created from all these participatory processes and interactions across the entire network, where the SOE plays a pivotal role at the centre of a web of prequalified agencies ready and able to respond to environmental changes among different public and private organisations, including SMEs. Consequently, this operating environment creates a platform that encourages understanding and provides a mechanism for the resolution of issues facing business initiatives from governments and the private sector in support of creating a diversified economy.

Economic Diversification in Oman

Economic diversification is a means to secure the stability and the sustainability of income levels in the future, which requires empowerment of the private sector to play a role in moving societies from being allocation states to being production states (Hvidt 2013). This necessitates the implementation of broader reforms at different levels. In Gulf Cooperation Countries (GCC), the governments are working seriously to build a diversified economic system as a means to create independence from the performance of the hydrocarbon sector. One of their efforts is investing in the private sector to make it more competent in creating jobs, building national capacity, generating knowledge and ensuring positive impact on the overall performance of the country (Amico and Hertog 2013; Fasano and Iqbal 2003). Up to now, unfortunately, the GCC's diversification activities have yielded insufficient results, as GCC governments are still leading their economies through the oil and gas industry (Fasano and Iqbal 2003; Hvidt 2013). Hvidt (2013) reported a number of external structural barriers to diversification in GCC states, such as the growth scenarios for the world economy, the duplication of economic activities among the GCC states and the sizable barriers to interregional trade. Additionally, lack of progress is attributed internally to a small degree of interaction and lack of communication channels with public organisations, inefficient allocation of resources, inefficient national labour force programmes and low productivity (Amico and Hertog 2013). As a result, the existing private sector is still playing a minor role in the GCC economies and continues to be reliant on the performance of the oil and gas industry. Investments in other industries are struggling due to the high risks associated with these investments, lack of experience and weak financial viability (Fasano and Iqbal 2003).

Like other GCC States, the Omani government is working towards economic diversification through several initiatives. These include establishing several SOEs to run a number of national strategic projects in different industries, such as tourism, electricity and water, telecommunication and infrastructure, fishing and agriculture. Besides these projects, the government has created several programmes to support SMEs and entrepreneurs, updated national regulations and strategies towards the 'Omanisation' policy, and subsidised local initiatives of self-employment. All these efforts aim to attract Omanis to join the private sector, participating in building national capacity and knowledge.

For the last 45 years, the government has continued to have a strong influence on the economy, mainly through the many SOEs created since 1970 (WTO 2013). By 2014, the government had full or partial ownership of 65 SOEs, delivering various services in various industries (Abdulaal 2014). Even though many of them do provide services that are needed for efficient development, others just became another bureaucracy overwhelmed by inefficiency, corruption and incompetence, draining resources from the public funds and capital. In 2014, the government declared that 17 companies had failed to deliver effectively the services for which they were created, and struggled to achieve their targets due to shortcomings in technical and managerial aspects (Abdulaal 2014). On the other hand, several public organisations are still continuing their efforts to form new business entities, particularly in those industries where the private sector has limited capability to do so, such as telecommunication, railways, heavy petrochemical industry and fishing.

In addition, the government has created distinct programmes to fund SMEs and entrepreneurs, which offer several advantages. For example, 10 per cent of public organisations and SOEs' purchases and projects should be dedicated and awarded to SMEs; a percentage of government lands and properties will be dedicated for investment in SMEs; entrepreneurial projects will be funded up to OMR 100,000 (nearly US$385,000) as soft loans, and so on. However, until now, the SMEs' contribution to GDP is estimated at less than 20 per cent, they employ 63 per cent of the labour force, of which only 36 per cent are local, and 40 per cent of SMEs are still concentrated in the wholesale and retail sector (ALshanfri et al. 2013). These figures imply that SMEs are still ineffective contributors to the national economy and are failing to strengthen the role of the private sector as a key part of the entire economy.

Furthermore, there is no doubt that unemployment rates are a real and worrying problem in all parts of the world, and perceived as one of the main obstacles to a diversified economy. Accordingly, the government has set up an 'Omanisation' policy and local employment programmes, as key instruments attached to the long-term national strategy, Oman 2020. They aim to generate a skilled and trained local workforce to meet the demands of the private sector, through a number of funded training and educational programmes that give knowledge and skills matching the Omani job market's needs. The World Trade Organization Report (2013) shows that Omanis still prefer to work in the government sector, as only 14 per cent of them are working for the private sector. This could be explained by the dependence on a large expatriate workforce, limited domestic supply of adequate skills, and an open-door policy and regulations to attract expatriate workforce (Fasano and Iqbal 2003).

In summary, the government has struggled to diversify its economy and make it a true success. From an organisational and managerial point of view, this is mainly due to the linear and piecemeal approach taken, in which each governmental initiative is treated separately from others, resulting in many cross-linkages being missed. There are also many inconsistencies relating to terms of regulation, communication, resources allocation and configuration, and so on. A systemic integration of these initiatives is needed to highlight opportunities for linking different activities, where the output of one becomes the input of another across different industries and programmes. Such an approach would upgrade the value-added produced locally by reorganising the activities and components attached to the various programmes of economic diversification.

Additionally, in such a context of interconnections across different industries, a systemic approach would enable the government to map the complex network design of its multiple systems and gain added benefits, such as expanding revenues and retaining or increasing value-added (Hvidt 2013). Also, it would shift the locus of innovation from a particular organisation to the network that it belongs to, as the latter would create a platform for co-creation and experience-sharing (Prahalad 2009). This would transform the business environment in such a way that private and public organisations can collaborate together and work collectively to generate value, assume risks and interact with their operating environment to ensure their long-term viability.

Design of SOEs

The definition of SOEs covers "a commercial, financial, industrial, agricultural or promotional undertaking—owned by public authority, either wholly or through majority share-holding—which is engaged in the sale of goods and services and whose affairs are capable of being recorded in balance sheets and profit and loss accounts. Such undertakings may have diverse legal and corporate forms, such as departmental undertakings, public corporations, statutory agencies, established by Acts of Parliament or Joint Stock Companies registered under the Company Law" (Basu 2008).

According to the above definition, governments have practised the creation of business entities, labelled state-owned enterprises (SOEs) or public enterprises (PEs), to execute business activities through entrepreneurial investments. They usually execute three types of economic activities provided wholly or partially by governments (Basu 2008): (a) socially profitable activities through Social Overhead Capital (SOC), such as road building and irrigation; (b) profitable activities of intensive capital provided with or without private investment, like heavy industry, power and transportation; and (c) activities which are natural monopolies, like those with very high fixed costs or those having restrictions to entry in a certain business. In addition to the economic aspects, many SOEs have non-commercial services that typically deliver social services and subsidised facilities to remote and rural areas, or to selected groups of customers (Amico and Hertog 2013; Rondinelli 2005).

In terms of the SOE design, the government's preliminary role is to form the organisational structures, policies, procedures and performance measures to guide SOE operations towards its objectives (Kennedy and

Jones 2003). The government is also responsible for assigning a state agency or an independent board of governors to supervise the performance of the SOE, ensuring that it operates efficiently in the public interest and that it is contributing to national development. Rondinelli (2005) discussed three common governance structures: (a) a Board of Directors (BoD) composed of members from the public and private sectors, provided that they do not have a conflict of interest or potential for illegal personal gain from serving on the board; (b) a responsible government body such as an SOE Commission or Agency with the responsibility for directing the enterprise's activities, auditing its finances and ensuring compliance with the legal system; and (c) a state enterprise holding company to which several SOEs report. To our knowledge, the first and third governance structures are very common in the Omani context. The first type is implemented in several companies, like Omantel in the telecommunications sector and Oman Air in the aviation sector, while the third structure is implemented in companies like the Electricity Holding Company, which looks after eight subsidiary companies in the electricity sector, and the Oman Oil Company, which is responsible for many companies in the oil and gas sector. These bodies are the final decision authorities that make strategic decisions, and ensure the control and monitoring of the overall performance of SOEs.

Nevertheless, it is a widely held view that SOEs have not delivered what was expected from them (Mulili and Wong 2011; Trivedi 2008). In many settings, governments exerted high influence on the design of SOEs through using traditional managerial approaches that make SOEs unable to operate in their complex environments. Consequently, they cannot cope efficiently and responsively to the increased competition and cooperation among agents in the networks to which they belong. The literature has addressed many complications attached to the organisational design of SOEs in terms of governance system and state-ownership, relationship with private sector organisations, and non-commercial services, as explained below:

- *Governance system and state-ownership*: benchmarking studies of SOEs conducted by Asian Development Bank (ADB) have shown that the state's legislative system and its governance frameworks heavily influence the design, organisational culture and performance of SOEs. As a consequence of this, SOEs have a vague vision and unclear objectives, along with impractical restrictions associated with state-ownership (Rondinelli 2005). In many cases, SOEs have less control over their strategic decisions, and less capacity to incorporate commercially oriented projects towards financial viability (Hertog 2010), and therefore they are seen as inefficient means for economic and social development.

- *The relationship with the private sector:* usually, the private sector should be encouraged and supported to deliver economic activities in a competitive framework through Directly Productive Investments (DPI) (Hertog 2012). In many contexts, SOEs are increasingly seen as pursuing private interests through their investments in profitable activities (Trivedi 2008), particularly when some governments have an interest in exercising control over the delivery of these activities through ownership of the assets. Therefore, such competitive actions may impact negatively on the performance and viability of the private companies concerned, and thus on their contribution to the entire economy.
- *Non-commercial services:* the social development attached to SOEs is actually very critical. First, in many cases, the subsidisation makes SOEs unable to maintain their financial viability without the governmental grants and funds. Second, overstaffing and use of SOEs as an efficient conduit for creating jobs and employing local people, regardless of the commercial aspects and capacity-utilisation, impact negatively on their performance and growth (Hertog 2010).

In view of this, we believe that one of the key factors to a successful SOE is to infuse SOEs with private sector discipline, business culture and competitive market pressures. One way to achieve this incorporation is through a systemic integration between SOEs and the private sector, particularly SMEs, via the national strategic projects (NSPs), as shown in the outer circle of Fig. 3.1. This integration will (a) join governmental and private initiatives towards a diversified economy, (b) give room for reducing legislative political intervention, (c) improve information-sharing channels across stakeholders, (d) allow targets to be reviewed continuously and collectively and (e) reframe those activities that are not commercially viable to meet the costs of capital.

The case study undertaken for this research, as will be explained in Sect. 6, demonstrates high complexity attached to the creation of a new SOE start-up resulting from the engagement of the potential stakeholders and highlights the necessity for a holistic approach to handle this complexity in

Fig. 3.1 The potential integration between NSPs, SOEs and SMEs

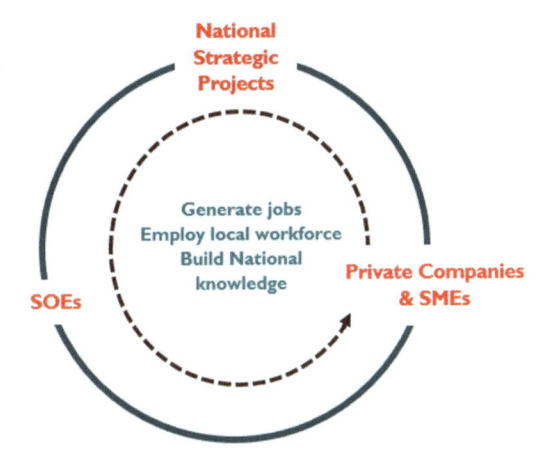

National Strategic Projects

*Generate jobs
Employ local workforce
Build National knowledge*

SOEs

Private Companies & SMEs

order to see the wide picture of the situation of such integration (NSP, SOE and SMEs). It also reveals a number of gains that could support other governmental initiatives towards economic diversification like generating jobs, employing local workforce and building national knowledge, as seen in the inner circle of Fig. 3.1.

System Thinking Approaches

The term 'system' has many varied definitions. One of these definitions defines systems as "constructs used for engaging with improving situations or real world complexity" (Reynolds and Holwell 2010). This definition addresses two main features of systems: holism and pluralism. Holism means unfolding the complexity of the system by looking at the relationships between things to discover how they affect what surrounds them, while pluralism means looking at things from different perspectives in order to define the problem concerned, to seek for improvement.

Most systems approaches are seeking systemic change in a complex situation through three orientations—(a) making sense of and simplifying relationships between objects, (b) surfacing and engaging contrasting perspectives and (c) exploring and reconciling power relations, boundary issues and potential conflict among various stakeholders (Reynolds and Holwell 2010).

Currently, the field of systems thinking has a considerable number of approaches, methodologies, methods and techniques (Jackson 2007;

Midgley 2000; Reynolds and Holwell 2010). Many scholars attempt to classify these approaches in groups based on their purposes or relations with other systems approaches. For example, Jackson (2007) attempts to classify some of these approaches into four categories according to the purposes they aim to achieve: improving goal seeking and viability, exploring purposes, ensuring fairness and promoting diversity.

The widely used traditional way of classifying systems approaches is based on three common categories: hard, soft and critical. Table 3.1 gives a list of examples of systems approaches using this schema.

Midgley (2000) used these categories to describe the evolution of system thinking through three waves. The first wave is exemplified by early hard systems theorists who described systems in physical and concrete terms, resorting to metaphors from physics or biology. It perceived unity of purpose, and therefore it was criticised for considering the system as a representation of a single reality rather than development of inter-subjective understanding. The second wave focused on wider soft perspectives of people; it emphasised dialogue, mutual appreciation and inter-subjective construction of realities. The two key concerns about this

Table 3.1 Three traditions of systems

Hard systems	General system theory (Bertalanfy 1956)
	First-order cybernetics (Ashby 1956)
	Operational research (Churchman et al. 1957)
	System engineering (Hall 1962)
	Socio-technical system (Trist et al. 1972)
	Rand-system analysis (Optner 1965)
	System dynamics (Forrester 1971; Meadows et al. 1972)
Soft systems	Inquiring systems design (Churchman 1971)
	Second-order cybernetics (Bateson 1971)
	Soft system methodology (Checkland 1972)
	Strategic assumption surface testing (Mason and Mitroff 1981)
	Interactive management (Ackoff 1981)
	Cognitive mapping for strategic options development and analysis (Eden 1988)
Critical systems	Critical system heuristics (Ulrich 1983)
	System of systems methodologies (Jackson 1991)
	Liberating system theory (Flood 1990)
	Interpretive systemology (Fuenmayor 1991)
	Total system intervention (Flood and Jackson 1991)
	Systemic intervention (Midgley 2000)

Source: adopted from Reynolds and Holwell (2010)

wave are insufficient attention to power relations within interventions and the lack of consideration of methodological pluralism (Midgley 2000). The third wave is critical systems thinking, which is concerned with power relationships, and how they affect the way problems are addressed.

In the third wave, many scholars suggest that in order to make system methodologies more effective in dealing with the richness of the real world, and match its complexities, it is desirable to go beyond using a single-system methodology to generally combining several methodologies, whether fully or partially (Jackson 2007; Midgley 2000; Mingers and Brocklesby 1997; Mingers and Rosenhead 2004; Zhu 2011). Therefore, the use of multiple methods has become a general theme in practice, and many practitioners tend to apply multiple methods in different levels of analysis based on their knowledge, experience and skills, as well as the nature of the problem and its organisational context, using a variety of strategies for choosing and mixing these methods.

Given that our focus is the organisational aspects associated with the design of an SOE, one powerful systemic approach that can assist and model the design of organisations is the Viable System Model (VSM), which was developed by Stafford Beer (Beer 1981, 1985; Espinosa and Walker 2011). Its concepts are grounded in cybernetics: "the science of communication and control in animals and machines" (Beer 1994). VSM studies and models feedback mechanisms and information flows within an organisation, improving its capability for self-regulation and control, aiming to maintain its viability (Espinosa and Walker 2011). Furthermore, VSM covers several features of complex settings, such as non-linearity, dynamic behaviour, emergence and self-organisation (Espejo and Kuropatwa 2011; Espinosa et al. 2007; Schwaninger 2006), which are very relevant given the globalised and open markets context in which most organisations operate nowadays.

The VSM is based on the dynamic interaction among three elements: environment, operation and management within a hierarchal structure containing five subsystems. System one is responsible for the operating units and refers to the primary activities producing goods or services (Beer 1985; Ríos 2012). System two is responsible for avoiding oscillations between these units, while system three supports these operating units to ensure that they self-regulated and develop their synergies. System four is responsible for creating the future of the organisation by developing innovative options for adapting to new circumstances in the environment (Christopher 2011; Espinosa and Walker 2011). Finally, system five is responsible for the identity and closure of the organisation, represents all the stakeholders and is the ultimate authority (Beer 1981).

Each viable system is made up of viable systems embedded within it and is itself embedded in other viable systems (Beer 1994). This design of systems and subsystems is a recursive structure that uses the same systemic laws and axioms and has common patterns and properties at each layer (Beer 1985; Espejo and Reyes 2011; Schwaninger 2006). However, recursions can be circular or 'self-referential', and they do not necessarily run from top to bottom, for example, virtual corporations that link several organisations by information to share skills, costs and access to new markets (Schwaninger 2006). Recursion is a powerful tool to assess the ability of organisations to build up their variety to cope with the complexity of their environment. We now apply the VSM to a case study of the design of an SOE, the Oman Broadband Company (OBC).

Research Design

The Case Study

In the past, the national telecommunications networks and services in Oman were managed by the Ministry of Transport and Communications (MoTC), and operated by the General Telecommunications Organisation (GTO). In 2000, due to Oman's commitments as a full member of the World Trade Organisation (WTO), the government started the liberalisation of the telecoms market by implementing a liberal telecom regime, opening the market to competition and gaining access to leading-edge technology. In fact, the government expected that the information and communication technology (ICT) industry would play a key role in its economic plans and strategies based on reforming the structure and economy of the ICT sector. Accordingly, in 2002, the government introduced a new telecommunication act followed by the establishment of a specialised authority called the Telecommunication Regulatory Authority (TRA) responsible for implementing telecommunications policies, regulating the telecoms market and balancing the interests of various stakeholders based on principles of non-discrimination, transparency and technology neutrality (TRA 2012). In 2006, the government set up a new entity called the Information Technology Authority (ITA) to implement national IT infrastructure projects and supervise all projects related to implementation of the Digital Oman Strategy, including e-government and e-payment services. Besides the above governmental bodies, the ICT sector is organised into a number of class I, II and III operators who provide the main telecommunication services to their consumers, including fixed-line telephones, mobile calls, internet services and other special telecom products. Additionally, it also includes vendors, technology providers and system integrators who offer a range of technologies and technical systems demanded by operators as well as consumers. As a consequence of this setup and structure, the ICT industry has become more complex, particularly when it incorporates and collaborates with other industries.

Currently, access to high-speed broadband networks is increasingly seen as a basic right of citizens, a key part of economic life, a critical factor in stimulating economic growth and a means of increasing productivity across other sectors. As a result, many countries have taken serious initiatives to promote the spread of broadband and make it accessible to all segments of society. At present, the broadband industry in Oman is facing a number of obstacles that limit its growth, including (a) low percentage of fixed broadband take-up with slower growth; (b) various constraints to expansion of mobile broadband coverage including spectrum limitations, provision of backhaul connectivity and securing rights of way for new towers; (c) high cost of broadband compared to GDP per head benchmarked across the region and globally; (d) limited competition among broadband providers; and (e) high cost to reach rural areas, which represent 23 per cent of the total population (MOTC 2013).

Given these obstacles, from 2011 to mid-2013, the government set up a committee from different public and private organisations to develop the National Broadband Strategy (NBS). It discussed many technical options, technologies, time frame, financial resources, risks and opportunities related to the broadband industry. One of NBS's initiatives is creating a commercial entity called the Oman Broadband Company (OBC), to be responsible for operating and managing broadband infrastructure across the country. Over the next three years, the size of this company is expected to reach 200 employees and US$500M capital.

Research Methodology

Due to the shared business/academic interests of this case study, the Cyclical Process Model (CPM) developed by Davison et al. (2004), as shown in Fig. 3.2, is used to organise this research. The model addresses our access to the organisation to conduct several cycles according to the

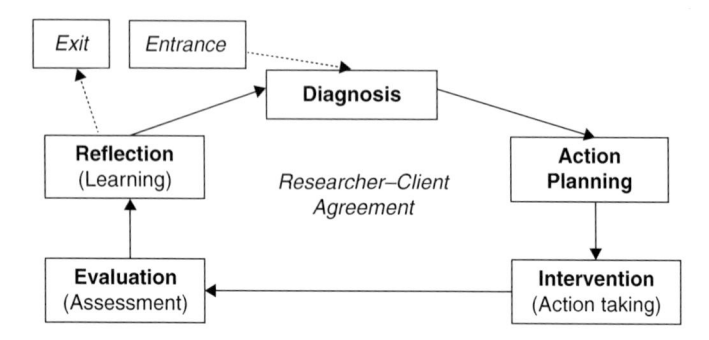

Fig. 3.2 Cyclical Process Model. Source: adapted from Davison et al. (2004)

project requirements, and allows both researchers and the OBC management to seek change through action and learning through reflection.

In addition, the CPM fits with the diagnostic framework grounded in the 'Inductive Top-Down Theorising Model' developed by Shepherd and Sutcliffe (2011). This combination allows us to use knowledge from literature, in particular those theories related to the main areas of this research, in addition to knowledge gained through experiences and perceptions of the problem concerned. It gives us greater flexibility to explore different stakeholders' perspectives, by seeing the phenomenon of concern through multiple theoretical lenses rather than a single one (Midgley 2000). This engagement of stakeholders could enhance the understanding of numerous non-linear interactions and interconnections among multiple factors in the wider system that modify the boundary judgement (Midgley 2000), organise the associated relationships (Checkland and Poulter 2006) and produce the outcome or change (Burns 2013).

This research has two main stages. Stage 1, environmental scanning, aims to scan the corresponding environments of various systems connected to the broadband industry at different recursion levels. Beer (1994) emphasised that an organisation has to understand different economic, social and environmental systems that are encountered by its internal subsystems. Stage 2, complexity mapping and adaptation: 'variety' is one of the key concepts in cybernetics; it is the way of measuring the complexity of a system. The system in focus has to build its capability to attenuate or amplify varieties in order to maintain its balance, and remain viable and self-regulated.

The output of these two stages would shape the identity of the SOE, and develop its strategy and operating model. Additionally, the design of the OBC, as an SOE specialising in broadband services, will impact on the reconfiguration and realignments of the whole ICT system and other related industries, which are expected, in turn, to influence the OBC design and its growth. The power associated to the dynamic interconnections across different autonomous agents gives high attention to the structural complexity and organisational cybernetics of the potential evolving networks. The implications of these networks would influence the operating model of their organisations to run a business, as well as impact on the performance of the entire economy.

Data Collection and Workshops

Three workshops were conducted, which helped to understand the context of the broadband industry, build the sensory representation and construct the problem situation. The organisers provided a number of documents showing historical data of the broadband industry and details about various steps taken to initiate the OBC. They enabled the authors to negotiate, discuss and reflect on the obtained data, and suggest future activities and actions to satisfy the academic objectives of this research as well as the business requirements of the OBC.

The first workshop aimed to review the National Broadband Strategy (NBS), which provided a large volume of historical data about the development of NBS and the initial steps taken by the government to set up the OBC. A partial environment scan was conducted, which unfolded a number of complexities related to the technology and economy, regulations and politics, social and culture. It became clear that NBS is a technology-driven strategy, as little consideration was given to linkages with other businesses related to the creation of local content, building national capabilities, engagement of private sector particularly SMEs, involvement of training and HR institutions, arrangements with social societies, and so on. Addressing these possible linkages could bring new opportunities, threats or issues related to supply and demand of broadband services.

The second workshop aimed to review the suggested operating model, which served three types of customers listed in NBS (residents, business and rural areas), through the use of different technologies (fibre, towers and satellite), serving three geographical regions (Muscat, urban cities and rural areas). Figure 3.3 illustrates the initial operating model for the OBC.

	OBC		
Technology	Fixed Fibre Infrastructure	Tower Infrastructure	Satellite & Wireless Infrastructure
Geographical Area	Muscat Urban cities	Urban cities Rural Areas	Rural Areas

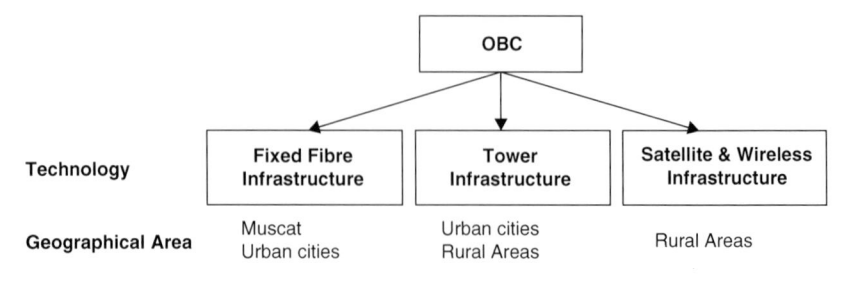

Fig. 3.3 OBC's Business Model

The first unit is the fibre infrastructure, which can accommodate the existing fibres owned by current operators, utility companies and other organisations, as well as manage new investments in fibre roll-out in other geographical zones to avoid overlapping and duplication. It will make use of underutilised national assets of fibre infrastructure, particularly those owned by electrical companies used for their Supervisory Control And Data Acquisition (SCADA) systems (SCADA is a system that operates with coded signals over communication channels so as to provide control of remote equipment). Similarly, the second unit, tower infrastructure, will manage the use and share of existing towers used for electrical networks and telecom mobile services, and drive the demand for new ones. Such towers could be utilised by different stakeholders for suspending fibres, antennas and other technical equipment. Lastly, the third operating unit is responsible for providing the wholesale satellite broadband service to rural and remote areas where any other infrastructure is not commercially justifiable. It also may play a key role in launching a future national satellite project.

The third workshop invited a focus group from the OBC and the ICT sector, and used VSM and recursion analysis (Beer 1985; Espinosa and Walker 2011) to explore the OBC's recursive layers, and distinguish various meta-systemic and operational functions attached to these layers. The exercise explored different views of the participants about the way the OBC was structured. The participants were keen to develop a model combining the technology, the geography and the OBC's primary activities. After lengthy but useful discussion, they were able to define System-1 operational activities at two recursive layers. At the corporate level, System-1 consists of the three business units (fixed fibre infrastructure, towers infrastructure and satellite and wireless reach), while at layer 2, System-1 includes four operations (design, build, connect and maintain). Figure 3.4 depicts these layers.

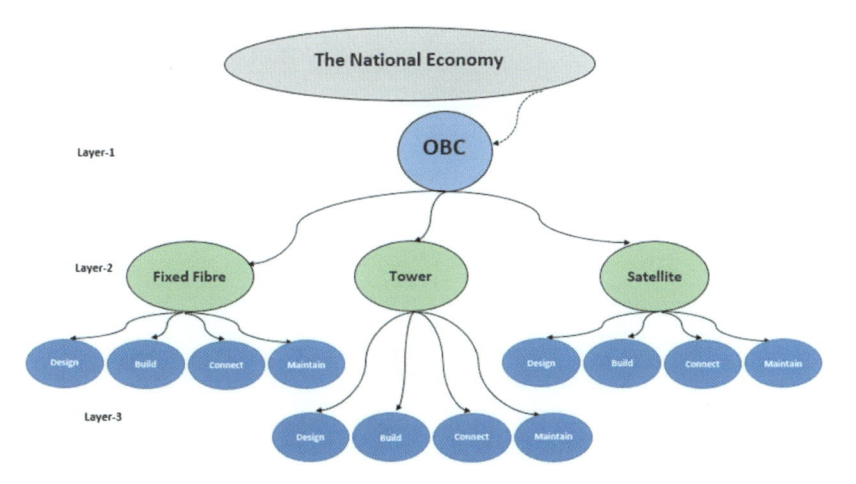

Fig. 3.4 The three layers of recursions in the OBC case

At layer 1, the OBC is seen as connected to the national economy, mainly through the ICT industry. It is responsible for managing the design, deployment and maintenance of broadband infrastructure across the country. At layer 2, the OBC is viewed as a holding company looking after three operating units: fibre, towers and satellite. Each one of these units is perceived as a viable system able to deal with its corresponding environment and addressing different complexities. At this layer, the OBC will deal with a number of private and public entities, such as policymakers, regulators, utility companies, telecom operators, and so on. All of them will interact with each other in order to maintain their resources and interests to influence the whole broadband industry. Undoubtedly, at all recursion levels, the OBC is practising meta-systemic functions required to manage and support its core purposes. For instance, at layer 1, the OBC's activities are strategic planning, resources allocation, commercial activities and governance actions, and so on, as shown in Fig. 3.5a.

Additionally, at layer 2, the three operating units are responsible to build their capacity in order to manage, execute and monitor their technical projects and work packages, as well as align their objectives with the OBC strategy and NBS. They will subcontract all projects attached to the four primary operations—*Design, Build, Connect and Maintain*—to specialised private companies and SMEs as shown in Fig. 3.5b. They will give the selected companies all required support to perform their jobs efficiently

66 A. AL-HINAI ET AL.

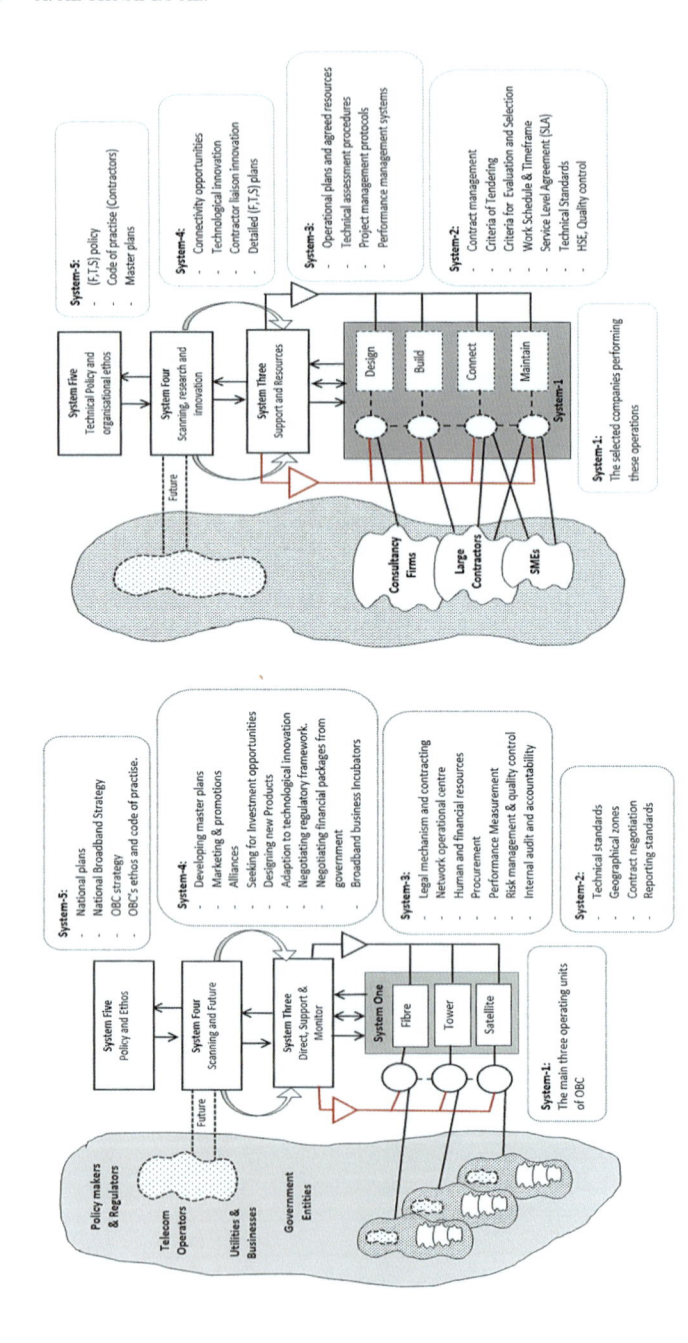

Fig. 3.5 (a) VSM of the OBC at the corporate level. (b) Generic VSM of fibre, towers and satellite

during the design and execution phases, and also in the course of the connection and maintenance to end-user customers. This support could be structured into three main functions: technical planning, project management and quality control.

Discussion and Data Analysis

Schwaninger (2006) argues that the design of a business system may face challenges related to positioning the company in the market and increasing relationships with all potential stakeholders. The three workshops revealed aspects of these challenges and constraints, and provide supporting evidence that this project—*creating an SOE start-up in the interorganisational domain*—is complex. Its complexity is associated mainly with the different interests and perspectives of stakeholders, and scopes, boundaries and components that were identified through different stages of this exercise.

This systemic investigation has revealed a high potential for the OBC to work as a nodal organisation, and operate as a context leader, connecting a number of public and private organisations across industries through collaboration and alliances. Figure 3.6 illustrates the potential of connections emerging at different layers of different functions. These connections allow different agents and nodes to have the possibility to exchange (a) tangible benefits, such as goods, services and revenue, (b) knowledge such as strategies and plans, and (c) intangible benefits such as loyalty and brand. This potential network of harmonious connections will assure technology and skills transfer, diffusion of a performance-oriented corporate culture and local multiplier effects (Hertog 2012). In addition, it becomes a significant source of value creation enabling some agents to be key players and powerful that may generate challenges, risks and opportunities for various businesses (Kleindorfer and Wind 2009).

Nonetheless, this network of connections could be reorganised in such a way as to increase flexibility, gain competitive advantage and maximise the outcomes of joint initiatives of the national economy. There is no doubt that this broadband initiative and its deliberate plans and projects could be capitalised to attract new connections of agents that may impact positively on the ICT industry as well as on other industries. For instance, the right side of Fig. 3.6 presents a possibility to link the OBC's business units with SMEs by subcontracting to them numerous projects,

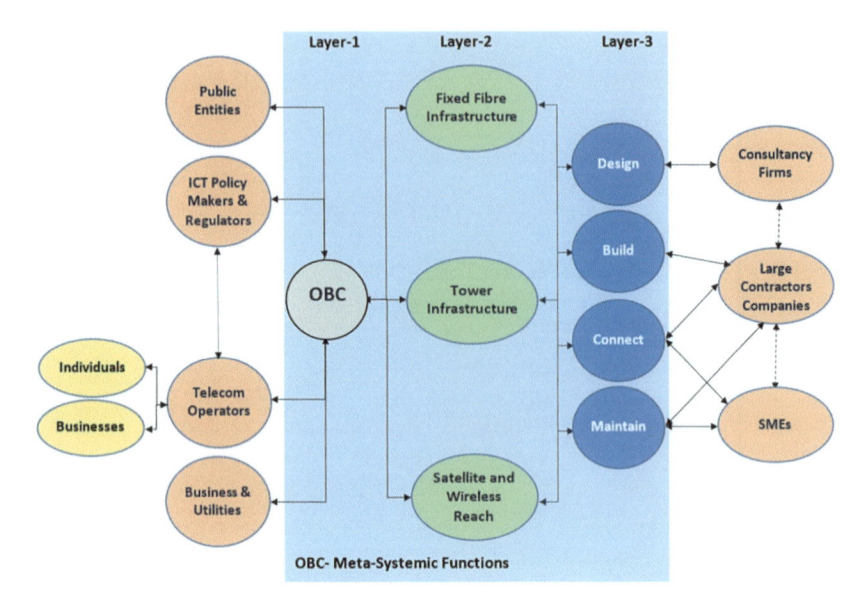

Fig. 3.6 OBC as a value integrator

work packages and operational jobs associated with the less complicated operations, for example, 'Connect and Maintain'. The vast size of these contracts within the next 10–15 years could be utilised to generate, guide and support SMEs across different regions of the country. These guaranteed contracts will sustain them to achieve growth and viability. The promising SMEs will have a potential to build advanced capabilities, transforming them gradually to perform complicated broadband operations, for example, 'Design and Build'. Additionally, these skills and capabilities will not be limited to implementation of SOEs projects, but will be extended to performance of similar projects and activities serving other business clients.

Additionally, the model reveals that an SOE can empower the private sector, particularly SMEs through their participation in national strategic projects, and become key players and strategic enablers in the national economy. This highlights two interrelated advantages. First, it will inspire local entrepreneurs to set up their own companies specialising in the primary operational activities of SOEs. This, in turn, will create national capacities focused on the core activities of national strategic projects, reduce risks of build-up capabilities associated mainly with reliance on external and overseas companies, and transfer various experiences to similar projects within the country or abroad. Therefore, the predefined quota (Currently, this quota is nearly 10 per cent of SOEs' projects awarded to SMEs in the form of subcontracts. Most of them are not related to the SOEs' core operations, and perceived as an added cost to SOE's investments) is not an economically viable condition for SMEs' growth, as for the national economy. There is no limit for this quota as long as SMEs have the ability and are stimulated to develop themselves in a way to compete for the complicated and less complicated activities of SOEs' operations. The second advantage is job creation, which is achieved by the formation of SMEs and their needs to hire a suitable workforce that matches their projects' size. In this case, SOEs will not be a direct source of employment, but will offer continuous projects and contracts to SMEs besides other private companies, in which a skilled and trained workforce will be hired frequently.

Furthermore, the OBC made an effort at this recursive layer to engage itself with other SOEs working in water and electricity, oil and gas, and telecommunication sector, by conducting a workshop on 9 June 2014, entitled "Integration and Partnership in Telecommunication Infrastructure and Broadband Projects". The workshop was successful in establishing new linkages with some potential organisations through joint technical projects. However, it was limited in engaging SMEs and entrepreneurs, showing them the market gaps and future business opportunities. These opportunities exceed the main four operations of the OBC, which include indirect activities such as logistics, HR and training, and so on. For instance, although the shortage in build-up capabilities was addressed clearly in the OBC's strategy, no further actions have been taken to deliberate this limitation with those organisations concerned. To our knowledge, since the OBC was established in January 2014, no training programmes related to the broadband industry have been announced by the existing training institutions, and no entrepreneurs have shown the effort to establish such programmes as a new business to fill this market gap. Thus, the aspects of human resources, training and educational programmes, employment regulations, and so on, require further deliberations to allow those interested organisations, *appearing in the recursive layer 1*, to establish new connections within the wider business ecosystem, to resolve all issues of the HR and employment aspects and to fulfil their needs.

- It is clear that the creation of an SOE to run a national strategic project could be exploited to reshape its wider system, in which many issues and aspects could be addressed and discussed among different agents. This encourages interested public and private organisations, including SMEs, to work jointly in handling different complexities and filtering their varieties to maintain their viability, by acquiring, generating and sharing knowledge within their wider system. It enables various organisations and entrepreneurs to generate new business ideas, allocate funds and configure resources, and produce innovative products. Accordingly, Fig. 3.1 in Sect. 4 could be revisited and enriched to illustrate the main meta-systemic functions attached to the three links between national strategic projects, SOEs, and private companies and SMEs, as shown in Fig 3.7.

In the main, this model suggests three groups of functions that have to take place in the integration between SOE and private companies/SMEs with the aim of achieving public purposes that are identified by the national

Fig. 3.7 Meta-systemic functions addressed in the wider system

strategic projects. All groups of functions are meta-systemic, but they appear in two different recursive layers—Groups A and B are associated with layer 1, while Group C is related to layer 2, as discussed in Sect. 8. The efficient execution of these functions collectively will definitely boost the efforts of generating jobs, employing skilled local labour and building national knowledge, which, in turn, will accelerate governmental programmes towards a diverse economy.

Additionally, the model insists on supplementing relationships between the SOE and the private sector companies, including SMEs, and ensures a fair and competitive framework for any potential and promising collaborations. To maintain this *non-competing* relationship, the model suggests a network governance system rather than hierarchical top-down control rules enforced by the government, to govern various activities taking place in the wider system, for example, the broadband industry in this case study. It involves various actors of public and private organisations who interact based on negotiation and procedural rationality, trust and political obligations. Such a system will reduce the legislative political intervention of governments and open new information-sharing channels across them. Over time, the wider system will be sustained by a flexible structure, dynamic behaviours and self-organised rules and norms.

Conclusion

To sum up, this chapter attempts to bridge the gap between SOEs and private companies, including SMEs, via the vehicle of national strategic projects. It discusses how the integration between these three entities could be achieved, how it would give all organisations access to social and economic development programmes and how they will participate collectively in building national knowledge, generating jobs and employing local workforces. All organisations will be enabled to assess and reshape their future environments at organisational, sectoral and national levels, which, in turn, will make them all play a vital role in the national economy and the drive towards diversification.

Acknowledgement We are grateful to Mr. Said Al-Mandhari, CEO of the OBC, for providing us this opportunity to align the business interests of this new company with our scholarly interests. This collaboration was instrumental in supporting an action research case study based on and motivated by the OBC. We extend special thanks to all the OBC members and all members from other ICT organisations, who participated in our workshops and contributed knowledge assisting in the development of this publication and its models.

REFERENCES

Abdulaal, N. (2014). Oman 2015 budget. *Alroya*. Muscat, 24 Nov 2014 [Online]. Retrieved June 8, 2015, from http://alroya.om/ar/discussions/shura/116175.html

Ackoff, R. L. (1981). The art and science of mess management. *Interfaces*, *11*(1), 20–26.

ALshanfri, D. A., Adham, Alsaid, F., & Albusaidi, S. (2013). *SME development symposium research summary* 2013. Retrieved from http://thefirm.om/Projects_and_Publications_files/SME%20Development%20Symposium%20Brief%20v2%20.pdf

Amico, A., & Hertog, S. (2013). *State-owned enterprises in the Middle East and North Africa: Engines of development and competitiveness?* OECD.

Ashby, W. R. (1956). *An introduction to cybernetics*. London: Methuen.

Basu, P. (2008). *Public enterprises: Unresolved challenges and new opportunities. Reinventing public enterprises and their management as the engine of development sand growth*.

Bateson, G. (1971). The cybernetics of "self": A theory of alcoholism. *Psychiatry*, *34*(1), 1–18.

Beer, S. (1981). *Brain of the firm: The managerial cybernetics of organization*. New York: Wiley.

Beer, S. (1985). *Diagnosing the system for organizations*. West Sussex: John Wiley & Sons.

Beer, S. (1994). *The heart of enterprise*. Chichester: John Wiley & Sons.

Burns, D. (2013). Systemic action research: Changing system dynamics to support sustainable change. *Action Research*, *12*(1), 3–18.

Checkland, P. B. (1972). Towards a systems-based methodology for real-world problem solving. *Journal of Systems Engineering*, *3*(2), 87–116.

Checkland, P., & Poulter, J. (2006). *Learning for action: A short definitive account of soft systems methodology and its use for practitioner, teachers, and students, 26*. Chichester: Wiley.

Christopher, W. F. (2011). A new management for enduring company success. *Kybernetes*, *40*(3/4), 369–393.

Churchman, C. W. (1971). *The design of inquiring systems basic concepts of systems and organization*. Basic Books.

Churchman, C. W., Ackoff, R. L., & Arnoff, E. L. (1957). *Introduction to operations research*. New York: John Wiley and Sons.

Davison, R., Martinsons, M. G., & Kock, N. (2004). Principles of canonical action research. *Information Systems Journal, 14*(1), 65–86.
Eden, C. (1988). Cognitive mapping. *European Journal of Operational Research, 36*(1), 1–13.
Espejo, R., & Kuropatwa, D. (2011). Appreciating the complexity of organizational processes. *Kybernetes, 40*(3/4), 454–476.
Espejo, R., & Reyes, A. (2011). *Organizational systems: Managing complexity with the viable system model*. London, New York: Springer.
Espinosa, A., Harnden, R., & Walker, J. (2007). Beyond hierarchy: A complexity management perspective. *Kybernetes, 36*(3/4), 333–347.
Espinosa, A., Harnden, R., & Walker, J. (2008). A complexity approach to sustainability–Stafford Beer revisited. *European Journal of Operational Research, 187*(2), 636–651.
Espinosa, A., & Walker, J. (2011). *A complexity approach to sustainability: Theory and application, 1*. World Scientific.
Fasano, U., & Iqbal, Z. (2003). *GCC countries: From oil dependence to diversification*. International Monetary Fund.
Forrester, J. W. (1971). *World dynamics*. Wright-Allen Press.
Gulati, R. (1995). Does familiarity breed trust? The implications of repeated ties for contractual choice in alliances. *Academy of Management Journal, 38*(1), 85–112.
Gulati, R. (1998). Alliances and networks. *Strategic Management Journal, 19*(4), 293–317.
Hall, A. D. (1962). *A methodology for systems engineering*. Van Nostrand.
Hertog, S. (2010). Defying the resource curse: Explaining successful state-owned enterprises in rentier states. *World Politics, 62*(2), 261–301.
Hertog, S. (2012). *How the GCC did it: Formal and informal governance of successful public enterprise in the Gulf Co-operation Council countries*. OECD.
Hoverstadt, P. (2008). *The fractal organization: Creating sustainable organizations with the viable system model*. Chichester: John Wiley & Sons.
Hvidt, M. (2013). *Economic diversification in GCC countries: Past record and future trends*.
Iacobucci, D., & Salter II, J. M. (2009). Social networks: You've lost control. *The network challenge: Strategy, profit, and risk in an interlinked world, 67*.
Jackson, M. C. (1991). Creative problem solving: Total systems intervention. In *Systems methodology for the management sciences* (pp. 271–276). Springer US.
Jackson, M. C. (2007). *Systems thinking: Creative holism for managers*. John Wiley & Sons.
Kennedy, R. M., & Jones, L. P. (2003). *Reforming state-owned enterprises: Lessons of international experience, especially for the least developed countries*. United Nations Industrial Development Organization, Small and Medium Enterprises Branch, Programme Development and Technical Cooperation Division.

Kleindorfer, P. R., & Wind, Y. (2009). The network imperative: Community or contagion. *The network challenge: Strategy, profit, and risk in an interlinked world*, 3–23.

Meadows, D. H., Meadows, D. L., Randers, J., & Behrens, W. W. (1972). The limits to growth. *New York, 102*, 27.

Midgley, G. (2000). *Systemic intervention: Philosophy, methodology, and practice. Contemporary systems thinking*. New York: Kluwer.

Mingers, J., & Brocklesby, J. (1997). Multimethodology: Towards a framework for mixing methodologies. *Omega, 25*(5), 489–509.

Mingers, J., & Rosenhead, J. (2004). Problem structuring methods in action. *European Journal of Operational Research, 152*(3), 530–554.

Mitroff, I. I., & Mason, R. O. (1981). The metaphysics of policy and planning: A reply to Cosier. *Academy of Management Review, 6*(4), 649–651.

MOTC. (2013). *The national broadband strategy*. Muscat.

Mulili, B. M., & Wong, P. (2011). Corporate governance practices in developing countries: The case for Kenya. *International Journal of Business Administration, 2*(1), 14.

Optner, S. L. (1965). *Systems analysis for business and industrial problem solving*. Englewood Cliffs, NJ: Prentice Hall.

Palmer, R. E. (2009). Cross-cultural leadership in networked global enterprises. *The network challenge: Strategy, profit, and risk in an interlinked world*, 49.

Park, S. H., & Ungson, G. R. (1997). The effect of national culture, organizational complementarity, and economic motivation on joint venture dissolution. *Academy of Management journal, 40*(2), 279–307.

Prahalad, C. (2009). Creating experience: Competitive advantage in the age of networks. *The network challenge: Strategy, profit, and risk in an interlinked world*. Wharton School Publishing, Philadelphia, 25–36.

Prashant, K., & Harbir, S. (2009). Managing strategic alliances: What do we know now, and where do we go from here? *The Academy of Management Perspectives, 23*(3), 45–62.

Reynolds, M., & Holwell, S. (2010). *Systems approaches to managing change: A practical guide*. London: Springer.

Ríos, J. M. P. (2012). *Design and diagnosis for sustainable organizations: The viable system method*. Springer.

Rondinelli, D. A. (2005). *Can public enterprises contribute to development? A critical assessment and alternatives for management improvement*. Prepared for United Nations Expert Group Meeting on Reinventing Public Enterprise Management.

Schwaninger, M. (2006). *Intelligent organizations*. Springer.

Shepherd, D. A., & Sutcliffe, K. M. (2011). Inductive top-down theorizing: A source of new theories of organization. *Academy of Management Review, 36*(2), 361–380.

Taket, A. R., & White, L. (2000). *Partnership and participation: Decision-making in the multiagency setting*. Chichester: Wiley.

TRA. (2012). *Telecom sector in Oman; 5-years at a glance*. Muscat.

Trist, E. (1972). Types of output mix of research organisations and their complementarity. In *Social Science and Government: Policies and Problems* (pp. 101–137). London: Tavistock Publications.

Trivedi, P. (2008). Designing and implementing mechanisms to enhance accountability for state owned enterprises. In United Nations (Ed.), *Public enterprises: Unresolved challenges and new opportunities*. New York: United Nations.

Ulrich, W. (1983). *Critical heuristics of social planning: A new approach to practical philosophy*. New York: John Wiley and Sons.

WTO. (2013). *Trade policy review, Oman*. Organisation, W. T.

Yoshino, M. Y., & Rangan, U. S. (1995). *Strategic alliances: An entrepreneurial approach to globalization*. Harvard Business Press.

Zhu, Z. (2011). After paradigm: Why mixing-methodology theorising fails and how to make it work again. *Journal of the Operational Research Society, 62*(4), 784–798.

CHAPTER 4

Implications of Public-Private Partnerships in Infrastructure Development for Economic Diversification

Michiko Iwanami

INTRODUCTION

Overture: The availability of infrastructure services is crucial to achieve economic development. In general, the provision of such services is the responsibility of governments, for they have natural monopoly features that may cause market failure if privately provided. Another reason for government responsibility derives from the fact that they are essential to daily lives and thus necessary to be accessible, provided at least minimum quality and affordable to all. However, past experience indicates that government provision of infrastructure services has generally failed, meaning that it has limited coverage and inefficient services. Such a condition is one of the reasons why the significance of public-private partnerships (PPPs) in infrastructure development has increased. Another reason is that governments lack financial resources for new investments so that they are available in line with the pace of economic development.

M. Iwanami (✉)
Sojitz Research Institute, Minato, Tokyo, Japan

© Gulf Research Centre Cambridge 2018
A. Mishrif, Y. Al Balushi (eds.), *Economic Diversification in the Gulf Region, Volume I*, The Political Economy of the Middle East,
https://doi.org/10.1007/978-981-10-5783-0_4

PPPs are said to improve managerial and financial efficiency and the quality of infrastructure services since private entities have commercial principles as well as set performance targets to monitor their achievements, and clear accountability to both customers and providers of capital. PPPs are also said to have other benefits such as the transfer of management and technical skills of the private company to the public entity. Therefore, PPPs achieve improved infrastructure services, which shall in turn result in economic development.

Approach to hypothesis: Up to date, there has been limited PPP experience in Gulf Cooperation Council (GCC) countries and as the review of the economic performances of GCC countries in section "Assessment of PPPs in Infrastructure Services and Economy in GCC Countries" shows, they have continuously relied on oil and natural gas sectors, and thus, it can be said that the structure of economy has not changed. Since the public sector leads the oil and natural gas sectors, it can be said that GCC countries have achieved public-sector-led economic growth. However, such situation is unsustainable since the economy is vulnerable to price changes of oil and natural gas and external economic conditions. Thus, for GCC countries to achieve sustainable economic growth, less reliance on such sectors and an increased role of the private sector is essential. To achieve this, both hard and soft bases need to be settled: infrastructure services and governance to regulate the private sector.

As such, it is hypothesized that GCC countries perform low in infrastructure services as well as governance due to limited economic activities of the private sector. From understanding the above and that PPPs have the potential to improve the performances of infrastructure services, the aim of this chapter is to reveal the implications of PPPs in infrastructure development for economic diversification of GCC countries. Thus, the hypotheses to be investigated in this chapter are the three as follows:

- Infrastructure services in GCC countries lack coverage and are inefficient.
- GCC countries have not achieved economic diversification.
- GCC countries have low government performance.

The significance of this chapter lies in investigating the relevance of the three hypotheses in the context of GCC countries.

Research questions and data sources: The objective of this chapter is to reveal the implications of PPPs in infrastructure development for economic diversification of GCC countries. To achieve this, the research questions to be addressed are as follows:

- What are the performances of infrastructure services of GCC countries?
- How have the economies of GCC countries evolved over time?
- What are the performances of the governments of GCC countries?

In order to address the above questions, this chapter examines and assesses the performances of infrastructure services, economies and governments. In doing so, it explains the process through which PPPs achieve economic diversification as well as the relevance of regulation for the successful implementation of PPPs. It also explains why GCC countries have performed as they have.

As for data, the chapter utilizes various documentary sources, the World Development Indicators published by the World Bank as well as the World Governance Indicators jointly published by the World Bank and Brookings Institution.

Structure of chapter: Followed by this introductory section, the next section defines PPP, explains the process of how PPPs in infrastructure services achieve economic diversification as well as highlights the relevance of the design and implementation of regulation for successful implementation of PPPs. The third section then examines the performances of infrastructure services and the economies of GCC countries. The fourth section then assesses government performance of GCC countries to examine how capable they are in managing PPPs. Finally, the fifth section provides an overall summary and conclusion of this chapter.

THEORETICAL PERSPECTIVES ON PUBLIC-PRIVATE PARTNERSHIPS

Definition of PPP

PPP is an institutional arrangement for delivering services, under which the private sector is involved in some form, at some stage of the service delivery process (Nickson and Franceys 2003; United Nations 2008). It is a general term used to cover a wide range of private sector involvement, including the formal and informal sectors (Plummer 2000). PPPs may take forms such as service contracts, management contracts, lease contracts, concession contracts, joint venture arrangements and Build-Operate-Transfer (BOT) contracts (Nickson and Franceys 2003; United Nations 2008). The difference lies in the extent to which the private company retains responsibility for the provision of services and is summarized in Table 4.1. The table compares the six forms and shows the kind of responsibilities distributed between the private and public sector.

Table 4.1 shows that the concession contract offers the most involvement of the private sector while retaining asset ownership within the public sector. It can be said that the concession contract has the most potential to achieve overall improvements of services before returning responsibilities to the public sector. This is because the concession contract is the form that transfers most of the responsibilities (i.e. operation, maintenance, capital investment/network expansion) and risk—compared with other forms of PPP contracts—to the private company, while the ownership of assets is held by the public sector. Thus, the private company has an incentive to improve services in order to minimize commercial risk and maximize profit.

The Benefits of PPPs: The Process for Improved Services

PPPs are said to improve the provision of infrastructure services as well as extend the network by improving managerial and financial efficiency. The underlying assumption is that public-private partnership (PPP) is a strat-

Table 4.1 Comparison of PPP arrangements

	Service	Management	Lease	Concession	BOT	Joint venture
Asset ownership	Public	Public	Public	Public	Private and Public	Public and Private
Operations and maintenance	Public and Private	Private	Private	Private	Private	Public and Private
Capital investment	Public	Public	Public	Private	Private	Public and Private
Commercial risk	Public	Public	Private	Private	Private	Public and Private

Source: Developed by author

egy that overcomes public sector failures in providing services. This means that PPP improves the performance of services with respect to efficiency, effectiveness and equity, which results in improved service to customers. It is also said that PPP brings in investment and reduces the burden on public resources. This is because private entities, unlike public entities, have commercial principles and have financial and managerial autonomy and clear accountability to both customers and providers of capital. Thus, it is argued that the private sector has incentives to provide customer-focused services while minimizing the costs of personnel, maintenance and other administrative tasks to achieve cost recovery (Nickson and Franceys 2003). Thus, private companies set targets to monitor their achievements, and such targets enable customers and providers of capital to utilize them in order to assess and decide how to improve service delivery.

PPPs are also said to transfer technical and management skills of the private company to the public entity. This is because the public utility shall gradually increase its capacity by being involved in the process of preparing and implementing the PPP arrangement. This then results in enabling the public entity to operate as efficiently as the private company.

The Benefits of PPPs: The Process for Economic Diversification
PPPs in infrastructure development open markets and brings in competition to areas of what was under government control. Put differently, PPPs in infrastructure development is the deregulation—reducing or removing the role of the public sector—of infrastructure sectors and facilitating competition.

Since PPPs in infrastructure development invest in large infrastructure systems, it requires the inflow of people, goods and finance from the international market as well as from the domestic market. Thus, PPPs in infrastructure development require the deregulation in trade and investment policies. This then, in the long run, opens and develops new markets, facilitates competition for goods and services and, as a result, creates new cross boarder flows of people, goods and services with existing and new partners, increasing further economic transactions.

Even "small" investments (e.g. service contracts: the PPP arrangement that has the least involvement by a private company) also creates competition, for it allows the public sector to tap private sector expertise for specific tasks and opens them to competition (Uitto and Biswas 2000). Furthermore, in large urban areas, several such "small" contracts may be awarded in different parts of the city for the same service, thus creating comparative competition (Nickson and Franceys 2003).

Competition is the key driver for diversification. This is because competition facilitates private companies to minimize costs and maximize profits as well as develop goods and services that shall be valued by customers. This results in the development and facilitation of markets where there are diverse providers of diverse goods and services and the elimination of lucrative private monopolies. This in turn creates a diverse domestic market.

The fact that the private sector has increased discretion over providing infrastructure service means that it is necessary for the private company to be monitored and controlled to ensure that the service quality is at an acceptable level and that tariffs are at an affordable level to the customers. With regard to PPPs, it is necessary for governments to ensure that private companies fulfil the PPP contract's objective to not charge whatever price they wish because some PPP arrangements require private companies to take commercial risk (i.e. cost recovery via tariff revenues). Therefore, increased role of the private sector in the form of PPPs in infrastructure development requires the governments to perform such roles, which is regulation and the focus of the next section.

The Relevance of Regulation

Governments first need to set the institutional environment to enable PPPs in infrastructure development. This is to monitor private company's competition for entering the market, which is, for example, organizing bidding processes. Another important role is to ensure service quality in the market. This is to monitor private companies' performance, which is, for example, to establish and enforce penalties in the case of breach of standards of the PPP contract. Ensuring service quality in the market is particularly important since infrastructure services have a feature of natural monopoly. Under such circumstances, the private sector is likely to abuse their monopolistic power and provide whichever service they want at any charge. Therefore, regulation is necessary to ensure competition, service quality as well as adequate pricing.

In order to carry out such aspects of regulation, the regulatory framework, which lays out who does which regulation, needs to be clear. This is so that institutions are able to carry out their regulatory aspects to improve services for existing and future customers. The importance of regulation can be highlighted by the fact that foreign direct investment (FDI) in infrastructure responds positively to an effective domestic regulatory framework (Kirkpatrick et al. 2006).

However, since regulating the private sector in infrastructure services is a new role for governments, governments lack the ability to carry out regulation effectively (Batley and Larbi 2004). Regulation is a challenging task for governments since they are the owner, operator and regulator—a situation creating conflict of interest. Regulation is also a challenging task since PPPs create businesses as well as losers, which tempts private companies to influence government officials to corrupt practices. Therefore, it is ideally important to have an independent regulator, meaning to separate the role of regulator and service provider, to ensure better services to customers and given discretion to perform regulation.

The importance of an independent regulator can be exemplified by the case of the Jakarta water concessions of Indonesia. Although there was a regulator, it had no authority to make changes to tariffs and service quality standards. The regulator was able to enforce penalties in the case of breach of standards in the contracts, but the authority to decide the content of such penalties was held by the contractual parties. Thus, the regulator was far from being independent since it hardly had any authority in making changes to the service providers to improve service to customers. Jakarta's water remains to have high losses of approximately 40 per cent in the transmission and distribution network and has intermittent water supply. Therefore, the Jakarta water concessions are under criticism for not improving water services, or to put it another way, for not achieving the contractual obligations (Iwanami 2009).

The Jakarta case indicates that the important aspects of regulation are (1) the ability to design, make changes and implement regulation and (2) to enforce penalties for breach of the PPP contract so that the PPP achieves its targeted objectives. For regulation to be performed effectively as such, there is a need for good governance. Lack of good governance results in distorted design of regulation, let alone the PPP contracts, resulting in underperforming services (Tremolet and Hunt 2006). Thus, it is central that the institution that carries out regulation has an important role in recommending changes and adapting the way the regulatory framework is implemented.

A study using case studies of 30 Asian countries revealed that there is positive and significant relationship between better governance and better infrastructure services (ADB 2012). Good governance for regulation ensures that the institutional environment of PPP allows sufficient functioning of infrastructure services via the PPP arrangement, which as a result, enables economic development (ibid).

Assessment of PPPs in Infrastructure Services and Economy in GCC Countries

This section shall first reveal the performances of infrastructure services—water, sanitation, electricity, road, port and telecommunications—and then the characteristic of the economy of GCC counties.

Infrastructure Services of GCC Countries

Water supply and sanitation: Improved water supply and sanitation is not only crucial to ensure better health but economic activities as well as to avoid environmental degradation. Due to such importance, the accessibility to improved water source and sanitation are two of the various indicators of the Millennium Development Goals (MDGs).

GCC countries already have a high performance in water and sanitation. As of 2012, even the least performing country, Oman, had accessibility of approximately 90 per cent for water and 95 per cent for sanitation.

Electricity: Electricity is crucial for both household and business activities. Moreover, increasing efficiency in service provision to reduce losses is important since it minimizes the unit cost for generation (i.e. fuel cost) as well as allows the efficient use of the energy source. Efficient use of energy source is important since electricity generation can be based on fossil fuels, which are the main cause of air pollution and global warming.

GCC countries have, with the exception of Saudi Arabia, steadily increased electricity production. Regarding production sources, natural gas is the main source of electricity. Bahrain, Qatar and UAE have been relying 100 per cent on natural gas, while other countries have a mixture of oil and natural gas.

However, GCC countries lack efficiency in the provision for electricity since they have relatively high losses, particularly Oman and Kuwait, as they have losses of over 10 per cent. Moreover, it can be said that losses show an increasing trend for Kuwait and Saudi Arabia and a decreasing trend for Oman and Qatar.

Road: Roads enable increased access to markets, facilities, and services by bringing in and out people and products (e.g. natural resources and manufacture products) as well as competition and information by being exposed to the outer environment. Roads have a clear impact on increasing productivity and employment and therefore, it is important that road networks are developed and made available.

Despite such importance of roads, there is a large difference of the availability of paved road. Oman and Saudi Arabia have less than 50 per cent of their roads paved, whereas other countries have over 70 per cent of their roads paved.

Port: The availability of ports as well as its efficient operation is crucial for timely export and import of goods, facilitating trade as well as reducing trade costs. The indicator "Quality of Port Infrastructure" is used to understand the performance of ports, which score ranges from one to seven, with the highest score being seven. The Quality of Port Infrastructure measures business executives' perception of their country's port facilities. Data are from the World Economic Forum's Executive Opinion Survey. A score of one means "extremely underdeveloped", and a score of seven means "efficient by international standards". Data were available for GCC countries from 2007 to 2013 (WB 2015).

Scores differ amongst GCC countries but have generally continued to be constant for the past seven years, with UAE scoring the highest and Kuwait scoring the lowest. As of 2013, UAE scored 6.4 and Kuwait scored 4.1. Since the world average was 4.2 for 2013, it can be said that GCC countries are performing above world standards.

Telecommunications: Being able to use the Internet nowadays has become vital since it facilitates the efficiency of all economic activities. It is important to design and build systems to help economies be more competitive in international markets.

GCC countries have been developing systems but there is a large disparity amongst GCC countries. As of 2013, the highest was Bahrain with 13.15 per 100 people, and the lowest was Kuwait with 1.39. Since the world average is 9.4, and developed nations such as Europe and the Americas are at 27.7, it can be said that GCC countries perform below world standards.

Summary: Table 4.2 summarizes the latest performance of infrastructure services of GCC countries as of 2013.

All countries show a high performance regarding water and sanitation. As for electricity, GCC countries have increased its production but have

Table 4.2 Comparison of infrastructure performances of GCC countries as of 2013

	Water (per cent)	Sanitation (per cent)	Electricity (kWh)	Elec. losses (per cent)	Road paved (per cent)	Port ($1 < a < 7$)	Internet (per 100 connections)
Bahrain	100	99.2	1.38 + E10	7.19	83.6	5.8	13.15
Kuwait	99	100	5.75 + E10	12.32	85	4.1	1.39
Oman	93	96.6	2.19 + E10	12.99	49.2	5.5	2.62
Qatar	100	100	3.07 + E10	2.03	90	5.2	9.936
Saudi Arabia	97	100	2.50 + E11	9.40	21.47	5.1	7.35
UAE	99.6	97.5	9.91 + E10	7.30	100	6.4	11.11

Source: WB 2015

high losses. As for road and telecommunications, there is a wide disparity amongst GCC countries, and thus further improvements are particularly necessary in these sectors. As for ports, GCC countries have similar performances.

By country, Oman performs lower in comparison to other GCC countries since it has high electricity losses, has fewer than half of its roads paved and has a low fixed broadband subscription rate. On the other hand, Bahrain and UAE are the higher performers amongst GCC countries.

Economic Performances of GCC Countries

This section now reveals the characteristics of the economy of GCC countries by looking at such countries' performance of gross domestic product (GDP), oil and natural gas rents, exports of goods and services, and fuel exports as well. Figure 4.1 shows the GDP of GCC countries during 1990–2013.

GDP has been expanding and its pattern of expansion reflects GCC countries' sensitivity to external economic conditions. That is, for example, the economic growth from 2005 to 2008 was associated with large oil rents, which is a reflection of increasing oil and natural gas prices shown in Figs. 4.2 and 4.3. The economic downturn thereafter was due to the global economic crisis as well as decreasing oil prices. Figure 4.2 shows the oil rents as a percentage of GDP as well as oil prices of GCC countries during 1990–2012. Figure 4.3 shows the natural gas rents as percentage

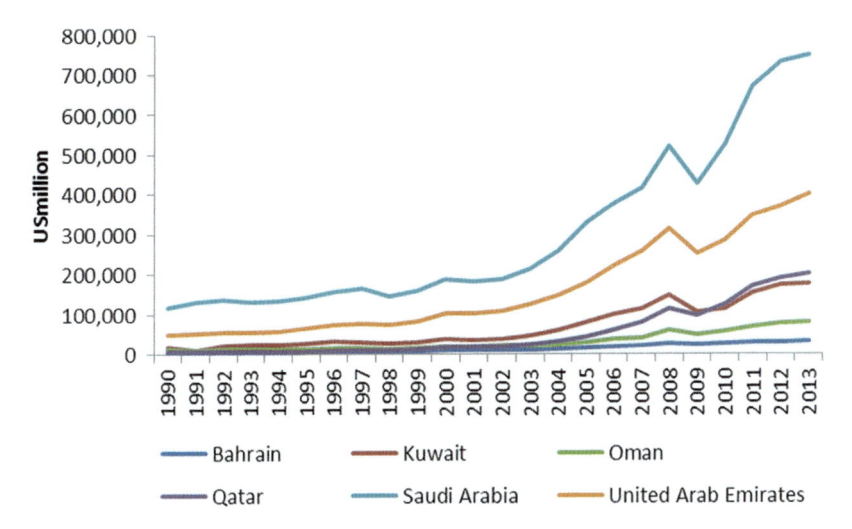

Fig. 4.1 GDP of GCC countries during 1990–2013. Source: WB 2015

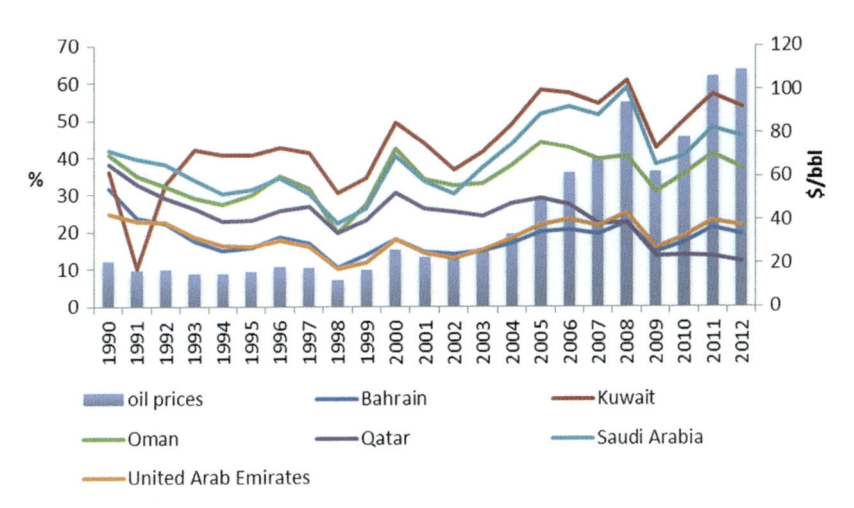

Fig. 4.2 Oil rents (per cent of GDP) and oil prices of GCC countries during 1990–2012. Source: IMF (International Monetary Fund) Primary Commodity Prices 2015 and WB 2015

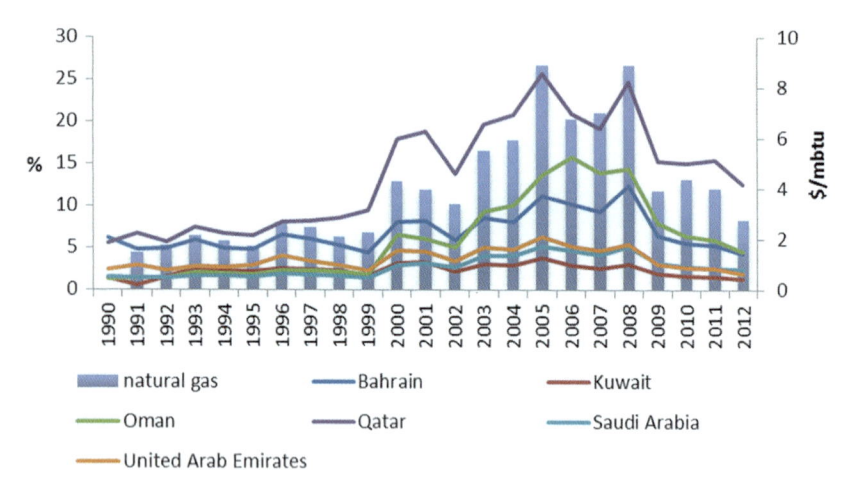

Fig. 4.3 Natural gas rents (per cent of GDP) of GCC countries during 1990–2012. Source: IMF Primary Commodity Prices 2015 and WB 2015

of GDP as well as natural gas prices of GCC countries during 1990–2012. Regarding their respective prices, Dubai crude is used for oil and Henry Hub for natural gas.

Both figures also show rents fluctuate in line to changes in their respective prices. It can be said that Kuwait, Oman and Saudi Arabia largely depend on oil and Qatar largely depends on natural gas.

Moreover, Figs. 4.4 and 4.5 show that GCC countries rely on exports and particularly on fuel exports (i.e. oil and natural gas) and this reliance has not changed over time. GCC countries rely approximately more than 50 per cent on exports and approximately more than 80 per cent consist of fuel exports or goods exports.

It can be said that countries that are abundant with natural resource have an advantage in being able to offer its existing asset rather than developing a new asset but have a disadvantage in that these countries are vulnerable to price changes and external economic conditions. Therefore, it is vital that they strengthen other sectors of their own economy by creating an institutional environment that encourages competition, thus increasing the efficiency of the market.

To do so, not only it is necessary to develop new industries, but rather it is necessary to open existing sectors of the economy that are reasonably developed and held responsible by the public sector, which is infrastruc-

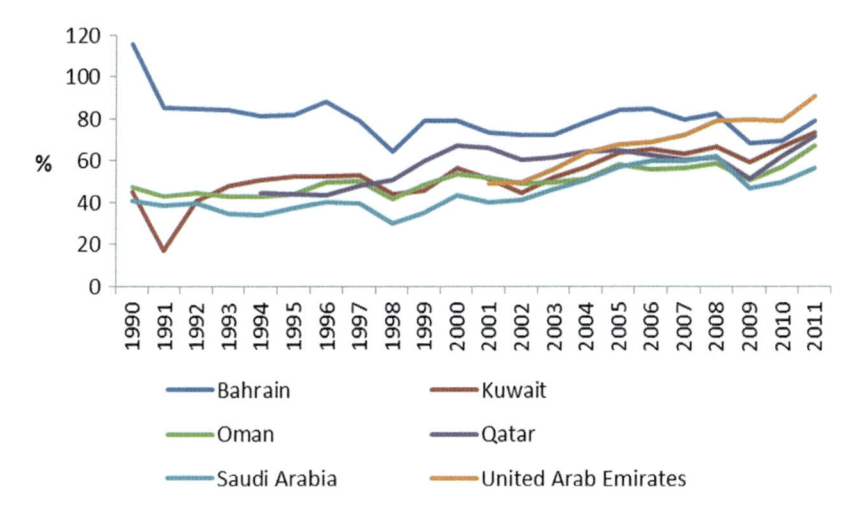

IMPLICATIONS OF PUBLIC-PRIVATE PARTNERSHIPS IN INFRASTRUCTURE... 89

Fig. 4.4 Exports of goods and services (per cent of GDP) from GCC countries during 1990–2011. Source: WB 2015

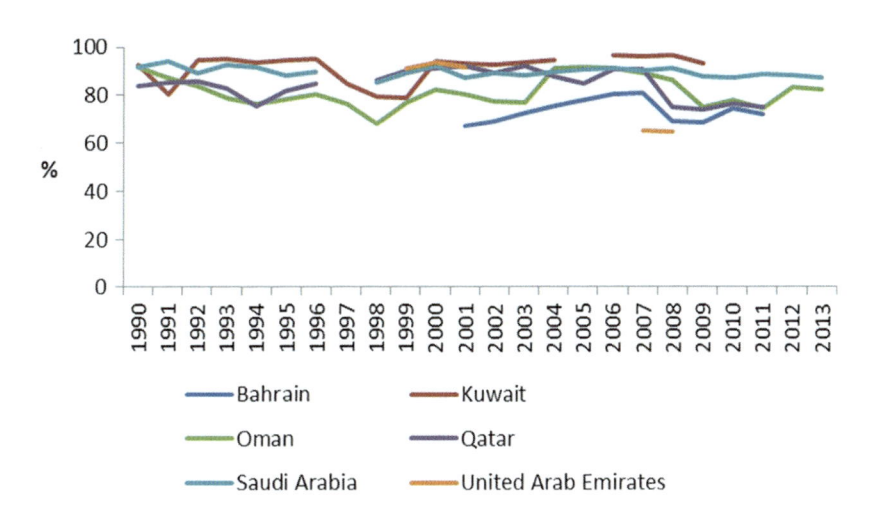

Fig. 4.5 Fuel exports (per cent of goods exports) from GCC countries during 1990–2013. Source: WB 2015

ture. As section "Infrastructure Services of GCC Countries" has shown, infrastructure services already have a relatively high performance, but there is room for expansion and for improving the quality of such services.

Assessment of Government Performances in GCC Countries

This section assesses the government performances of GCC countries to reveal the extent to which they are able to manage PPPs. To do so, the Worldwide Governance Indicators (WGIs)—developed by Brookings Institution and the World Bank—are used since they portray aspects of quality of governance. The definitions of each indicator are extracted from Kaufmann et al. (2010). There are six of them: (1) control of corruption, (2) government effectiveness, (3) political stability and absence of violence/terrorism, (4) regulatory quality, (5) rule of law and (6) voice and accountability. WDIs cover a 15-year period from 1996 to 2013.

Followed by describing GCC countries' government performance by each indicator, the average overall government performance during 1996–2013 of each GCC country and the status of 2013 (the lasted available) is shown.

Control of corruption: Control of corruption shows the extent to which public power is exercised for private gain, including both petty and grand forms of corruption, as well as "capture" of the state by elites and private interests.

Corruption negatively affects the economy and society. It is considered one of the major obstacles to do business, having a clear negative correlation between both investment and economic growth. It also brings in resentment amongst citizens, in some cases causing fall of governments. Amongst GCC countries, Qatar and UAE rank high while Saudi Arabia and Kuwait rank low.

Government effectiveness: Government effectiveness shows the quality of public services, the quality of the civil service and the degree of its independence from political pressures, the quality of policy formulation and implementation, and the credibility of the government's commitment to such policies. As of 2013, Qatar and UAE rank relatively high and Kuwait and Saudi Arabia rank relatively low.

Political stability and absence of violence/terrorism: Political stability and absence of violence/terrorism shows the likelihood that the government will be destabilized or overthrown by unconstitutional or violent means, including politically motivated violence and terrorism.

Instability of a country is a constraint in performing business activities since changes in governments may be accompanied with policy changes in the business environment. There is a large disparity amongst GCC countries with a widening trend with Bahrain showing a decreasing trend. Once again, Qatar and UAE are the high performers, with Qatar showing an improving trend and performing well, while UAE's performance has remained stable.

Regulatory quality: Regulatory quality shows the ability of the government to formulate and implement sound policies and regulations that permit and promote private sector development. As mentioned in previous sections, the ability to design, make changes and implement regulation is central to ensure the realization of the PPPs' intended objectives; therefore, regulatory quality is an important governance aspect with regard to PPPs. Oman, Kuwait and Qatar show an improving trend, whist other countries have performed steadily.

Rule of law: Rule of law shows the extent to which agents have confidence in and abide by the rules of society, and in particular the quality of contract enforcement, property rights, the police, and the courts, as well as the likelihood of crime and violence. The enforcing of the rule of law is important to ensure security and protection in carrying out business and individual activities. GCC countries have perform similarly and remained stable.

Voice and accountability: Voice and accountability shows the extent to which a country's citizens are able to participate in selecting their government, as well as freedom of expression, freedom of association and free media. People having more voice narrows the gap between people and governments, which in turn allows governments to create policies which are responsive to the needs of the society. A declining trend can be seen in this aspect across GCC countries, with Saudi Arabia having the least voice and accountability and Kuwait having the most voice and accountability.

Overall government performance: Now that the above has revealed each of the six aspects of government performance of GCC countries, Fig. 4.6 shows the trend of the average percentile rank of the six aspects of GCC countries to understand how countries have performed overall during the monitored period of 1996–2013. The lower the percentile rank, the lower the performance.

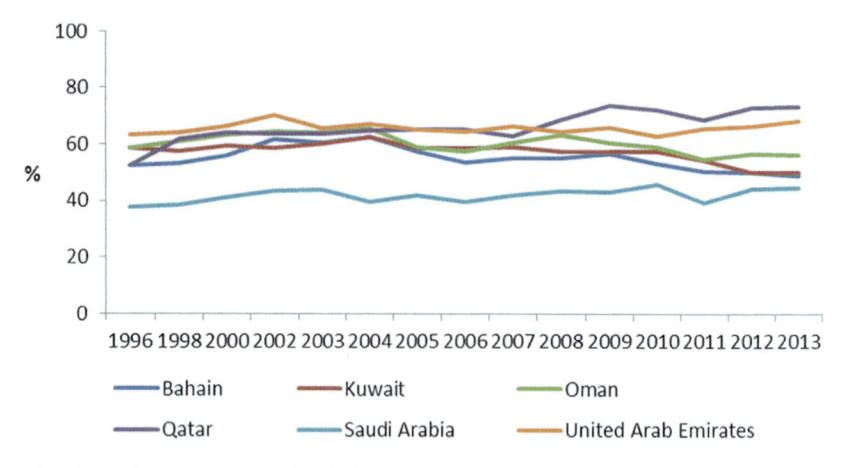

Fig. 4.6 Average percentile of all six WDIs of GCC countries during 1996–2013. Source: WB and Brookings Institution 2015

Table 4.3 Government performances of GCC countries as of 2013

	Bahrain	Kuwait	Oman	Qatar	Saudi Arabia	UAE
Control of corruption (per cent)	69	54	60	85	58	88
Government effectiveness (per cent)	70	52	61	81	57	83
Political stability and absence of violence/terrorism (per cent)	9	52	63	92	34	76
Regulatory quality (per cent)	71	50	67	74	55	75
Rule of law (per cent)	62	63	67	83	61	71
Voice and accountability (per cent)	12	28	19	24	3	18
Total (per cent)	293	300	337	439	268	411

Source: WB and Brookings Institution 2015

Overall, it can be said that GCC countries' performance has not significantly increased nor decreased over time. As of 2013, Qatar was the highest performer and Saudi Arabia was the lowest performer.

Latest government performance as of 2013: As Table 4.3 shows, all GCC countries which performed low in terms of voice and accountability have a large disparity in political stability and absence of violence/terrorism. Initially, there was a large difference in control of corruption, but they show a narrowing trend. Regarding government effectiveness and rule of law, GCC countries performed similarly. As for regulatory quality—the key governance aspect with regard to PPPs—Bahrain, Qatar and UAE are the high performers. Moreover, the table reveals that overall low government performance is not necessarily associated with low performance in each of the governance aspects.

Summary and Conclusion

Summary of Findings

The objective of this chapter was to reveal the implications of PPPs in infrastructure development for economic diversification.

To achieve this objective, section "Theoretical Perspectives on Public-Private Partnerships" first defined what PPP is and explained the process of how PPPs in infrastructure development enables economic diversification. It also explained the importance of design and implementation of regulation for its successful implementation.

Section "Assessment of PPPs in Infrastructure Services and Economy in GCC Countries" then examined the performances of infrastructure services as well as the economy to understand how GCC countries have developed. As a result, it revealed that GCC countries already have a relatively high performance of infrastructure services, but is subjected to expansion and improvement of service quality and its efficiency. Oman performed lower in comparison to other GCC countries since it has high electricity losses, has fewer than half of its roads paved and has a low fixed broadband subscription rate. On the other hand, Bahrain and UAE were the higher performers.

Section "Assessment of PPPs in Infrastructure Services and Economy in GCC Countries" also revealed that GCC countries achieved economic growth rather than diversification. GCC countries continue to rely on oil and natural gas sectors; such situation becomes a risk since GCC countries shall be vulnerable to external economic conditions and to price changes of oil and natural gas. Therefore, to reduce such risk, GCC countries need to create a business environment that enables competition by opening existing sectors of the economy that are responsible by the public sectors to the private sectors, which is the infrastructure sector. This is because, as mentioned above, there is room for expansion and improvement of quality of such services.

Section "Assessment of Government Performances in GCC Countries" then reviewed government performance of GCC countries to assess how capable they are in managing PPPs. Government performance was assessed using the WGIs, which covers six aspects of governance: (1) control of corruption, (2) government effectiveness, (3) political stability and absence of violence/terrorism, (4) regulatory quality, (5) rule of law and (6) voice and accountability.

As a result, overall government performance shows that Qatar and UAE have the highest potential of being able to manage PPPs but Bahrain also for its high regulatory quality.

But what raises concern is that "voice and accountability" was low for all countries with a decreasing trend, indicating that GCC countries are less able to meet the needs of their society—a fundamental role—and thus raises concern whether they shall be able to perform a new role involving regulation.

Conclusion

Drawing from the findings, this chapter concludes that GCC countries have the potential to benefit from PPPs in infrastructure development, not only through improvement of such services but also by achieving economic diversification via increased competition. Nevertheless, GCC countries do not necessarily have or have developed the ability to carry out regulation effectively, which is a challenge for GCC countries with respect to successful implementation of PPPs. This is not only because regulation is a new role for governments, but also because voice and accountability for GCC countries is low; this indicates that there are not sufficient channels of mechanisms to shape policies to better reflect society's needs. The explanation for low voice and accountability can be derived from the structure of the economy of GCC countries. That is, as was explained in section "Assessment of PPPs in Infrastructure Services and Economy in GCC Countries", GCC countries largely rely on their oil and gas sector and thus weaken the incentives to reform their economy, since they are able to gain from its endowments without endeavouring to strengthen the non-oil sectors of the economy. To put it another way, to increase voice and accountability, GCC countries need to exercise in partnership with businesses and citizens to shape policies which address their needs. Thus, in the long run, PPPs in infrastructure development strengthen governments through the process of preparation and implementation of PPPs, increasing voice and accountability, in addition to infrastructure development and economic diversification.

REFERENCES

Asian Development Bank (ADB). (2012). *Infrastructure for supporting inclusive growth and poverty reduction in Asia*. Mandaluyong City: Asian Development Bank.

Batley, R., & Larbi, G. (2004). *The changing role of the government: The reform of public services in developing countries.* New York: Palgrave Macmillan.

International Monetary Fund (IMF). (2015). *Primary commodity prices.* Retrieved April 9, 2015, from http://www.imf.org/external/np/res/commod/index.aspx

Iwanami, M. (2009). *Ensuring improved service delivery for customers: The case of the Jakarta water concessions.* Ph.D. dissertation, University of Birmingham.

Kaufmann, D., Kraay, A., & Mastruzzi, M. (2010). *The worldwide governance indicators: Methodology and analytical issues.* Policy Research Working Chapter 5430. Washington, DC: The World Bank.

Kirkpatrick, C., Parker, D., & Zhang, Y. (2006). Foreign direct investment in infrastructure in developing countries: Does regulation make a difference? *Transnational Corporations, 15*(1).

Nickson, A., & Franceys, R. (2003). *Tapping the market. The challenge of institutional reform in the urban water sector.* New York: Palgrave Macmillan.

Plummer, J. (2000). *Municipalities & community participation—A sourcebook for capacity building.* London: Earthscan Publications.

Tremolet, S., & Hunt, C. (2006). *Taking account of the poor in water sector regulation.* Water Supply & Sanitation Working Notes No. 11. Washington, DC: The World Bank.

Uitto, J. I., & Biswas, A. K. (2000). *Water for urban areas. Challenges and perspectives.* Tokyo: United Nations University Press.

United Nations (UN). (2008). *Guidebook on promoting good governance in Public-Private Partnerships.* Geneva: United Nations.

World Bank (WB). (2015). *World development indicators.* Retrieved April 6, 2015, from http://databank.worldbank.org/data/views/variableSelection/selectvariables.aspx?source=world-development-indicators

WB and Brookings Institution. (2015). *Worldwide governance indicators.* Retrieved May 7, 2015, from http://info.worldbank.org/governance/wgi/index.aspx#home

CHAPTER 5

Quality of Education and Labour Market in Saudi Arabia

Ashraf Mishrif and Amal Alabduljabbar

INTRODUCTION

Education plays a central role in preparing individuals to enter the labour force, as well as equipping them with the skills to engage in lifelong learning experiences. The speech by King Salman, as he ascended to the throne in early 2015, reinforced his government's commitment to improving the opportunities and quality of education (Abdulaziz 2015). Despite such commitment, progress has been slow in the Saudi education system. This chapter examines the relationship between the quality of the education system and the efficiency of the labour market in Saudi Arabia, with particular focus on the impact of this relationship on the success and failure of the country's economic diversification strategy. It examines the extent to which the significant investments and increases in the budget have improved the quality of primary and higher education, and whether this has improved the efficiency of the labour market. Initial assessment reveals a mismatch between the needs of the labour market and the type of graduate coming out of the education system.

A. Mishrif (✉) • A. Alabduljabbar
King's College London, London, UK

© Gulf Research Centre Cambridge 2018
A. Mishrif, Y. Al Balushi (eds.), *Economic Diversification in the Gulf Region, Volume I*, The Political Economy of the Middle East,
https://doi.org/10.1007/978-981-10-5783-0_5

To explain such mismatch, this chapter explores the Saudi societal, cultural and macroeconomic contexts, which influence the school-to-work transition and the decision-making in the education system. This system is hugely affected by the characteristics of all stakeholders, including children, their families, schools, community and society. Although government has direct supervision over the majority of schools, one could argue that an individual's family and community, school characteristics, time spent in the education system and the type of education determine the quantity and quality of education. In addition, a general versus a technical educational path has strong repercussions on labour market entry. Thus, important educational outcomes should include cognitive and technical skills, general and specific knowledge, and values that help prepare individuals to enjoy healthy, productive and fulfilling lives. The acquisition of such attributes may differentiate between the holders of good degrees and educational or professional training who end up in good jobs and those who have low or no education and remain professionally inactive or unemployed.

The above discussion raises a critical question on how and to what extent does the quality of education affect the efficiency of the labour market? This question is addressed through a case study approach, where we examine the nature and determinants affecting the relationship between the education system and labour market in Saudi Arabia. Why has the Saudi education system failed to provide high-quality education for its citizens? What is the outcome of the huge capital investment in education? Why has the quality of education remained low, despite having one of the highest education budget, estimated at around 30 per cent of GDP in 2013–2014? Why has the Saudi education system been unable to produce competent and productive generations that can meet the demand of the private sector and compete in the increasingly globalized marketplace? While examining these critical questions, this chapter also attempts to look into whether the low quality of the educational system and the labour market, with its high dependence on foreign labour, a by-product of the rentier state mentality and Saudi culture. The institutional settings and the levels of coordination between the Ministry of Education and the Ministry of Labour, as well as the Saudization programme, are also examined.

Previous studies on Saudi Arabia underscore the weak link between the education system output and the needs of the economic sectors, especially the private sector that requires high skilled labour (Achoui 2009; McEvers 2009). This assumption receives some attention here with the aim of analysing how the failure of previous efforts to improve the education system contributed to lack of efficiency of the labour market and hampered the success of the Saudization programme. The effects of recent investments in education between 2009 and 2015 are also analysed in light of their objectives to improve the quality of the Saudi labour force and its employability nationally and internationally. The aim is to identify the various ways in which the quality of education is linked to the quality of the labour market, and how this could enhance the country's capacity to implement successful economic diversification.

One significant aspect of this study is that it underlines the imbalances between the education output and labour market needs in a country where 84 per cent of all Saudi PhD holders are women, yet the rate of unemployment is also the highest among women. This kind of deficiency raises the question of whether the quality of the education system is the only reason behind Saudis' lack of participation in the workforce, or whether questions of culture, tradition, oil wealth and the rentier mentality are also involved. Another aspect that could hamper economic diversification is the preference of Saudi employers to employ foreign workers at the expense of Saudi citizens. Such preference by the private sector raises doubt on whether Saudi citizens are properly prepared for the job market. Meanwhile, analysis indicates that the rentier mentality, job security, Saudi labour laws and subsidies have rendered the public sector and made it more attractive for Saudi citizens. Addressing such deficiencies and imbalances requires more than just investment in physical infrastructure in education; it requires investment in human development in terms of knowledge, transferable skills, work ethic, reliability, dedication and efficiency.

EDUCATION DEVELOPMENT IN SAUDI ARABIA

Formal education in Saudi Arabia began with elementary education in the 1920s, while secondary and intermediate schooling opened in the early 1940s. Higher education started in 1953, and technical and vocational education only began in 1961 (Mahdi 2000). Education in Saudi Arabia is free at all levels. The school system is composed of elementary, intermediate and secondary schools. A large part of the curriculum at all levels is devoted to religious studies; and at the secondary level, students are able to follow either a religious or a technical track. The rate of literacy between 2008 and 2012 reached up to about 99 per cent among males and is about

97 per cent among females (UNICEF 2013). Classes are segregated by gender. Higher education has expanded rapidly, with large numbers of universities and colleges being founded particularly since 2000. Institutions of higher education include the country's first university, King Saud University founded in 1957, the Islamic University at Medina founded in 1961, and the King Abdulaziz University in Jeddah founded in 1967. Other colleges and universities emphasize curricula in sciences and technology, military studies, religion and medicine. Institutes devoted to Islamic studies, in particular, abound. Women typically receive college instruction in segregated institutions. Education in Saudi Arabia has until recently been synonymous with religious education and was seen as a vehicle for spreading the teachings of Islam.

In 2010, *The Chronicle of Higher Education* argued "the country needs educated young Saudis with marketable skills and a capacity for innovation and entrepreneurship. That is not generally what Saudi Arabia's educational system delivers, steeped as it is in rote learning and religious instruction." This is reiterated in a BBC report (2010) over lessons to Saudi students in the UK and in a report by Freedom House (2006), which argued that the "Saudi public school religious curriculum continues to propagate an outdated, even medieval ideology. Education only slowly became secularized, with the rapid rise in literacy rates being an enormous achievement. From 15 per cent in men and 2 per cent in women in 1970, literacy increased to 73 per cent and 48 per cent respectively in the 1990s."

Thus, the aim of the Saudi government is to tackle the inadequacy of the country's university education by slowly modernizing the education system through the Tatweer education programme. The commitment to such modernization is seen in the increase the Tatweer programme budget from approximately US$2.5 billion in 2009 to US$21 billion in 2014, with the aim of shifting teaching away from the traditional methods of memorization and rote learning towards analysis and problem-solving. It also aimed to create an education system that provides a more secular and vocationally based training (Chronicle of Higher Education 2010).

As Saudi Arabia embarked on its educational journey, quantitative development was a top priority for government. As a result, large numbers of students joined the education system. Over the years, the surge in the number of students, teachers and schools was hailed as a great success. As was the case in all GCC countries, the provision of education was part of the social contract between the government and its citizens. Education is viewed as a good way to invest the oil wealth; in Saudi Arabia about 26 per cent of the annual budget is dedicated to education and training. The substantial investment in education resulted in significant increases in the number of Saudi students in primary, intermediate and secondary schools. Over the past 40 years, the number of students increased by about 1200 per cent prior to 2009, the number of teachers increased by more than 1850 per cent and the number of schools by almost 1050 per cent (Al Munajjed and Sabbagh 2010). This enormous quantitative development is a great success, another being the massive increase in literacy among the youth (those aged from 15 to 24).

This increase in numbers brought concomitant problems relating to the quality of primary education, enrolment and quality of graduate and postgraduate education and the job market in the country. Attempts to address deficiencies in the quality of several aspects of education have yet focused on curricula, teaching methods, information technology, and soft and hard skills (Al Munajjed and Sabbagh 2010). However, repetition and dropout rates remain very high, reaching an average of 18 per year in boys and 15 in girls. Achoui (2009) argues that the "rapid growth in the number of secondary stage graduates is a major challenge, with serious economic and social implications." There have been a growing number of poorly prepared graduates entering the job market. In addition, the rise in secondary-level graduation needed to be accompanied by an increase in higher educational opportunities for graduates, especially in the case of girls (World Economic Forum 2010). This was successfully addressed by Higher Education Institutions, which offered places to more than 90 per cent of secondary school graduates in 2009 (Ninth Development Plan 2009).

As of the quality of educational leadership, there have been some concerns relating to the quality and composition of the teaching staff and the quality of the curriculum and instruction. Instruction methods that put more emphasis on memorization or rote learning rather than analytical skills have failed to equip graduates to effectively participate in today's world with its rapid advances in technology. The overall administration of education is unwieldy and top-heavy, with the Ministry of Education being congested with former teachers and administrative staff. This situation has arisen from a perception that teaching is a profession with low status. This probably was the reason why the teaching profession had been predominantly occupied by non-Saudi teachers and administrators in the past. The quality of technical and vocational training was quite poor, and did not keep pace with developments in primary and secondary education. A variety of programmes including industrial, commercial and agricultural training was offered, and all suffered from high dropout rates. Of the

80,000 enrolled in industrial education at the start of the plan, only 24 per cent graduated.

Saudi Labour Market

In Saudi Arabia, the labour market is largely formal as the government encourages small and medium enterprises. The economic structure of the country that is dominated by the oil industry makes this industry a major sector for employment. This is followed by the agricultural sector, comprising both traditional and modern farms, which gets a great deal of public finance and subsidies. Other sectors for employment are construction, transport, communication and other infrastructure projects. In fact, about 48 per cent of the Saudi labour force are now employed in managerial and defence in the public sector. Teachers are mostly female. Agriculture employs significant numbers of Saudis, but not many are employed in manufacturing. As for non-Saudis, the majority of foreign workers are employed in the private sector, mainly construction, domestic services and vehicle maintenance. There are a number of foreign teachers, although the numbers are declining. About 12 per cent of non-Saudis are employed in manufacturing (Mahdi 2000).

The Saudi labour market is highly segmented, as the demand side is not balanced by the supply of labour. This is also true in terms of unequal distribution of jobs between men and women. Saudi graduates tend to prefer jobs in the administrative sectors, whereas the market requires numbers of workers qualified in technical subjects, particularly given the rate of technological change in today's world. High dropout rates combined with restricted university enrolment and the poor quality of public and university education have created a problem for the labour market. The public sector is unable to accommodate the numbers of prospective employees into administrative jobs, while the private sector is unwilling to take on the cost of recruiting and training the under-skilled Saudi staff. This resulted in most citizens employed in the public sector, whereas expatriates hold most of the private sector jobs. Such segregation caused the uncompromising position of nationals to take up less prestigious jobs and the preference of the private sector companies to employ foreign workers at wages and employment conditions that are unattractive to Saudis (G20 2011). Statistics show that expatriate labour makes up two-thirds of the workforce, with over 88 per cent being in the private sector. The country loses significant revenue in remittances, as foreign workers repatriate large portions of the money they earn.

The Ministry of Labour is working towards amending the labour laws and modifying regulations regarding the issuing of expat working visas and the minimum wages offered to them. However, the issue of skills and training is still a long way from being overcome. Private sector employers mention many issues relating to the employment of Saudis, most of which are connected to their skills and training, and the lack thereof. They identified lack of specializations, lack of practice and insufficient soft skills as issues that prevent them from employing Saudi citizens. Rapid technological change means that the Saudi job market lacks science and technology graduates and is over-supplied with graduates from the humanities and social sciences. Science and technology are essential for the development of key industries, including water engineering and alternative energy sources. Transport planning and logistics can benefit from specializations.

Moreover, graduates are generally not given enough practical experience to fit them for the business world. There are few work placement and training opportunities and collaboration between educational institutions and the private sector is very weak. The educational system does not equip students with the soft skills required in the job market, as "graduates from all levels of the education system lack training in soft skills such as leadership, team motivation, project management, problem solving, communication, and negotiation" (Human Capital Challenges in Saudi Arabia 2009).

The effect of lack of specialist knowledge and experience on nationals in the private sector is significant, as many Saudis are losing jobs to better skilled and less costly expatriates. The social impact of such outcome has prompted the Ministry of Labour to apply stringent Saudization rules on private enterprises to increase the number of Saudis on their payrolls. This solution does not really address the main reasons why Saudis remain unemployable. Forcing Saudization policies on unwilling employers can only be a short-term solution and will not increase productivity. Hertog (2006) argues that "while the policy's intentions are commendable, it is incompatible with moves towards increasing the international competitiveness of the Saudi private sector." What is actually needed is to provide the Saudi labour force with the appropriate education and training that could give them the capability to compete with foreign workers over private sector jobs. Another challenge to the labour market is the demographic structure of the country, where over 60 per cent of the Saudi population is under 18 years of age. This significant demographic change, together with oil dependency, poses serious challenge for the Saudi workforce and the education system. In fact, the education system is faced with the need to accommodate a rapidly growing number of students, while maintaining the quality of the service. The deterioration of the system, along with a consumer culture and a rentier mentality, has created an employment crisis in the country.

Indeed, the challenges to overcome labour market deficiencies are huge. The educational system is expected to improve its services and outputs in order to facilitate economic diversification and develop human resources in order to be able to compete in the global marketplace. As labour organizations and trade unions are non-existent in Saudi Arabia, it is the government's responsibility to devise new policies that allow for institutional development and effective communication and coordination between the Ministry of Education and Ministry of Labour in a way that improves the quality of educational outputs and labour force. This is necessary if the diversification strategy is to succeed. Saudi government has also begun to feel the pain of the decline of oil price, which, together with the subsidies and benefits system, has created fiscal pressures and expectations of what governments should deliver at a time when the current political and economic system is not sustainable (Kinninmont 2015). The government has spent its resources on stabilizing political pressures rather than investing in growth and development to the extent that it could overtake both revenue and output.

Mismatch Between Education Output and Labour Market Needs

The commitment and determination to human capital development is evident in the details of recent Saudi national development plans. The Ninth Development Plan (2010–2015) has had a clear mandate to develop a "knowledge based economy and consolidate the basis of an information society" (Ninth National Development Plan 2009). Half of the expenditure of the Plan's US$385 billion was devoted to human resources development, including education and training. What impact has this kind of investment made on the efficiency of Saudi labour force?

Despite the considerable investment made in education and training, the degree of harmony between the education system and the labour market has been modest. This is evident in a survey done by Booz & Company in 2010 measuring young people's satisfaction with their educational systems in the GCC. The survey shows that when it comes to the quality of their education, "the primary beneficiaries of the GCC's education expansion are not happy. Today's youth are deeply concerned about financial insecurity and unemployment" (Al Munajjed and Sabbagh 2010). Many of these individuals believe that their education is not preparing them properly for future jobs, indicating an overall perception of a mismatch between the educational system and the market place. This creates a sense of frustration with the education they are receiving (Fasih 2008). Employers express similar concerns about not only shortcomings in the technical and business skills of potential employees but also issues concerning professionalism and work ethics.

Attempts to bridge the gap between secondary school and university level requirements have led to the introduction of foundation-year programmes in many public and private universities. These programmes are equivalent to the first year of university education, but tend to focus more on soft skills such as communications, languages, computer and self-development (Asmari 2008). Such skills are necessary for university as well as preparation for the workplace. The programmes rely on private education providers outside the university teaching staff, but under the supervision of the university administration. Students are given placement tests at the beginning of the programme, and they take part in international certification examinations to measure their level of improvement on completion. At the university level, students lack opportunities to gain practical experience in their subjects; the educational curriculum is not in line with the requirements of the job market, and the teachers still use traditional teaching methods which emphasize repetition and memorization or rote learning. Skills like creative thinking, problem-solving and personal initiative—that are of value in the workplace—are not cultivated in the classrooms (Al Munajjed and Sabbagh 2010).

Achieving harmony between educational and training curricula and the requirements on the ground at the workplace has been one of Saudi Arabia's biggest challenges for human development. The labour market requirements are changing rapidly, and "the economy is increasingly driven by competition, information and knowledge, particularly in scientific and technical areas" (Achoui 2009). This makes this challenge of developing Saudi human resources even more pressing, as it is vital to its economic security. The government's plans to expand higher education, especially for women, have not matched the requirements of the private sector job market. Employers complain about the large number of academics and the lack of capable technicians. In addition, employees are great at day-to-day tasks but have inadequate problem-solving skills. This is illustrated by a comment made by a Saudi executive, who argues, "our universities graduate good accountants, but not financial managers" (Human Capital Challenge 2009).

The Crisis of Youth Unemployment

Another issue facing the country is youth unemployment. By 2012, over a million Saudis were unemployed, and of these, at least 29 per cent are women (Nagraj 2012). This is why the government had to introduce the *Hafiz* programme of unemployment benefits in 2011. Indeed, the rise in youth unemployment is a historical issue since the drop in oil revenues, which occurred in the second half of the 1980s and caused employment rates to stagnate. This problem is accelerated by the advancement in technology and changes to the production processes, which in turn require new skills. In an interview with Wall Street Journal, Mishrif (2013) argues that such skills are not provided by Saudi schools (Knickmeyer 2013). Eventually, the government has been unable to employ all the poorly skilled graduates within the public sector. Planning to deal with this issue has not also been based on informed decision-making (Hertog 2006).

However, one has to stress here that the issue of youth unemployment is not due largely to lack of jobs, but largely to social consideration. In fact, young Saudis have grown up amidst vast oil-boom wealth and high expectations of job opportunities in the public sector or well-paid, high-status private-sector jobs, which are no longer to be found (Kinninmont 2015). The oil wealth has given rise to a mentality whereby young people expect to have jobs, which are undemanding. Saudi Arabia bases part of its claim to legitimacy on its role as a provider of welfare and benefits for its citizens. With sharp decline in oil prices since the start of 2015, the country is beginning to have trouble in meeting the expectations of the younger generation and maintain its generous welfare system. In light of high population growth and relative decline in hydrocarbon resources, the government is concerned about its capacity to deliver in the long run (Al-Nujaidi 2013). It may argue that the longer economic benefits are established, the more likely they are to be seen as a right. Meanwhile, the rise in the cost of living is a pressing concern among Saudis, and especially the youth. As the Chatham House states in its Future Trends in the GCC workshop, "63 per cent of the young people surveyed in GCC countries said they were 'very concerned' about the rising cost of living. Such concerns are most pressing in Bahrain, Oman and Saudi Arabia, where incomes are lower" (Kinninmont 2015).

Serious efforts to address youth employment are evident in the US$36 billion (SAR135 billion) financial benefits package initiated by King Abdullah Bin Abdulaziz in early 2011. This package intended to support youth education, housing and employment and included compensation for up to a year for unemployed Saudis, many of whom are youth. The Saudi government also funded between 200,000 and 250,000 scholarships for students to obtain degrees abroad, many of them are pursuing scientific and technical subjects. This could reduce the negative effects of the previous education policy that resulted in two-thirds of all higher education graduates in Saudi Arabia being in the humanities and related fields that do not match the labour market needs (Achoui 2009). The main challenge, however, is to create the right kinds of jobs that these individuals will pursue upon graduation; and that failure to plan or do so will worsen youth unemployment rates and may lead to economic, social and political instability in the country.

Saudi Arabia's Council of Ministers adopted the Saudi Employment Strategy in July 2009, with the aim of diversifying the economy through its focus on improving the employability and productivity of Saudi nationals. One of the key aspects of this strategy is the preparation of young people for employment in emerging sectors of the economy (OECD/ILO 2011). This goes in line with the official policy of creating around four million jobs to absorb the new labour market entrants over the coming five years (Chatham House 2015), as well as rigorous implementation of a policy of Saudization or nationalization of the labour force. Despite the evident desire to implement the regulations, the country has struggled to attain the stated objectives. Successful economic diversification and infrastructure growth has instead attracted even greater numbers of expatriate workers. The implementation of the *Nitaqat* programme in 2013, which intended to reinforce the implementation of the Saudization policy, resulted in large-scale deportations of foreign workers from the country (Knickmeyer 2013). According to the Ministry of Labour, almost a million foreign workers were deported from the country, and that 250,000 Saudis took up new jobs as a result. This leaves almost 750,000 jobs unfilled. This is in addition to the failure of the Eighth National Development Plan to achieve its objective of creating four million jobs by 2009, which resulted in a shortfall of 21 per cent.

Indeed, the enforcement of the *Nitaqat* policy, which rewarded companies for recruiting more Saudis by limiting the renewal of work permits for non-Saudi employees increased the percentage of Saudis in the private sector from 10 per cent in 2011 to 20 per cent in 2013 (Zuhdy 2013). However, impressive this may look, the fact of the matter is that many companies used "fake Saudization" in order to get around the regulations and obtain more foreign work visas for their companies. Company executives resort to fake Saudization in order to ensure that their companies can continue to operate without hindrance. Not meeting Saudization quotas means risking the loss of a number of privileges, not least the possibility to recruit expatriate workers from abroad. Fake Saudization simply means employing Saudi men and women on minimum salaries in order to inflate the percentage of Saudis in the company. The number of young Saudis receiving monthly salaries while sitting at home has increased, and this explains to some extent the rise in the employment figures after the enforcement of *Nitaqat*. It has also been alleged that "Saudis negotiate their salaries with employers and demand high amounts for essentially doing nothing" (Saudi Gazette 2015). This is a clear example of the need to introduce a work ethic into the educational system. Young Saudis have become accustomed to find easier ways to earn a living other than by honouring the values of hard work and honest labour.

Saudi citizens have better access to legal protection than migrants do. Migrants lack job security, are liable to deportation and are dependent on their employer to sponsor their presence in the country. This makes the expat worker more attractive as an employee in the private sector, as they are easy to hire and fire. The issue of dependency on foreign workers cannot be addressed by simply improving the training and development of the local workforce; rather it requires comprehensive development of the entire education system in tandem with the employment system. It also requires radical reform of the labour laws and different approaches to deal with issues of mindset, knowledge, training and employee and employer rights.

Moreover, Saudi human resources policy has not yet considered the country's demographic changes. Unlike other Arab Gulf countries, whose nationals are becoming a minority in the overall population, Saudi Arabia's demographic indicators show that about one-third of the country's total population is not of Saudi origin. Nevertheless, this number has increased significantly over the past decade, despite the policy of Saudization (Kinninmont 2015). The labour market is the best way to measure this change. For example, between 2000 and 2010, almost 5.4 million jobs were generated in the private sector in the GCC; however, about 88 per cent of these jobs went to foreigners, with nationals remaining dependent on the expansion of the public sector for their jobs. The private sector continues to hire significant numbers of foreign workers, despite the obstacles in the recruitment process. Between July 2011 and July 2012, 1.1 million work visas were issued, whereas only 83,000 Saudis were hired by the private sector during this period (Shams 2013). The immediate reaction of the government was to expel 900,000 illegal migrant workers in 2013, which led to a decline in the number of expatriates. However, this reaction is seen as a "by-product of such policies and not the end goal. Saudi Arabia has only made a small dent in its nine-million-strong expatriate community" (Kinninmont 2015).

The societal aspect in youth unemployment is apparent in the so-called consumer mentality, by which most Saudis are accustomed to depend on expats for their services. Many Saudis see domestic and infrastructural services jobs beneath their social status and hence given to foreign workers. Despite concerns about rising poverty level in some Saudi villages and towns, most people refuse to engage in manual or domestic jobs because of the stigma surrounding this kind of work. Cultural issues such as tradition, religion and values play a significant role in limiting Saudi involvement in the private sector. The predominance of these traditional norms affects female participation in the labour force, which was estimated at 29 per cent in 2013 (Achoui 2009; Shams 2013). Although Saudi citizens play the role of consumer in their own country, it is not certain whether this consumer mentality comes about through traditional norms, tradition, popular belief, education and the media or is merely a by-product of the oil wealth.

Blurry Vision in Reforming the System

Saudi human development strategy lacks a satisfactory level of engagement by key stakeholders such as students, educators, employees, employers, professional associations and other civil society organizations. They were designed by management consultancies and international financial institutions, and based in international best practices, in isolation of the

Saudi context and its social norms, culture and tradition. This creates a degree of misperception and misunderstanding of the objective of the policies and miscommunication, or rather lack of it, among the concerned government departments and ministries. Lack of communication between decision-makers in education and the labour market on the kind of skills required in the market often results in outdated plans. For example, lack of communication and collaboration between the Ministry of Education and Ministry of Higher Education had been a major challenge to the development of the educational system. One researcher argues that the two ministries had long "suffered from insufficient standard setting, coordination, communication, and constant blaming of the other for the poor quality of educational outcomes" (Al-Abduljabbar 2015).

Current and past human development policies have suffered from a fragmented approach. While many of the problems facing Saudi youth today are interrelated, education has an impact on employment, leisure time and community engagement; hence, solutions require the involvement of an entire society (Al Munajjed and Sabbagh 2010). Such approach is beginning to emerge in the government on a limited scale. Al-Abduljabbar (2015) argues that the recent ministerial changes and reshuffles that took place in January 2015 have addressed this problem by merging the ministries of education and higher education into a single ministry and administration. The new Ministry of Education presents an opportunity to create a much-needed unified vision and purpose. It enables the education system to develop the student from pre-school up until entry into the job market. It may overcome issues of unified standard setting and data sharing, which has long been an issue in the various Saudi ministries. This re-engineering provides a chance to look closely at the Ministry's strengths and weaknesses, to make the changes to the system and the various steps required to improve performance and outputs and to provide solutions to existing issues that were not adequately addressed in the past due to poor communication and collaboration (Al-Abduljabbar 2015).

Another major issue emanating from the lack of collaboration between ministries is the lack of credibility between assessment systems. There is an inconsistency between official indicators and the actual quality of the education provided—seen in the poor knowledge base of newly recruited graduates into the workforce. Companies recruiting Saudis often need to conduct extensive internal training in basic skills. This is not only apparent in undergraduates, but is even more so among those coming out of higher education. Unemployment in this sector is rising, due to the mismatch between the output of education and training systems and labour market requirements, particularly in the private sector (Human Capital Challenges 2009). For example, the substantial growth in the Saudi tourism industry has not been met with an associated growth in the number of tourism professionals among nationals due to inadequate education programmes or failure to overcome social stigmas attached to vocational training that is considered fit only for poorly performing students and less privileged individuals.

The breakdown in coordination and correspondence is also seen in the Saudization programme. In 2014, the Saudi Gazette reported that one of the targets of the kingdom's Ninth Development Plan (2010–2015) was to "bring down the unemployment rate to 5.5 per cent and revive the Saudisation strategy" had not been realized. Statistics show Saudis account for 92 per cent of public sector employees, but only 13 per cent of private sector workers. This underscores the inability of the government to increase the number of Saudis in the workforce and that the nationalization of the labour market has had little success.

What is apparent is that Saudi national development plans are very broad and lack specific, well-defined milestones. The Vision 2020 aims at economic diversification, development of human resources, expansion of the public services, expansion of the private sector and streamlining and modernizing the governance structures in the public sector in order to meet the challenges of implementation (Hanushek and Wossmann 2007). Although the development of human resources is clearly stated, the vision fails to mention what kind of Saudi labour the education system should produce. How competent are the citizens be to work in the private sector and the highly competitive marketplace? How efficient is the education system in building human capacity and providing the right transferable skills that are required in the marketplace? Is the expected candidates capable of contributing to economic diversification utilizing their transferable and specialist knowledge from one company to another and from sector to sector? How pragmatic is the government in devising human resources policies that take into account the national cultural and social norms and values?

While addressing these critical questions, the government ought to seek means to resolve political division over the pace of reform at the leadership levels. It should also engage the private sector in the development process and provide real incentives to private enterprises to overcome their averseness to embrace the human development strategy (Hertog 2006). One must acknowledge that the role of the private sector is crucial for successful human capital development, simply because enterprises can easily bypass the regulations through clientelism and patronage or by being well connected to the political establishment. A more comprehensive vision will not only require greater involvement of all stakeholders in developing the country's human resources' development strategies but also better communication and coordination between the education and business communities when it comes to building the country's human capacity.

Conclusion

The above discussion shows that the Saudi government is aware of the shortcomings of the educational system and has undertaken a number of initiatives to rectify the situation. This is true in the 2009 King Abdullah Project for Development, which allocated significant financial resources to improve the qualification of teachers, curriculum development, learning environment and extra-curricular activities. The government has also recognized the need to develop science-based education in order to meet the needs of the labour market. Analysis shows that the initiatives and efforts made by the government have not yet produced the desired outcome from education reforms. This finding is simplified in the reluctance of the private sector to employ Saudi nationals, despite the enforcement of the Saudization policy.

The study identified a number of challenges that affected negatively the development of both the education system and labour market in Saudi Arabia. Chief among these challenges is the lack of coherence between the strategies set in place to combat unemployment and the educational system itself. Improved communication and coordination between the government and the main stakeholders can pave the way to finding solutions to the problem of employment among Saudi nationals. The main education providers should seek partnerships with the business community, especially the private sector, and aim at meeting the demands of the labour market.

The study also finds that throwing money at the education-labour market problem does not provide a solution. Serious efforts at reform should start by rectifying the root problems in society, starting from the family and primary education. As a key stakeholder, family plays an important role not only in providing the very first stage of learning but also in selecting the kind of education that is suitable for their children and participating the decision-making when it comes to education reform. Changes in the attitudes of youth towards work must begin at home and develop formally in the primary and secondary education, if the Saudi educational policy is to succeed. The mindset of the country's younger generations must change, so that the youth recognize the value of work and its importance in life. This is the responsibility of the education system, in which young people are offered the opportunity to experience the value and ethics of work through practical and empirical teaching and learning methods and work placements.

While much of the blame of the modest improvement of Saudi human development policy rests on the shoulders of the government, the private sector is responsible for the problem due to lack of engagement in the decision-making in reforming the education system and reluctance to employ or provide adequate training and support for Saudi citizens. The participation of the private sector as a key stakeholder in the reform process of both the education system and labour market is necessary, as insights of company executives could shed light on the needs of their companies and hence shape the direction and pace of reform process. Eventually, the oil boom will end, and that the need for a competent and highly competitive workforce will be the only way to sustain reasonable levels of social and economic development. Now is the time to engage in radical reforms so that the youth may grasp these opportunities and thereby create new and vibrant society of which they may be proud.

References

Abdulaziz, S. (2015). *Appointment speech*. Riyadh: Government of Saudi Arabia.

Achoui, M. (2009). Development in Gulf countries: An analysis of the trends and challenges facing Saudi Arabia. *Human Resource Development International*, 12(1), 35–46.

Al-Abduljabbar, A. (2015). *New Ministry of Education: Big opportunity or big problem?* Pscinnovativegov.org. *Government Insights* series, March.

Al Munajjed, M., & Sabbagh, K. (2010). *Youth in GCC countries: Meeting the challenge*. New York: Booze & Co.

Al-Nujaidi, A. (2013). *Youth employment initiatives and services in Saudi Arabia: Cross-channels strategies and programs*. Riyadh: Human Resources Development Fund.

Anonymous. (2009). *Human capital challenges in Saudi Arabia and suggested solutions*. Retrieved May 2015, from https://www.google.com/url?sa=t&rct= j&q=&esrc=s&source=web&cd=1&cad=rja&uact=8&ved=0ahUKEwigscPc5e

7JAhWGkY4KHUj7ClcQFggdMAA&url=http%3A%2F%2Fwww.academia. edu%2F9197698%2FHuman_Capital_Challenges_in_Saudi_Arabia_and_ Suggested_Solutions&usg=AFQjCNF7GqcoQswyO0BAAQF2t-h3ABk2TQ&sig2=1MH1VX6ZwwwTh-IN9c7m5w&bvm=bv.110151844,d. c2E

Asmari, A. (2008). *Integration of foreign culture into pre-service EFL teacher education: A case study of Saudi Arabia*. Ph.D. thesis, Faculty of Arts, Language and Linguistics, University of Melbourne.

BBC News. (2010). *Saudi school lessons in UK concern government*. 22 November.

Chatham House. (2015). *Saudi-British relations: Second bilateral workshop*, London.

Chronicle of Higher Education. (2010). *Saudi Arabia's education reforms emphasis training for jobs*, October.

Fasih, T. (2008). *Linking education policy to labour market outcomes*. Washington: World Bank.

G20 Country Policy Brief. (2011). *The Saudi employment strategy*. Geneva: OECD/ILO.

Government of Saudi Arabia. (2009). *Ninth development plan 2010–2014*, Riyadh.

Hanushek, E., & Wossmann, L. (2007). *Education quality in economic growth*. World Bank Policy Research Working Paper 4122, Washington.

Hertog, S. (2006). Segmented clientelism: The political economy of Saudi economic reform efforts. In P. Arts & G. Nonneman (Eds.), *Saudi Arabia in the balance: Political economy, society, foreign affairs*. London: Hurst & Co.

Kinninmont, J. (2015). *Future trends in the Gulf Report*. London: Chatham House.

Knickmeyer, E. (2013). Saudis crack down in foreign workers. *Wall Street Journal*, 1 April 2013. Retrieved December 26, 2015, from http://online.wsj.com/article/SB10001424127887324883604578396603434399588.html

Mahdi, S. (2000). *Saudization and structure of the labour market in Saudi Arabia*. University of Hertfordshire Business School. Working Paper Series 24.

McEvers, K. (2009). *Changing the way Saudis learn*. Retrieved May 2015, from http://www.slate.com/articles/news_and_politics/dispatches/features/2009/changing_the_way_saudis_learn/reforming_saudi_education.html

Nagraj, A. (2012). Over 1.3m Saudis on unemployment benefit. *Gulf Business*, 23 September. Retrieved from http://www.gulfbusiness.com/articles/jobs/over-1-3m-saudis-on-unemployment-benefit/

Saudi Gazette. (2015). *Fake Saudization: A threat to national economy: Experts*, January.

Shams, A. (2013). *The mismatch between labour market needs and Saudi workforce*. Your Middle East Foundation [website].

Shea, N., et al. (2006). *Saudi Arabia's curriculum of intolerance*. New York: Freedom House 2010. This medieval Saudi education system must be reformed. *The Guardian*, 26 November.

UNICEF. (2013). *UNICEF Annual Report 2013: Gulf Area Sub-Regional Programme*. Retrieved from https://www.unicef.org/about/annualreport/files/Gulf_Area_Subregional_Programme_COAR_2013.pdf

World Economic Forum. (2010). *Global gender gap report*. New York.

Zuhdy, N. (2013). Education and employment in the Arab world. *Harvard Journal of ME Politics and Policy*, December.

CHAPTER 6

Policy and Regulatory Frameworks for Foreign Direct Investment in Saudi Arabia

Ahmad Al Daffaa

INTRODUCTION

This chapter seeks to investigate similarities and differences in the regulatory pattern between inward and outward investments to and from Saudi Arabia. It is based on the assumption that the Saudi regulatory system does not afford equal treatment between inward and outward direct investment. It argues that it is important to have equal regulatory and policy treatment for both inward and outward investment. This will attract international organizations that are interested in the Kingdom of Saudi Arabia (KSA), especially that the Kingdom is one of the top Arabic countries regarding the foreign direct investment inflow stock to United States standing at 215 billion US dollars until 2014 (Iaigc.net 2016).

This chapter also demonstrates the ability of the Saudi economy to rely equally on inward and outward investment as policy instruments, which will assist in creating an environment encompassing stability and certainty in domestic and international trade. Moreover, it shows the potential role

---

A. Al Daffaa (✉)
University of Hull, Hull, UK

© Gulf Research Centre Cambridge 2018
A. Mishrif, Y. Al Balushi (eds.), *Economic Diversification in the Gulf Region, Volume I*, The Political Economy of the Middle East,
https://doi.org/10.1007/978-981-10-5783-0_6

and function of the Saudi government in the formulation of a policy and regulatory framework for the promotion of outward investment from both public and private operations in Saudi Arabia.

Determinants of FDI

The definition and treatment of FDI as determined by scholars and international organizations, is reflected in the literature review. Foreign investment involves "the transfer of tangible or intangible assets from one country into another for the purpose of their use in that country to generate wealth under the total or partial control of the owner of the assets" (Sornarajah 2004). The Organization for Economic Co-operation and Development (OECD) provides a more specific explanation of the term "foreign direct investment", stating that it "reflects the objective of establishing a lasting interest by a resident enterprise in one economy (direct investor) in an enterprise (direct investment enterprise) that is resident in an economy other than that of the direct investor" (Organisation for Economic Co-operation and Development 2009).

Furthermore, the International Monetary Fund (IMF) clarifies direct investment as "the category of international investment that reflects the objective of a resident entity in one economy obtaining a lasting interest in an enterprise resident in another economy" (IMF 1993). In addition, a definition of foreign investment has been provided by the United Nations Conference on Trade and Development (UNCTD), as "an investment involving a long-term relationship and reflecting a lasting interest of a resident entity in one economy (direct investor) in an entity resident in an economy other than of the investor" (Unctad.org 2013).

Academic research has focused its impact on the effects of international trade in the form of investment liberalization. Pertinent theories formed a paradigm and a theoretical framework which is based on the principle of competitive advantage for investment movements globally (Dunning 1994, 1998, 2006). The research has been also influenced by the theories of control in investment, in particular, mobility of international trade, namely the work of Buckley and Casson (2003).

The control of all aspects of foreign investment, either inward or outward, is a sovereign right. With regard to inward investment, host state control may be broken down into three key fields. Firstly, there may be limitations that dismiss certain investments from the state as a whole, or otherwise from particular industries and/or sectors. Secondly, foreign direct investment may be allowed following a review, which may result in a number of conditions being imposed upon the investor in return for consent to enter the host state. Thirdly, upon the establishment of foreign direct investment, the investor's activities will be subject to the general policy and regulatory framework of the state in question. Importantly, the first two areas function upon the entry phase in relation to inward investment and the exit phase in relation to outward investment. During these phases, the host state exerts its sovereign right to control the manifestation of unknowns within its borders. The third phase signifies the post-entry stage, when the investor has become subject to compliance with the host state laws. Overall, the laws applied during this phase are those implemented within domestic organizations.

Nevertheless, the application of such laws may be impacted by the overall type of the activity and business organization of the multinational enterprise, and may subsequently bring about the formation of new legal reactions directed towards multinational enterprises in particular. Once more, in relation to the principle of state sovereignty established within international law, the host state holds unrestricted discretion in terms of controlling and policing foreign investor activities. As a result, the host country can protect the investment environment within the country through the right of control, which is achieved through the sovereignty right. On the other hand, the protection of investment is not only important for the host country, but also for the investor. Thus, the foreign investor will require protection against any dangers or risks that may arise and which may be influential on investment decisions. The existence of such risks arises as a direct result of either change to presently adopted economic and political policies of the host state or a regime change. Such changes pose a threat to foreign investment. Importantly, any state holds the right to change its economic policy, although such a right may ultimately come to be restricted through the growing number of treaties pertinent to international trade and investment, as identified by the work of Sornarajah (2010).

Methodology

As mentioned, this chapter seeks to investigate similarities and differences in the regulatory pattern between inward and outward investments to and from Saudi Arabia. It is based on the assumption that the Saudi regulatory system does not afford equal treatment between inward and outward direct investment. Accordingly, it sets three numbers of questions: (1) What is the relationship between the domestic regulatory framework and the inward and outward FDI flow patterns? (2) What is the effect of specific elements within the domestic regulatory framework such as specific rules and regulations on the inward and outward flow FDI patterns? (3) What is the impact on FDI patterns of international determinants such as international investment conventions (IIC), bilateral investment treaties (BIT) and double taxation treaties (DTT)?

It adopts a desktop, analytical and comparative approach to critically investigate and assess the regulatory investment framework in the Kingdom of Saudi Arabia. It follows a developmental perspective to trace the evolution of the Saudi framework on investment. Improvements made and difficulties created in this process will be critically evaluated. It will also contain a comparative dimension, whereby the regulatory investment framework of Saudi Arabia is compared with international frameworks. Hence, various aspects of the investment regulatory framework of Saudi Arabia will be compared with international conventions on investment.

The analysis performed in this study was facilitated by the author's good access to various primary and secondary sources of data on this subject. Primary data were gathered through semi-structured interviews with a number of leading Saudi companies, from different sectors, that have a history and experience with outward foreign direct investment. The selected companies are a representative sample of the Saudi economic and industrial base.

The transcripts of the interviews served as the primary data source. This data was coded, examined, verified and confirmed. The process of transcribing the interviews gives the researcher additional knowledge and understanding of the subject. After the transcribing the researcher coded the data. The coding process is essential as a part of the qualitative research (Collis and Hussey 2009). The codes of the data helped the researcher to identify the main themes; as the researcher recognized several different themes, this is an indicator of the research problem by distributing the data into themes based on the framework. Then the data were analysed.

Relationship Between the Saudi Regulatory System and FDI

Due to the discovery of oil in the KSA, and the resulting inflow of foreign direct investment, a series of regulations for foreign capital investment for the non-oil sector were enacted. The first regulation of foreign capital investment was in 1956, the second regulation replaced the first in 1962, and the third regulation was promulgated in 1979. The recent framework of foreign investment was issued in 2000. The last one focused on the theme of the relationship between the domestic regulatory system and FDI and in particular the Regulatory Regime on Foreign Direct Investment in the KSA. Moreover, it facilitates and regulates foreign investment through agencies to create a healthy environment for investment (Sornarajah 2010).

These investments are categorized into two categories. The first category is where a firm is wholly owned by a foreign investor as an individual owner without a partner who is a Saudi citizen. The second category includes the ownership of an investment project which is shared between a Saudi partner and a foreign investor. Nevertheless, no specific percentage of ownership by foreign and Saudi investors is stipulated for investment projects (Saudiembassy.net 2000). In addition, there are two key supervisory authorities for foreign direct investment in Saudi Arabia: the Saudi Supreme Economic Council, and the Saudi Arabian General Investment Authority. These authorities are the key policymakers and regulators of the privatization of public services, which opens new doors for FDI.

The Saudi Supreme Economic Council

The importance of the Saudi Supreme Economic Council can be seen through the duties and functions of this authority, which deals with all economic policies in the country by supervising and recognizing the government ministers and commissions relating to the economic sector. In addition, this authority controls the performance of Saudi Cabinet decisions relating to economic issues and then sends reports to the Saudi Cabinet explaining the performance of the implementations of these decisions. Moreover, the authority works by studying and reviewing all economic matters in the state, such as development plans, financial policy, reports that are submitted by government ministers and commissions which relate to economic affairs, and issuing annual reports about the economy of the country. Furthermore, the importance of the Saudi Supreme Economic Council comes not only through the duties and responsibilities of this administrative body, but also from its role in assisting the business of the Saudi Cabinet in all economic issues and matters. The Saudi Supreme Economic Council is the only body which has the authority to regulate and control any type of investment activities in the country. Since the Saudi Supreme Economic Council assists the Saudi Cabinet in economic issues, the constituents of this authority are the highest members of the Saudi Government: the Chairman of the Saudi Supreme Economic Council is the King, and the members are the Crown Prince and several of the government ministers, including the Ministers for Labour, Trade and Industry, Petroleum and Mineral Resources, Finance, Economy and Planning, Water and Electricity, and the Governor of the Saudi Arabia Monetary Agency (SAMA).

The Saudi Arabian General Investment Authority (SAGIA)

The Saudi Arabian General Investment Authority (SAGIA) was established in 2000, to create a healthy climate for investment in the country while providing comprehensive services for investors and attracting investment (Sagia.gov.sa 2002). This was intended to achieve the aspirations of the government regarding rapid economic growth, which would be reflected in its impact on the country and population by acquiring high-quality services with reasonable prices. Furthermore, creating SAGIA as an independent governmental authority that was not under any ministry's control, offered the opportunity for creativity, excellence and development in the field of foreign investment in the country.

SAGIA has many functions which aim to create an investment environment for both national and foreign investors. These functions include the preparation of state policies in the field of development, improving domestic and foreign investments, and submitting economic reports to the Supreme Economic Council. Moreover, SAGIA proposes implementation plans and rules to create an investment environment in the Kingdom and submits them to the Supreme Economic Council. In addition, the authority studies and evaluates the performance of domestic and foreign investment in order to report thereon. Finally, SAGIA is responsible to ensure that investors have met all the requirements and conditions for obtaining a licence before starting work on an investment project.

The Privatization System in the Kingdom of Saudi Arabia

In 1997, the Council of Ministers in the KSA issued eight objectives for the implementation of privatization in the country in Decree No. 60 (Saudiembassy.net 1997). In 2001, it also decided in Decree No. 257 that the Supreme Economic Council would have government authority to take responsibility for a privatization programme, controlling the programme and organizing the public authorities which would be involved in activities that would be transferred to the private sector. Furthermore, privatization was defined as a term by the Supreme Economic Council in Resolution No. 1/23 in 2002, as follows: "The process of transferring the ownership or management of government or public projects, services and enterprises to the private sector relying on market mechanisms and competition through a number of methods including management contracts, operating, leasing, financing, or selling all or part of the government's assets to the private sector" (Mep.gov.sa 2002).

A Privatization Committee was established under the umbrella of the Supreme Economic Council to be responsible for considering the privatization programmes and procedures in the country; the members of the Privatization Committee are the President, who is the Secretary-General of the Supreme Economic Council; Members Representatives from the Ministry of Finance, the Ministry of Economics and Planning, the Ministry of Water and Electricity and the Ministry of Commerce and Industry; and two members of the Advisory Board for Economic Affairs. There are eight objectives of privatization issued in Resolution No. 1/23 in 2002 which are the following:

- To increase the smooth-running of the country's economy and improve its abilities to compete in domestic and international markets.
- To facilitate investment in the private sector and its participation in the national economy and to increase its production in order to achieve growth in the economy as a whole.
- To increase the proportion of productive assets in the hands of Saudi citizens.
- To encourage domestic and foreign investors to invest capital in the Saudi economy.
- To widen employment opportunities, make maximum use of the Saudi work force, and ensure the continued rise in individual income and general standard of living.
- To provide appropriate services for citizens and investors in a cost-efficient way.
- To rationalize public expenditure and reduce government budget levels by providing the private sector with the means to fund, conduct and maintain the services it offers (Mep.gov.sa 2002).

Consequently, the privatization influences the private sector to have more autonomy to manage and control their investments on those activities that were predefined by the government. In addition, the private sector has built a confidence to invest in complex projects of high capital. It also enforces competition among key players which call for high-quality standards. All of these consequences impact positively on the regulatory framework of IFDI by engaging different stakeholders to participate in the development and the coevolving of different procedures, strategies and governess polices concerned.

International Agreements on Investment

The Kingdom of Saudi Arabia acknowledges the importance of foreign investment in the development of the country and the growth of its economy. As a result, there are many kinds of agreements that have been signed by the Saudi government, which deal with protecting foreign investment. In the earlier agreements, made in 1975, the Saudi government signed with the United States an agreement on protection and investment guarantee (Zergers 2009). Subsequently, the Kingdom of Saudi Arabia signed many bilateral investment treaties with different states, such as Austria (2001), Belgium and Luxembourg (2001), China (1996), Egypt (1990), France (2002), Germany (1996), India (2006), Italy (1996), Malaysia (2000), Spain (2006), Philippines (1994), Turkey (2006) and Switzerland (2006).

Such agreements reflect the Saudi government's belief regarding the importance of international agreements, through which agreements, the Saudi government is facilitated in improving public services and developing the country in different sectors. Consequently, the Saudi government has signed a number of multilateral agreements and conventions, all of which relate to foreign investment. One of these agreements was in 1980, when the Kingdom of Saudi Arabia joined the Convention on the Settlement of Investment Disputes between States and Nationals of Other States (the Washington Convention), which settles any investment disputes between member states and nationals of different states who are parties to the Convention, under the protection of the International Centre for the Settlement of Investment Disputes (ICSID).

Foreign direct investment is promoted by the Multilateral Investment Guarantee Agency (MIGA) under the World Bank, which provides political risk insurance for foreign investment (Miga.org 2016). Since 12 April

1988, the government of the Kingdom of Saudi Arabia has held a membership of the Multilateral Investment Guarantee Agency to attract foreign investment and to guarantee the foreign investment against political risk. The Saudi government, through signing this kind of convention, has sought to provide more legal protection for foreign investment within their country.

Furthermore, the Kingdom of Saudi Arabia has a number of different types of membership in international organizations that deal with the oil and gas sectors, such as the World Petroleum Council (World-petroleum.org 2016) and World Energy Council (Worldenergy.org 2016).

The Kingdom of Saudi Arabia has joined on the 11th of September 2005 the World Trade Organization (WTO), as member number 149. In addition, the Kingdom of Saudi Arabia has a membership in the Group of Twenty (G-20) Finance Ministers and Central Bank Governors. The Group of Twenty (G-20) comprises 20 major economies around the world, namely, the Kingdom of Saudi Arabia, the European Union, Argentina, Brazil, India, Mexico, South Africa, Russia, China, Republic of Korea, the United Kingdom, Turkey, the United States of America, France, Germany, Canada, Indonesia, Japan, Australia and Italy.

As any foreign investor should obtain a licence from SAGIA, the importance of international treaties can be seen in the conditions attached to the granting of the licence. One of these conditions is that SAGIA should ensure that by granting a licence to a foreign investor, the authority will not be in breach of any type of international agreement to which the Saudi Government is a party (Sagia.gov.sa 2002).

Saudi Investment in Agriculture Abroad: Enhancing Saudi Food Security

This section describes the only supported initiative for the outward investment. It is well known that the issue of food security (FS) is one of the top five issues at the global level, as some states monopolize the production and exportation of food commodities, especially strategic ones, with the aim of exerting political and economic pressure on developing and underdeveloped countries. The Kingdom of Saudi Arabia seeks to achieve a certain level of food security by maintaining a strategic food stockpile sufficient to meet consumption needs for at least six months. This stockpile is established through local production, importation and foreign agricultural investment to meet emergency conditions, especially as the Middle

East region has witnessed events and developments which make it an unstable region militarily, politically and economically. This reserve was established because the Saudi economy enjoys sufficient resources as a result of high oil prices, and the financial surplus representing 32.5 per cent of Gross Domestic Product GDP (Saudi Arabian Monetary Agency 2010).

To ensure domestic supply of wheat and other key staples, in 2009 the authorities launched the King Abdullah Initiative for Saudi Agricultural Investment Abroad, which provides incentives to Saudi firms to invest in farming in around 35 foreign countries, in particular (but not limited to) those in Africa, Eastern Europe and East Asia such as Sudan, Egypt, Ethiopia, Turkey, Ukraine, Kazakhstan, the Philippines, Vietnam, Brazil and other suitable countries with agricultural investment potentiality. In February 2014, the director-general of the initiative, Saad Khalil, said that to date 31 countries had approached the Kingdom to discuss hosting Saudi investments in the sector.

The initiative targets eight agricultural products, namely wheat, rice, feed barley, yellow corn, soybean meal, oil seed, sugar, and livestock and poultry. The government is allocating around US\$22.1 billion of funding towards the plan, and in 2011 it established a new firm—the Saudi Agricultural and Livestock Investment Company, which is controlled by the country's sovereign wealth fund, the Public Investment Fund—with paid-up capital of US\$800 million to support the initiative. As of 2012 the authorities said that Saudi firms to date had invested US\$10.66 billion in agricultural projects in Latin America, Africa, Eastern Europe and Canada under the initiative.

According to a mid-2012 report released by Standard Bank, 70 per cent of major investments by Saudi firms in foreign agricultural projects were in African countries, amounting to around 800,000 ha of farmland. North and East African countries, notably Sudan and Ethiopia, have seen particularly heavy investment; for example, Saudi Arabian firms are estimated to have invested around US\$3.47 billion in farming projects in Ethiopia, which has made a total of 4 m ha of land available to foreign investors from a range of different countries. Companies participating in the initiative include the Saudi firm Iktifaa, which in January 2014 announced plans to establish several projects in Sennar and Northern States in Sudan.

Other recent major deals include the acquisition of land in northern Sudan by four companies from the Kingdom—Almarai, Al Safi, Tabuk Agriculture and Al Jouf Company—also in January 2014. According to the former agriculture minister, the government supports the private sector by providing the two most important things an investor looks for: financing and security for their investment. The government recently agreed to expand the mandate of the agricultural development fund from providing loans for domestic agriculture projects to also covering overseas investment.

Such efforts face a number of challenges, as both Saudi investors and those pursuing similar plans, such as China and India, have found, in particular in relation to African projects (which account for the bulk of Saudi investments so far). The state of infrastructure in Sudan, Egypt, Ethiopia and other countries targeted by Saudi Arabia and neighbouring Gulf States with similar initiatives, for example, has proven to be an obstacle, as noted by a 2011 report from the Ministry of Industry and Commerce, which also pointed to other problems, such as barriers to investment in many countries.

In May 2013 the Saudi Arabian company Hadi Property Investment suspended plans to produce wheat in Sudan because of restrictions applied in practice by the Sudanese central bank to the repatriation of profits, and in December 2013, several investors from the Kingdom were reported to be withdrawing from projects in Ethiopia, saying they could not meet the lending conditions. Foreign agricultural projects in Ethiopia—both Saudi and otherwise—have also faced a number of problems, including financial difficulties, which have resulted in delays to development plans, and opposition from local people to the large-scale allocation of land to foreign farming operations.

Analysis and Discussion

Since the establishment of the recent body of policy and regulation for FDI in 2000, the definition of such foreign investment is seen as "investment of foreign capital in an activity licensed and authorized by a KSA government administrative authority" (Saudiembassy.net 2000). Additionally, this body uses privatization as one of the tools to help the state to attract foreign direct investment through encouraging private sector investors to invest in public services. These regulatory and policy changes have resulted in the Kingdom to undergo radical transformation. It also combines natural energy with a long-term vision and strategic planning, which in turn have created today's stable, robust economy that positions KSA as a new global force. Therefore, the design of the questions has been centripetal towards three thematic. First, the institutional structure of regulation of inward and outward FDI in Saudi Arabia; second, the sectoral presence of investment interest in Saudi and overseas markets; and third, overt or covert barriers to inward and outward investment actors within Saudi Arabia.

Inward FDI

In 2003, there were 2118 licensed projects that brought SAR 56.8 billion, including 551 new licences granted by the Board of Directors with a total amount of 6.5 billion Saudi Riyals (SAR), 183 industrial licences that raised SAR 4.93 billion, 336 services licences bringing SAR 1.52 billion, and two agricultural licences bringing SAR 92 million. Foreign investment inflow reached 59 per cent of the total financing of licensed projects during that year, which constituted approximately SAR 3.9 billion.

In 2004, SAGIA issued 460 licences for joint projects with foreign and Saudi investors, which gave a total amount of SAR 15.2 billion, including 192 industrial licences with SAR 14,498 million, 226 services licences with SAR 675 million, and two agricultural projects with SAR 50 million. The Board of Directors issued 1389 licences with the total foreign investment inflow amounting to SAR 68 billion.

In 2006, the granted licences included 409 industrial licences and 979 services licences, but only one agricultural project (Saudi Arabian General Investment Authority 2010). In 2008, 1197 applications were approved and given licences, which included different types of investment activities, involving public sectors such as education, transport, telecommunication and real estate. Nevertheless, comparing the numbers for 2006 and 2008, it can be observed that the number of licences issued by SAGIA in 2008 was lower than in 2006. However, the total amount of foreign investment inflow increased in 2008 to SAR 143 billion.

In 2010, the total amount of foreign investment inflow was less than in 2008, which in that year was SAR 105 billion (Saudi Arabian General Investment Authority 2010). The reason for this is the global financial crisis which started from the United States and affected it significantly and United States is the major source of FDI inflows to the Kingdom of Saudi Arabia as foreign direct investment. This can be shown through the inflows between 2007 and 2010 of SAR 87 billion. However, the investment licences issued by SAGIA till 2013 was 9265 licences.

It is clear from the above discussion that the inward FDI increased dramatically due to the well-organized policy and regulatory framework. The growth of the Saudi Economy was evident; it was ranked as the world's 19th largest economy in 2013, according to the World Bank, based on a GDP of US$764 billion and 9.3 per cent growth on non-oil sector.

These figures demonstrate that the main success factors for the efficient IFDI regulatory framework were the wide and diverse experiences of FDI investments and cooperation on the Saudi market. These experiences generated a matured policy and regulatory processes that fit with the Saudi economy's needs. In addition, this long-term experience in attracting IFDI, since oil production, has shaped clarity on the main key sectors at the three different institutional layers: policy agencies, regulations and operating units. Furthermore, the potential growth in non-oil and gas investments has persuaded key stakeholders and the decision makers of the significance of such investments to maintain the sustainability of the Saudi economy apart from the conventional oil and gas investments.

The connecting patterns between IFDI and OFDI are mainly related to potential and growth. The high rewards from the IFDI to the entire economy will reflect positively on the OFDI due to the similarity in experiences and capacities generated, considering distinguished features of the concerned markets and industries. Such capacities could be invested to develop a regulatory body for OFDI, which currently does not exist in the Saudi structure. These capacities are good enough to create efficient policies, processes and monitoring procedures that can shift OFDI from its current position to the desired position within the Saudi economy.

Outward FDI

On the other side, outward investment has not been treated as efficiently as inward investments. According to the interviews, there is no authority to regulate the facilitation of outward investment. Therefore, a gap emerges which positions outward investment outside the Saudi policy and regulatory investment framework of the 2000 Foreign Investment Law. Nevertheless, despite the lack of regulatory coverage, outward investments from Saudi Arabia have witnessed remarkable progress.

Since the enactment of the 2000 Foreign Investment Law, outward investments from Saudi Arabia during the period from 2001 to 2011 amounted to US$40 billion (SAR 150 billion). Such outward investment flows are depicted by the World Investment Forum (Unctad.org 2013), which stated that between 2001 and 2010, the outward investment from the Arab nations was US$169 billion, with Gulf Council states accounting for 82 per cent of these outward investment flows, primarily through non-private organizations, sovereign investment funds and other state-owned businesses as investment vehicles.

In spite of the number of trade international agreements that have been made with different countries in developing as well as developed countries, exports as a percentage of GDP are still low. However, trade might not boost OFDI if the domestic firms are not able to invest abroad, and the success in attracting IFDI in the economy of Saudi Arabia has not yet impacted positively on OFDI. It does not encourage the domestic firms to go abroad and benefit the KSA economy. There is no doubt that such engagement in international business would encourage Saudi firms to operate in a foreign environment, which could be enhanced through import and IFDI.

The domestic determinants (policy and strategy) could be invested to promote both IFDI and OFDI among the Saudi investors, particularly those who have existing investments and joint ventures with international companies in the Saudi market. Such investments would give spaces for Saudi investors to invest abroad in order to maintain their growth, as well as enhancing the diversity of the Saudi economy.

International agreements and the regulatory bodies in KSA do not help state companies to invest abroad. Nevertheless, the state company Saudi Basic Industry Corporation (SABIC) has entered Europe and the United States with a strong motive of market seeking and technology seeking with Brownfield investment to acquire additional technology, and SABIC has R&Ds in different locations in the world. This has been done without any support from the government. However, this is a good step in order to build location advantage, like skills (technical, managerial and general) and build an efficient strategy to expand and operate overseas.

The liberalization of the Saudi Arabia government's policy with respect to OFDI is still not implemented. This constrains further expansion of the Kingdom's companies. Rapid rise of OFDI is important for any country, with increasing globalization, which causes uncertainties and risk. Saudi's companies must be able to adapt themselves to any challenge coming in the future. Therefore, Saudi's firms need to build up technology, bring out product innovation, make their products different from those of competitors and build large R&D to help them to acquire competitive advantage and strength.

Policy and Regulatory System, FDI and Economic Diversification

The Saudi government had believed that to develop the country and its economy, not only should it not be dependent on the oil industry, but it was also important to diversify the economy by allowing foreign and national investors to invest in the different sectors in the Kingdom. Therefore, in 1970, the Saudi government issued the first development plan as part of its economic strategy for the country. Since 1970, the Saudi government has issued nine development plans, which are a kind of public commitment on the part of the government to demonstrate and implement its economy strategy every five years. The Development Plan should be studied by the Ministry of Economics and Planning, and should then be passed through different authorities in the country before being issued, such as the Shura Council, the Supreme Economic Council and the Saudi Cabinet. Finally, after the project of the Development Plan has been agreed by these authorities, the Prime Minister of the Saudi Government can sign the project as an official Development Plan for the following five years (Al-Obuid 1994).

However, it cannot be said that planning for development started in 1970 because before that time the Saudi government had passed through four stages until reaching 1975. The first stage was from 1955–1957; during this time, the Commission for Economic Development was established by the Saudi government to solve the financial crisis in the Saudi economy because government expenditure was increasing without underlying stability in oil prices. The second stage was in 1961 with Royal Decree No. 50, whereby the Saudi government established the planning board after receiving recommendations from the World Bank. The nature of the work of the planning board was to provide recommendations to the Saudi Cabinet relating to the annual budget. The third stage came in 1965 when the Saudi government created the Central Planning Commission following suggestions by the United Nations to create such a body to prepare and issue economic development plans, the first plan to be for the next five years. The fourth stage started when the Saudi government changed the Central Planning Commission to the Ministry of Planning in 1975 after the Central Planning Commission had failed in respect of the proposed development plans. However, the work of the Central Planning Commission was the first serious attempt at planning by the Saudi government (Baker 2003).

Diversification helps countries in attracting foreign direct investment through allowing private sector investors to invest in non-oil sectors or industries. This has an effect on the economic and social environment in the country; for example, (1) it creates jobs and employment; (2) provides high-quality services; (3) transfers capital resources from the home country of the foreign investor to the host country; and (4) helps governments to achieve economic objectives through strengthening of the private sector and the development of public services (Habish 2011). However, the regulatory instruments of privatization in any country are one of the important elements in attracting foreign and national investors because privatization leads the parties involved to safeguard their rights, including their responsibilities, and the rights of consumers and citizens.

Administrative regulation has, therefore, played a primary role in privatization in the Kingdom of Saudi Arabia, whereby private sector investors, whether foreign or Saudi, can invest in any public institution service or activity (Anthony 2003).

The importance of diversification can be seen through different aspects in any country, such as the political, social and economic arenas. There are many advantages to diversification. One of these advantages is reducing the economic burden on the government through lowering pressure on its administrative and financial responsibilities, with the private sector sharing the economic responsibility and aims (Goyal and Goyal 2010). In addition, through diversification, the quality of services and competition can be improved, which will enable citizens to receive a higher standard of different services in the country. Moreover, by diversification, economic growth rates will also increase in the country. The rate of achieving the objectives of all or most of the development and economic plans in the country will also be increased by diversification (Kanoua 2005). Furthermore, the advantages of diversification for the citizens of a country are not only in receiving a higher quality of services but also in having the chance to gain jobs in the private sector and to be granted opportunities about the ownership of companies through the stock market. Moreover, one of the main advantages of diversification in a country is encouraging the private sector, including national and foreign investors, to increase their investment in development and services projects in the country, for example, in the telecommunications sector, transportation, education, health and tourism. In addition, with diversification, the economy of a country will grow through a variety of methods. One of these methods involves foreign investors wanting to invest in the public services of a country because they will need to transfer some of their capital from their countries of origin to the host country. However, the host country has to create a healthy investment environment and protect investments, including national and foreign, because the economy and the country's reputation will be affected negatively if it fails to give adequate protection to investors (Goyal and Goyal 2010).

Conclusion

Investment, whether inward or outward, enjoys massive economic, social and even political importance, as it is the central pillar of development. In this chapter, evidence demonstrates that the Kingdom of Saudi Arabia is not meeting the ambition of the government for both inward and outward investment flows. Each sector is behind the desired level. Saudi Arabia needs a clear vision supported by firm strategic action from the highest authority of the government.

The researcher identified three thematic in the empirical stage of the research; institutional regulation of inward and outward FDI, sectoral presence and barriers to investing. These thematic were corroborated by responses of interviewees.

The data from the empirical stage of the research revealed a picture which is consistent with the analysis of the literature and the international instruments of inward and outward investment applicable to the Kingdom of Saudi Arabia.

Institutional frameworks and existing policy and regulation are useful and helpful for investors; the problem is with lack of effective implementation. Regarding the sectoral presence, the tendency of the government is not clear, and the role of the SAGIA does not offer appropriate treatment for investors, so investors do not have an interest to do business in this environment. Therefore, there are barriers that prevent inward and outward investments, which has prompted the Saudi government to approve a plan for broad economic reforms, called "Saudi Vision 2030".

References

Al-Obuid, A. (1994). *Egtsadalmamlukhalarabuahalsoudah: nathrahtahlulah*. Riyadh: Dar el-ma al-maktbuit (In Arabic).

Anthony, O. (2003). Comparing regulatory systems. In A. David & S. David (Eds.), *International handbook of privatization*. Cheltenham: Edward Elgar Publishing.

Baker, N. (2003). *Al-egtasad al-saoudyfeahada al-malukfahedashrounalammn al-enjazat*. Riyadh: King Saud University Publication (In Arabic).

Buckley, P. J., & Casson, M. (2003). The future of the multinational enterprise in retrospect and in prospect. *Journal of International Business Studies*, 219–222.

Collis, J., & Hussey, R. (2009). *Business research: A practical guide for undergraduate and postgraduate students* (3rd ed.). Basingstoke: Palgrave Macmillan.

Dunning, J. H. (1994). Re-evaluating the benefits of foreign direct investment. *Transnational Corporations, 3*(1), 23–51.

Dunning, J. H. (1998). Location and the multinational enterprise: A neglected factor? *Journal of International Business Studies*, 45–66.

Dunning, J. H. (2006). Comment on Dragon multinationals: New players in 21st century globalization. *Asia Pacific Journal of Management, 23*(2), 139–141.

Goyal, A., & Goyal, M. (2010). *Environment for managers*. New Delhi: V.K. (India) Enterprises.

Habish, N. (2011). *Al-kasuksahwaaturuhi ala houqoua al-amulun be-alqatai al-ama*. Beirut: Mansourt al-habe al-houqoua (In Arabic).

Iaigc.net. (2016). *The Arab Investment and Export Credit Guarantee Corp. (Dhaman)*. Retrieved from http://www.iaigc.net/UserFiles/file/SnP_rating_2012.pdf

IMF. (1993). *Balance of payments manual*. Retrieved from https://www.imf.org/external/np/sta/bop/BOPman.pdf

Kanoua, N. (2005). Alkaskashalekatsadehbeshakelaeamejabuatahwasalbutah (In Arabic). *Tishreen University Journal for Studies and Scientific Research—Economic and Legal Sciences Series, 27*(2), 60.

Mep.gov.sa. (2002). *Privatization strategy of the Kingdom of Saudi Arabia*. Retrieved from http://www.mep.gov.sa/inetforms/themes/clasic/article/articleView.jsp;jsessionid=FC8AE57EEB156FC88F6A3D5639842206.alfa?Article.ObjectID=25

Miga.org. (2016). *Home | Multilateral Investment Guarantee Agency | World Bank Group*. Retrieved February 6, 2016, from http://www.miga.org/

Organisation for Economic Co-operation and Development. (2009). *OECD benchmark definition of foreign direct investment 2008*. Paris: Organisation for Economic Co-operation and Development.

Sagia.gov.sa. (2002). *The Executive Rules of the Foreign Investment Act*. Retrieved from https://www.sagia.gov.sa/Documents/Laws/The%20Executive%20Rules%20of%20the%20Foreign%20Investment%20Act_En_2.3.pdf

Saudi Arabian General Investment Authority. (2010). Retrieved April 21, 2015, from AlTagruareAlsanoueLlHuaihAlAmahLlesthmarLleam.

Saudi Arabian Monetary Agency. (2010). *Report*. Retrieved September 23, 2013, from http://www.sama.gov.sa/sites/samaen/ReportsStatistics/ReportsStatisticsLib/5600_R_Annual_En_48_2013_02_19.pdf

Saudiembassy.net. (1997). *Council of Ministers Meeting*. Retrieved from https://www.saudiembassy.net/archive/1997/news/page118.aspx

Saudiembassy.net. (2000). *Foreign Investment Act and Executive Rules [2000]*. Retrieved from https://www.saudiembassy.net/about/country-information/laws/Foreign_Investment_Act_and_Executive_Rules.aspx

Sornarajah, M. (2004). *The international law on foreign investment*. Cambridge: Cambridge University Press.

Sornarajah, M. (2010). *The international law on foreign investment*. Cambridge University Press.

Unctad.org. (2013). *unctad.org | Foreign Direct Investment (FDI)*. Retrieved from http://unctad.org/en/Pages/DIAE/FDI%20Statistics/Foreign-Direct-Investment-FDI.aspx

Worldenergy.org. (2016). *World Energy Council*. Retrieved February 6, 2016, from http://www.worldenergy.org/

World-petroleum.org. (2016). *World Petroleum Council (WPC)*. Retrieved February 6, 2016, from http://www.world-petroleum.org/

Zergers, J. (2009). Foreign investment protection. In A. Shoult & H. Anwer (Eds.), *Doing business with Saudi Arabia: A guide to investment opportunities and business practice* (4th ed.). London: GMB Publishing Ltd.

CHAPTER 7

Organisational Effectiveness of Private Enterprises and Diversification in the Gulf Countries

Shazia Farooq Fazli and Ayesha Farooq

INTRODUCTION

In his address to the 2002 World Summit on Sustainable Development, Kofi Annan argued that 'without the private sector, sustainable development will remain only a distant dream'. He stressed the pivotal role that private sector enterprises can play in the development process and the need for these enterprises to operate differently (Annan 2014). One aspect of operating differently is to create a link between the external and internal environment of enterprise in such a manner that could develop core competencies through leadership, strategy, processes, culture and human resources, all of them make the enterprise competitive in the market.

S. Farooq Fazli
Department of Sociology, Maulana Azad National Urdu University, Hyderabad, Andhra Pradesh, India

A. Farooq (✉)
Department of Business Administration, Aligarh Muslim University, Aligarh, Uttar Pradesh, India

© Gulf Research Centre Cambridge 2018
A. Mishrif, Y. Al Balushi (eds.), *Economic Diversification in the Gulf Region, Volume I*, The Political Economy of the Middle East, https://doi.org/10.1007/978-981-10-5783-0_7

In the context of Gulf countries, it becomes more important that business must redefine its boundaries and play its role effectively, as this region is undergoing an extraordinary economic and social transformation—a transformation that has an impact on the global economy. In terms of both economic growth and individual wealth, the Gulf region as a whole ranks among the world's top emerging markets. The six-member Gulf Cooperation Council (GCC) including the Kingdom of Saudi Arabia (KSA), United Arab Emirates (UAE), Kuwait, Qatar, Bahrain and Oman represent one of the wealthiest country groupings in the world. Blessed with extensive oil and gas reserves, development and investment in the sector is substantial (Gulf Cooperation Council 2015).

This chapter is an attempt to study the link between country-level macro-dimensions and the managerial aspects prevailing within the organisations. The organisations serve as a bridge, which connect these two ends. We propose that the best performing companies must be the ones deploying the best practices. Hence, the objectives to be achieved are as follows:

- To review the role of private sector in the development of GCC countries.
- To discuss business practices that enhance organisational effectiveness and productivity, thus providing the organisations an edge to contribute significantly towards the economic and social development of the country.

The Role of Private Sector in Diversification Strategies in GCC Countries

During the new oil boom of 2002–2008, GCC countries developed clear long-term diversification strategies. Visions, such as Abu Dhabi 2030, Bahrain 2020 or Oman 2020, fix long-term economic development objectives and priorities for future diversification. Although GCC governments themselves are cash rich, their development strategies increasingly rely on the local private sector for diversification, job creation and building of a more productive and less oil-dependent 'knowledge economy' (Government of Abu Dhabi 2009; General Secretariat for Development Planning 2008).

According to International Monetary Fund (2014b), the GCC economies have been among the best performing regions in the world in recent years.

Particularly, growth in the non-oil sector is expected to remain strong at about 6 per cent, driven by large investments in infrastructure and private sector confidence. Lately, Employment and job creation have taken centre stage. For several GCC countries, job creation for nationals is a key priority (International Monetary Fund 2014a). Other than growth, measures to strengthen education and training, better job placement services and steps to improve the relative attractiveness to employees of private versus public sector employment will be needed.

Gulf business has a chance for greater developmental role and political autonomy only if it increases its interdependence with society at large through providing employment and investment opportunities for GCC citizens. Of these, employment is very important and could decide the political fate of private businesses in this region in the long run. Hertog (2013) emphasised that GCC business now plays a deeper role in sectors like education, health, telecom, heavy industry and air transport, which until the 1990s were partly or completely state controlled. The various long-term development visions that GCC governments have published since the early 2000s state a clear willingness to delegate increasing development tasks to private sector. Fasano and Zubair (2003) argued that the availability of imported skills at internationally competitive wages has been crucial to keeping the cost of production down. Most of the national labour force has been employed in government sector with higher wage expectations than expatriate worker.

Economies of GCC countries are mainly oil dependent, though over the years GCC countries tried hard to diversify their economies and increase the share of non-oil and private sectors in the GDP. Saudi Arabia has an oil-based economy with strong government controls over major public sectors. It possesses about 16 per cent of the world's proven petroleum reserves. The petroleum sector accounts for roughly 80 per cent of budget revenues, 45 per cent of GDP, and 90 per cent of export earnings. Saudi government is encouraging the growth of private sector in order to diversify its economy and to employ more Saudi nationals. Diversification efforts are focusing on power generation, telecommunications, natural gas exploration and petrochemical sectors (CIA World Factbook 2015).

The United Arab Emirates is the world's eighth largest oil producer and upholds a free market economy. Although oil has been the main support for UAE economy and continuous to contribute significantly to economic affluence of the country, non-oil sectors accounted for around 69 per cent of the GDP in recent years. According to the Abu Dhabi's

Economic Vision 2030 and Dubai's Strategic Plan 2015, the strategy of UAE government is to increase investment in industrial and other export-oriented sectors, including heavy industry, transport, petrochemicals, tourism, information technology, telecommunications, renewable energy, aviation and space, and oil and gas services (uaeinteract.com).

Qatar is the third largest economy in the GCC after Saudi Arabia and UAE, accounting for 12 per cent of the regional GDP. Despite a slowdown in real GDP growth because of the timely hold on the liquefied natural gas expansion programme of the country, Qatar has prospered in the last several years with continued high real GDP at 6.1 per cent in 2012 due to non-oil sector. The non-oil industrial and services sectors are estimated to have exhibited strong growth of 10.1 per cent and 9.1 per cent, respectively, according to Qatar National Bank Group. This compares to just 2.1 per cent for the oil and gas sector. Economic diversification plans of Qatar focused on increasing private and foreign investment in non-energy sectors.

Kuwait is a small GCC country but has 6 per cent of the crude oil reserves (around 102 billion barrels) of the world. Petroleum accounts for nearly half of the GDP, 95 per cent of export revenues and 95 per cent of government income. In 2010, Kuwait passed an economic development plan that assured to spend up to US$130 billion over five years to diversify the economy away from oil, attract more investment and boost private sector participation in the economy (World Factbook 2015).

Oman is a middle-income economy and not as wealthy as its nearby GCC countries. Oman's economy is heavily dependent on decreasing oil resources. For the reason of declining reserves and rapidly growing national youths in employment age group, the country actively proposed a development plan that focuses on economic diversification, industrialisation and privatisation, with the objective of reducing the oil sector's contribution to GDP up to 9 per cent by 2020 and creating more jobs to offer work for the rising numbers of Omanis entering the workforce. Tourism and gas-based industries are key components of the government's diversification strategy.

Bahrain has made great efforts to diversify its economy; its geographical location along with highly developed communication and transport facilities and most importantly free economic atmosphere make Bahrain home to numerous multinational firms with business in the Gulf. Although hydrocarbon reserves of Bahrain are decreasing very fast, but Bahrain's economy continues to depend heavily on oil. In 2013, petroleum production and refining accounted for 73 per cent of Bahrain's export receipts, 88 per cent of government revenues and 21 per cent of GDP. As a part of its economic diversification campaign, major economic activities are production of aluminium—Bahrain's second biggest export after oil—finance and construction. Bahrain continues to seek new natural gas supplies as feedstock to support its expanding petrochemical and aluminium industries.

Being oil-dependent economies, the main economic sector of GCC countries is industry. However, substantially high share of service sector indicates towards economic diversification efforts of GCC countries. Bahrain is on the top with 53 per cent share of service sector in the total GDP of Bahrain, Kuwait 49 per cent and Saudi Arabia 43 per cent are in the top league of economic diversification plans of GCC countries.

Lately, GCC countries have become strong. There has been a recognition in these countries that to support the growth momentum and create sustainable development, they need to diversify their sources of income beyond hydrocarbons. They have, therefore, used their sizable surpluses to finance large projects with the aim of diversifying their economies and creating additional pockets of growth. As a result, the contribution of non-hydrocarbon sector to growth has increased in recent years and is currently the main driver of growth in most of these countries, said the QNB Group in a recent report. It says a significant part of investments is going into infrastructure projects such as the building of new cities, roads, transport networks, real estate and power and water stations. This is partially to accommodate the region's growing populations but mainly to create infrastructure that enables the private sector to play a bigger role in the economy (arabnews.com).

In the long run, the dynamism and innovation of private sector is expected to drive growth and development with the government focusing on formualation of right physical and legal environment to encourage that process. While this 'horizontal diversification' away from hydrocarbons is the main common theme behind the large capital spending in GCC countries, there is also a 'vertical diversification' that is taking place. This represents investments in petrochemicals and other industries to move up the hydrocarbon value chain. Notwithstanding the diversification aim common across all GCC countries, there are important differences in the vision of each country and how they go about executing their visions. Saudi Arabia's ninth development plan for 2010–2014 aimed to diversify the economy away from dependence on hydrocarbons and create jobs for the large and growing population. The Kingdom's development strategy is built around the creation of four new economic cities, each with its own strategic focus, such as knowledge-based industries and services, metals and food production, automotive products, logistics and agribusiness.

To encourage the development of the private sector, the government has assigned leading role to private companies as the master developers for the economic cities. The largest economic city is the US$93 billion King Abdullah Economic City (KAEC) being developed by Emaar, added the report. KAEC plans for 2 million inhabitants by 2025 and includes the largest port in the Red Sea region and a logistics and industrial area. It intends to leverage large-scale industrial complexes nearby to target industries such as petrochemicals, pharmaceuticals and automotive. KAEC also aims to provide high-quality living conditions near the recently completed King Abdullah University for Science and Technology, supporting the Kingdom's development of human capital. In Qatar, the National Vision 2030 focuses on diversifying the economy away from hydrocarbons by building a knowledge-based economy through investing in human development and education. For example, the US$7.5 billion Education City project aims to create a regional educational centre of excellence by building schools and attracting branch campuses of renowned global universities. It also hosts Qatar Science and Technology Park, which commissions applied scientific research and turns them into commercialised products.

Similarly, Abu Dhabi's Economic Vision 2030 also foresees diversifying away from hydrocarbons by building a knowledge-based economy through investment in education. For example, Abu Dhabi has established a number of branches of leading universities, such as New York University, Abu Dhabi, and INSEAD Abu Dhabi. Meanwhile, with limited hydrocarbon resources, Dubai has diversified its economy into service sector, such as retail, tourism, exhibitions, events, re-export and finance. It has invested heavily in infrastructure and logistics, such as large port and warehousing facilities and a range of free trade zones with minimal regulation and taxes.

This has helped to create regional business hubs in different industries, such as manufacturing and service. Dubai continues to invest heavily in making the Emirate an attractive destination for visitors, retail and to live. For example, the US$147 billion Dubai Land project, a tourism, leisure and residential development, is the largest real estate development in the GCC. In Kuwait, the Kuwait Development Plan is a series of five-year plans starting in 2010 and stretching to 2035. The aim is to modernise and expand the country's infrastructure with the strategic goal of turning Kuwait into a financial and trade hub. A few priority projects such as Az-zour power station, water waste management projects and building of schools and hospitals are already underway. The development of Bobiyan Island Port is central towards transforming Kuwait into a regional commercial and trade hub. Overall, capital expenditure will continue to gather momentum throughout the GCC. This should underpin the process of diversification and moving towards a sustainable growth model in accordance with the national visions of each respective country (arabnews.com).

Theoretical Perspectives on Organisational Effectiveness and Management Practices

Organisational Effectiveness and Productivity

Throughout history, economic growth has been fuelled by two factors: the expanding pool of workers in organisations and their increasing productivity and performance. From the perspective of rising prosperity, however, it is productivity that makes all the difference. Disparities in Gross Domestic Product per capita among countries—or between the past and the present in the same country—primarily reflect differences in labour productivity and performance. That in turn is the result of production and operational factors, technological advances, and managerial skills. As managers improve efficiency, invest and innovate to be competitive, their collective actions expand the global economy.

For nearly a quarter century, the McKinsey Global Institute (MGI) has focused on the role of productivity growth in economic performance. Along the way, MGI's findings have challenged conventional thinking about the sources of productivity growth and clarified two primary lessons for policymakers and executives. The first is to accept no sweeping generalisations regarding the state of a country's competitiveness or the prospects for its future economic performance. Macro-level insights can be generated only by rolling granular examination of individual businesses up to the industry, sector and country levels. The second is to recognise productivity improvements as the primary source of sustained and long-term economic growth. According to Manyika et al. (2014), in order to raise economic performance, there is a need to focus on the causes of productivity differences among companies, sectors, industries, and countries.

Etzioni (1964) stated that organisational effectiveness is the concept of how effective an organisation is in achieving its vision, mission and purpose. Organisational effectiveness captures organisational performance plus the myriad internal performance outcomes normally associated with more efficient or effective operations and other external measures. These measures relate to considerations that are broader than those simply associated with economic valuation (either by shareholders, managers or customers), such as 'corporate governance' and 'corporate social responsibility (CSR)'. An organisation's effectiveness is dependent on its strategy, structure, processes, culture, communicative competence and ethics. The relationship among these is simultaneous. Farooq and Hussain (2011) argued that many of the organisations competing in the fast-changing business environment are in a constant search for a robust strategy to help survive the new global economic order, making achieving improved performance continuously imperative.

To compete and contribute to the country's economic development, organisations continually need to improve their performance by reducing cost, innovating products, processes and services, and improving quality, productivity and speed to market. Muogbo (2013) emphasised that achieving a competitive advantage position and enhancing firm performance about their competitors are the main objectives that business organisations, in particular, should strive to attain.

Despite strong GDP growth and high oil prices, several of the GCC economies have experienced falling labour productivity for some time, a trend that accelerated after 2009. Promisingly, the amount of output produced per worker is improving in the UAE with marginal productivity growth recorded in 2011 and 2012. Saudi Arabia, Oman and Qatar have also recorded improvements in productivity over the five years to 2012 (Augustine 2014).

Looking at the GCC countries over the past two decades, capital investment and labour force growth have been the main drivers of growth in the non-oil sector, while total factor productivity (TFP)—a measure of how efficiently capital and labour inputs are being used in the production process—has generally declined. For the period since 1990, TFP growth has been negative for all the GCC countries, with only Saudi Arabia experiencing some positive TFP growth in non-oil sector. Comparing the 1990s to the period since 2000, TFP growth in non-oil sector was positive for some GCC countries in the 1990s but has deteriorated and turned negative over the last decade. In Saudi Arabia, TFP growth in non-oil sector has improved and became positive in the 2000s, compared to the 1990s (International Monetary Fund 2014).

Management/Business Practices

The term world class manufacturing (WCM), is a set of practices, including quality management, continuous improvement, training and investment in technology (Hayes and Wheelwright 1984). WCM means continual and rapid improvement in all areas of the company, where training act as a catalyst. Schonberger (1986) regarded improving material flow in the production as one of the most important issues, which could be enhanced through implementing just-in-time (JIT), total quality control and total preventive maintenance (TPM). He argued that many lessons could be learned from the Japanese manufacturing industry.

In the late 1970s and early 1980s, the 'best practice' approach to manufacturing strategy seriously entered the industrial and academic agenda with recognition of the extraordinary process and product improvement success of Japan Inc. Western industries and academics alike began to look at Japanese companies' achievements to understand the principles behind that. 'Best practice' achievement has since become a driving force among the industry. According to Voss (1995a), the best practice approach to manufacturing strategy encapsulates the world class manufacturing (WCM) philosophy and benchmarking and is based on the assumption that 'The continuous improvement of best practice in all areas of the organisation will lead to superior performance capability leading to increased competitiveness'.

The basic principle of the best practice thinking is that operations philosophies, concepts and techniques should be driven by competitive benchmarks and business excellence models to improve an organisation's competitiveness through development of people, processes and technology (Greswell et al. 1998; Voss 1995b). The implementation of these 'best practices' would lead to superior performance (Flynn et al. 1998).

Davies and Kochhar (2002) argue that best practices are those that lead to improvement in performance. That is, they help a low-performing company become a medium performer, a medium performer become a high-performing company and a high performer stay successful. Laugen et al. (2005) assume that the best performing companies deploy the best practices. To find out what are those practices, the highest performing companies in the 2002 International Manufacturing Strategy Survey database were identified by them, and the role 14 practices play in these companies was investigated. Laugen et al. (2005) concluded that process focus, pull production, equipment productivity and environmental compatibility appear to qualify as best practices. Quality management may have been best practice previously, but lost that status. E-business, new product development (NPD), supplier strategy and outsourcing are relatively new, cannot yet be qualified as, but may develop into, best practice.

Bloom et al. (2007) have examined practices and performance of more than 4000 medium-sized manufacturing operations in Europe, the United States of America and Asia. The findings of the study support earlier research which asserts that firms across the globe that apply accepted management practices perform significantly better than those that do not. This suggests that the improved management practice is one of the most effective ways for a firm to outperform its peers. Greater competitive intensity drives improved management practice, while labour market flexibility leads to particularly good people management habits.

Bloom et al. (2007) found that better-managed firms also have a more highly educated workforce, among managers and non-managers alike. For companies, this research is good news, suggesting that they have access to dramatic improvements in performance simply by adopting good practices used elsewhere. For policymakers, it lays down a challenge. The overall performance of most countries is determined not by the performance of its leading companies, but by the size of its 'tail' of poor performers. By developing environments that promote good management practices across all firms and by devoting as much attention to the followers as to leaders, governments can drive the competitiveness of their entire economies.

Thus, it becomes imperative that organisations play a pivotal role and must look externally as well as internally. On one hand, with CSR practices, corporate governance and marketing their products and services, organisations can relate and contribute to society and national economy. On the other, organisations have to look inside and focus on its strategy, leadership, systems, functions and processes and human resources. To contribute substantially towards the economic growth of the region, the organisations have to attain competitive advantage, therefore, must also focus on those business practices of the organisation that lead to a competitive environment.

Methodology

Research Design

This is a qualitative and secondary data based chapter which studies the extent to which economy has been diversified in GCC countries and the contribution of different sectors in economic growth. The chapter concentrates on understanding and explaining management practices in an organisation across Gulf countries presented as a case study. This has addressed questions such as: What is the contribution of different sectors in GDP of GCC countries? To what extent management and organisational practices matter for effectiveness, productivity and growth, both directly and through their role in innovation, human resource management, the use of information technology, knowledge management and the response to the demands of external environment? Better business practices are significantly associated with higher productivity and effectiveness, and other indicators of corporate performance. Improving management practice is also associated with rise in productivity and output.

McKinsey's 7S Framework

The present chapter is based on the conceptual model that incorporates McKinsey's 7S Framework.

Figure 7.1 exhibits business practices as independent variable, organisational effectiveness as mediating variable, and economic and social

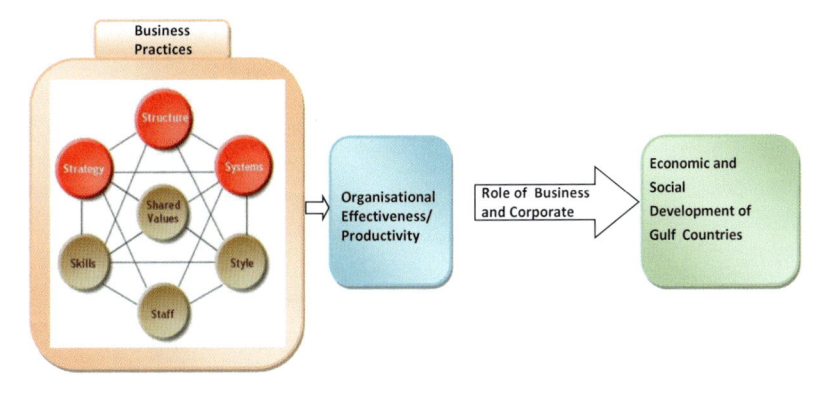

Fig. 7.1 Conceptual model: McKinsey's 7S Framework (adapted by the authors)

development as the dependent variable. Peters and Waterman (1982) argued that management practices pertain to 'hard and soft S' as provided by McKinsey's 7S Framework. Various management practices which successful and effective companies follow are derived from 7S, namely, superordinate goals/shared values, strategy, structure, style, systems, staff and skills. Management practices falling under the categories of leadership, human resource management, production and operations, marketing and finance are covered by 7S. Business and organisational effectiveness provided in the conceptual model serve as linking pins.

The McKinsey 7S Framework has been chosen to suggest as an implementation model as it combines rational and hard elements with soft and emotional elements, which are interconnected and interrelated. The model is most often used as an organisational analysis tool to assess and monitor changes in internal situation of an organisation. We try to look at the existence of an organisation through its purpose or objectives. In order to achieve that purpose or objectives, these 7Ss are vital.

'**Strategy**' represents the major approaches adopted by an organisation to achieve its vision and goals. It derives from assessment of organisation's internal strengths and weaknesses, and external opportunities and threats (SWOT analysis) and includes environment influences, nature of competition, company distinctive competencies and company's key success factors. The basic argument is that strategy must be dynamic not static that is, responsive to internal and external environment.

'**Structure**' prescribes formal relationships among various positions and activities. Now, the question is why should you prescribe a formal relationship among various positions and activities? What are the reasons for doing so? A structure helps in reducing internal uncertainty arising out of variable, unpredictable, random human behaviour within the organisation through control mechanism. Structure provides the roles and responsibilities in the organisation and gives to the individual certain amount of authority, in order to execute his roles and responsibilities. So, he can exercise certain amount of authority in the organisation. This authority in the organisation, what does it do? It reduces the internal uncertainty about his role in the organisation. The structure enables focus and coordination of organisation's activities. In other words, the structure is something which makes the organisation to have a focus to exist, that is why does it exist in the first place?

Practices Related to Structure

Communication: Communication is the key to fostering empathy and building relationships of openness, trust and honesty with team. The first step for effective communication is to create time and space for people to talk and ask questions. After all, people cannot be motivated until they understand the outcome. Objectives should be set clear for both the organisation and its people, to discuss and negotiate them, people should know what support and resources they have access to and rewards should be clearly link to objectives. Providing timely and meaningful feedback to staff is crucial, as is determining how best to give them this feedback. Leaders must tailor their approach to each individual, with some people requiring regular assurance and support while others preferring more autonomy.

Non-verbal behaviour is just as important as what people say. So effective managers need to be keen observers to gauge how people are responding to a work situation at an emotional level. Communication needs to flow in all directions, from managers to their staff, from staff to managers and between team members. An effective leader is a good listener and fosters an environment where people get to know each other and understand each other's strengths, weaknesses and styles. Good managers are open to the input of their staff and learn from their feedback (Josie Chun, careerfaqs.com).

The next S in the organisation refers to **'Systems'** that are rules, regulations, processes and procedures—formal and informal that complements the organisation structure. This is also referred to as the infrastructure in the organization.

Management Practices Related to Lean Manufacturing (System) often simply 'lean', is a systematic method for the elimination of waste within a manufacturing process. The role of the leaders within the organisation is the fundamental element of sustaining the progress of lean thinking. Some commonly mentioned goals are:

Improve quality: To stay competitive in today's marketplace, a company must understand its customers' wants and needs and design processes to meet their expectations and requirements.

Eliminate waste: Waste is any activity that consumes time, resources or space but does not add any value to the product or service.

Reduce time: Reducing the time it takes to finish an activity from start to finish is one of the most effective ways to eliminate waste and lower costs.

Reduce total costs: To minimise cost, a company must produce only to customer demand. Overproduction increases a company's inventory costs because of storage needs.

The next S in the organisation is what we call 'style'. What is style? Style is the lever to bring about organisational change, pattern of action taken by top management over a period of time. Style is reflected in the form of leadership and governance practices, which creates the climate for the organisational members.

Management Practices Related to Leadership and Governance (Style): The GCC countries are ruled by traditionally organised family groups, with varying underlying executive, legislative and judicial models. Leadership and governance will therefore, be instrumental in determining the path that the GCC countries will take over in future. Although, much is being undertaken today in terms of reforms to improve the efficiency and openness of these systems, the strategies chosen and the rates of change vary between GCC countries. In managing both internal stability and reforms, leadership plays a critical role at all levels of GCC government as well as in the private sector.

Show empathy: Empathy is the ability to listen to people, relate to their emotional experience and let them know that you are doing so. It is the most important core competency for managers and leaders. Developing the ability to understand people and connect with them in a genuine, meaningful way is a key determining factor in how effective you can be at influencing them, setting them objectives that motivate them and rewarding them in a way they each actually find rewarding (Josie Chun, careerfaqs.com).

Encourage innovation: It's important for leaders to think outside the square and know when to take risks, take risks with your employees—often they bring pleasant surprises. By giving people the latitude to work through problems and solutions themselves, you will encourage innovation, creativity and resourcefulness. Lee advises, 'Let your team think for themselves, don't strangle their creativity. Encourage innovation—Google allows one day a week for every employee for innovation (Josie Chun, careerfaqs.com).

Be flexible: Good managers have a flexible approach and adapt their style to individual employees, allowing them to work to their own style. Flexible workplace practices have also emerged as an increasingly important priority for many employees. A recent survey by Leadership Management Australasia lists flexible work arrangements/hours as the fifth most important influence on employee performance and fourth most important reason for employees to stay with an organisation. In other words, flexibility pays (Josie Chun, careerfaqs.com).

The next S is *staffing*. Staffing refers to selection, placement, training and development of appropriately qualified employees. The example that I have taken is that of Hindustan lever. This organisation, Hindustan Lever, places an enormous amount of effort in recruitment, so, the process of recruitment itself. If you really see, when they come for recruitment to different campuses in the country at different levels, they make it a point to explain to the candidate concerned. Last S, in the organisation is *skills*. Skills are the most crucial attribute or capability of an organisation; it is also referred to as the distinctive competence in the organisation.

Management Practices Related to Human Resource Development (Staffing and Skills)

Human resource planning focuses on the process of analysing an organisation's human resource needs and developing the activities necessary to satisfy these needs under changing conditions.

Select the right people: It all starts with getting the right team in place—together, the whole can be greater than the sum of its parts. Organisations need to select the right people for the right jobs, build a complementary team, and align your people with your organisational goals and culture. 'The development of key people may be the single greatest determinant of an organisation's ability to deal with uncertainty and succeed. Central to development is a leader's ability to engage people and align the needs of individuals with those of the organisation to deliver a united and cohesive front', states Grant Sexton, managing director of Leadership Management Australasia (Josie Chun, careerfaqs.com).

Develop your staff: Help your employees to succeed—their success is your success. Be patient. Coach them and coach them and coach them ... they'll remember one day. The best way to coach your people is to help them focus on process rather than content. As a manager you will have people coming to you with issues and problems, but instead of getting bogged down in the detail, coach people by asking them to outline the problem, describe the impact the problem is having, describe what they've tried already, define an ideal outcome, explore the resources they might use to get there, consider possible next steps, have them try it and come back with the results. This turns the problem into a great learning opportunity and empowers the person to solve the problem themselves (Josie Chun, careerfaqs.com).

Career management related to the process of designing and implementing goals, plans and strategies to satisfy the organisational needs while allowing individuals to achieve their career goals.

Performance evaluation is focused on measuring and evaluating an employee's past performance against a standard of performance.

Rewards focuses on repaying equitably for a service based on the quality of service.

Shared Values or Super Ordinate goal in an organisation refers to the set of values and aspirations that goes beyond the conventional formal statement of corporate objectives or fundamental ideas around which a business has built its main values.

Case Study of the Private Enterprise in the GCC Countries

This case study is based on interview conducted with Chairman and Managing Director of Manappat Group of Companies, Mr. Ameer Ahamed. An appointment was taken from him and a face-to-face interview was conducted which went on for 80 minutes. The data collection methodology adopted to develop this case was an open-ended interview. A list of guiding questions was preplanned. Interviewing method was flexible to an extent that the interviewer had the freedom to formulate questions as the interview progressed around the investigated central phenomenon, but it was inflexible with regard to asking only the preplanned questions. The interview was recorded and it was listened to by the experts. Salient aspects were extracted from the interview and it was organised into a case study.

- Case study is a qualitative method based on a strategy of enquiry. Creswell (2009) has observed that the qualitative research cannot be carried out by random sampling; rather a purposeful sampling strategy is adopted. The objective is to explore a central phenomenon and not to generalise the findings to the representative sample. The objective is to learn from the people who are information rich with respect to a central phenomenon under study. Some of the characteristics of qualitative method are (Creswell 2009):

- It allows direct interaction with the person studied in the context, through interview and behavioural observation.
- Data is collected through examining documents related to the person under study.
- More than one sources of data are reviewed, made sense of and organised into themes.
- Emphasis is laid on the meaning which the interviewee provides, and not the researcher's meaning.
- As a result, a complex picture is developed by putting together different perspectives and identifying several factors involved in the problem.

Mr. Ameer Ahamed, the Chairman and MD of Manappat Group of Companies, is a vibrant, versatile business house with an unrivalled portfolio of interests and investments. The group has its turnover to the tune of approximately INR 700 Crores (2015). The group has its business spread across the Sultanate of Oman, United Arab Emirates, India, Saudi Arabia and United Kingdom (Fozia et.al. 2016).

The group has interests in the following five industries (Exhibit 7.1).

Engineering: They undertake wide-ranging civil, electromechanical and fire engineering projects throughout the Persian Gulf and the Indian subcontinent. Using technical expertise and specialist resources, they undertake major commercial, residential and specialist construction projects. They undertake designing and installation of the latest fire protection products and services; install and commission electromechanical works, including building electrification, plumbing, drainage, air-conditioning, power installation and lighting; and carry out complete interior decorative and design works.

Trading: Organisations and individuals working in the construction, oil and gas, petroleum and petrochemical, manufacturing, marine and agricultural and fisheries industries, among many others, rely on their specialist applications and solutions to maintain their day-to-day operations and to work productively and efficiently.

Foods: Manappat Group distributes popular frozen food products to more than 1500 shops, restaurants, supermarkets, hotels and catering companies. They also market in-demand brands of carbonated drinks, fruit juice and beverages, including leading international brands and well-established own brands.

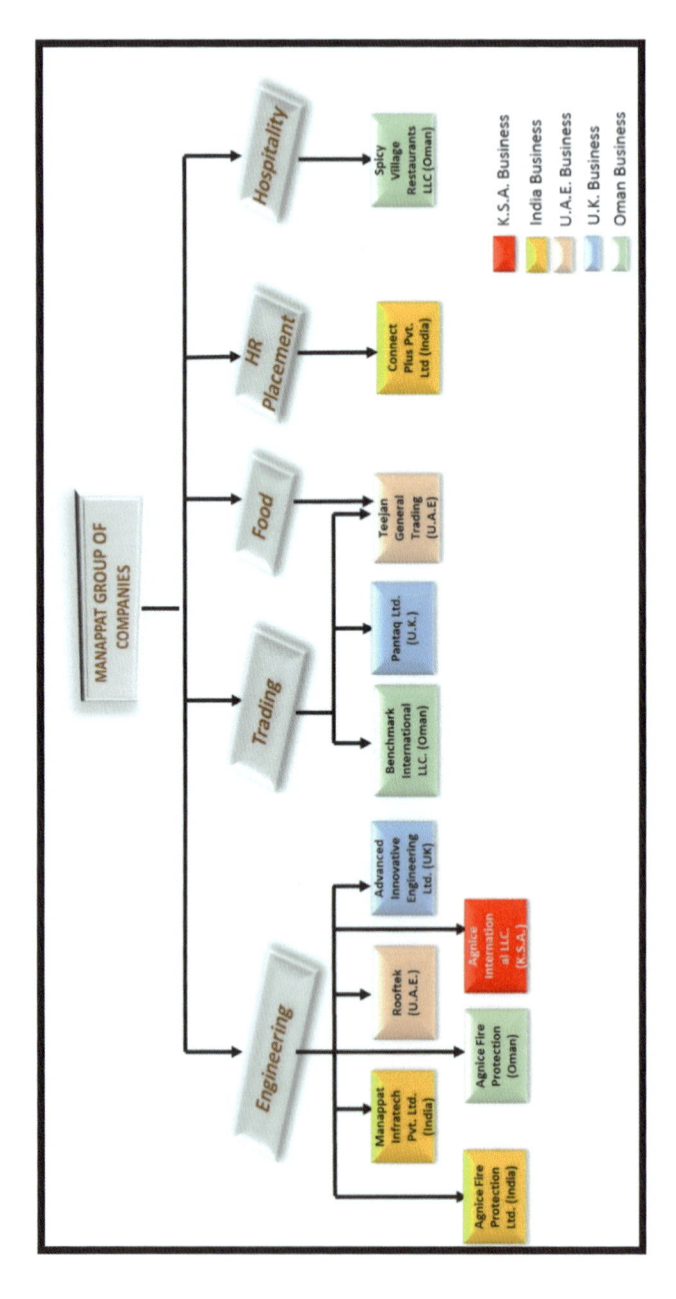

Exhibit 7.1 Industry-wise distribution of Manappat Group of Companies

Human Resources: They provide organisations of all sizes with high-calibre personnel drawn from across India. They also supply permanent, temporary and contract staff and specialise in finding the right candidates for the right jobs in the construction, engineering, oil and gas, IT, hospitality, finance and healthcare industries.

Hospitality: They provide end-to-end services and facilities for parties, conferences or executive lunches for corporations and individuals.

The description of various companies and corporate structure (Exhibit 7.2) in different countries is as under.

Sultanate of Oman

Benchmark International LLC.: Incepted in 2009, Benchmark International is a market-leading supplier of specialist products and services to the construction, oil and gas, petroleum and petrochemical, environmental, manufacturing, marine and agricultural and fisheries industries. From fire curtains to flooring systems, shutters to seating systems, moveable walls to complete state-of-the-art mobile storage systems, our products, systems and solutions are essential for maintaining day-to-day operations and processes and working productively and efficiently in quality-conscious industries throughout Oman.

Spicy Village Restaurants LLC.: Incepted in 1987, The Spicy Village restaurants are famous throughout Oman for their exquisite food, welcoming, congenial atmosphere and fast and friendly service. Offering lip-smacking Indian, Chinese and Continental cuisine at affordable prices and superb service, they are the perfect location for an unforgettable night out with family and friends, a productive business lunch with colleagues and clients or to celebrate a birthday or special occasion in style.

Agnice Fire Protection: Incepted in 2009, this prominent fire engineering company custom designs, engineers and installs superior fire protection systems and helps organisations throughout the Middle East manage fire risk.

United Arab Emirates

Teejan General Trading: Teejan General Trading is one of the leading distributors of specialised building materials in the United Arab Emirates since 1992. They exclusively distribute ESSCOFOAM extruded polystyrene insulation boards in the UAE, which have been used to insulate in

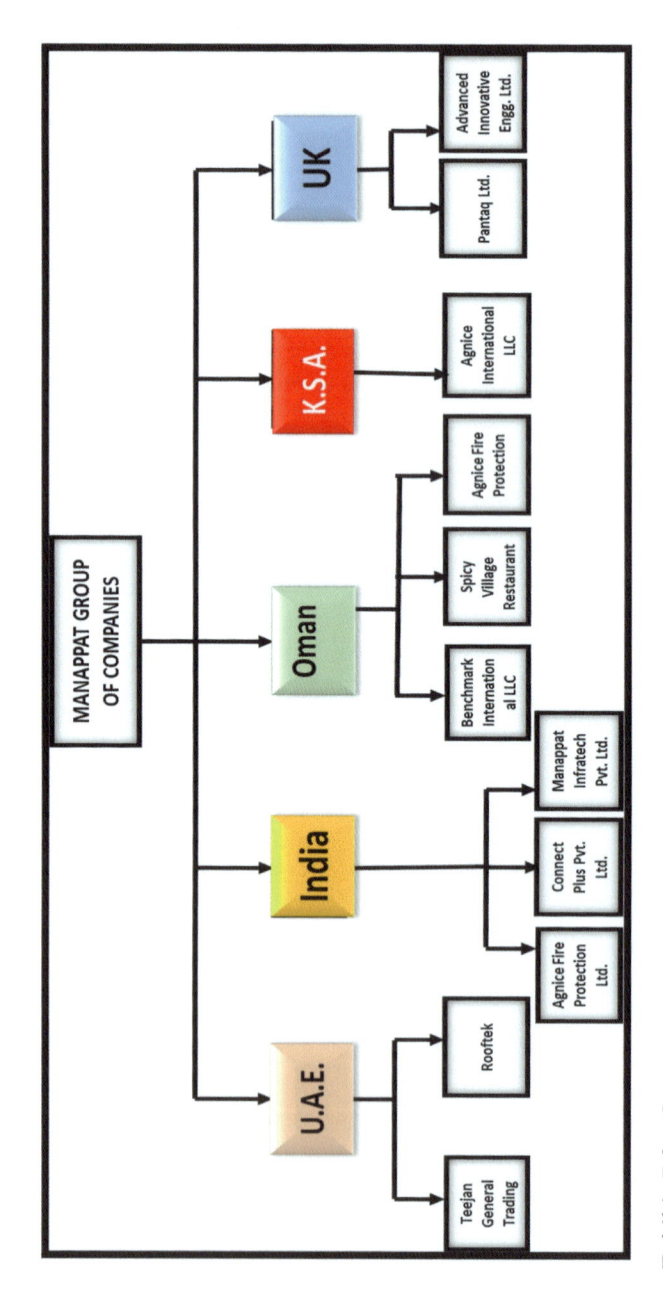

Exhibit 7.2 Corporate structure

various prestigious projects in Dubai International Airport, City Centre Deira, Dubai International City, Dubai Festival City, Dubai Internet City, Dubai Marina, Emaar Towers, Mall of Emirates Hotel, Dubai World Trade Centre Hotel and so on.

Rooftek: Rooftek is one of the major suppliers and contractors specialising in waterproofing, industrial coating and allied services in UAE. Established in 2004, they have emerged as a key player in the industry within a short span of time. Their solutions include waterproofing, insulation, GRP lining and all types of functional flooring for specified usage. Their trading division supplies specialised products required for the waterproofing industry. They have completed projects of various dimensions from as small as AED 50k to AED 13 million. Rooftek is committed to providing the highest quality of products and services to their customers, no matter how large or small. This is of fundamental importance for the continuous success of the organisation.

Saudi Arabia

Eram-Agnice International LLC: This joint venture company was formed in 2012. It is a fire engineering company custom-designs, engineers and installs superior fire protection systems, and helps organisations throughout the Middle East manage fire risk. The company has its operations in India and the United Kingdom also which are not considered for the present case.

IMPACT OF ORGANISATIONAL EFFECTIVENESS AND MANAGEMENT PRACTICE ON MANAPPAT ENTERPRISE IN THE GULF COUNTRIES

Manappat Enterprise has been analysed for organisational effectiveness based on seven key internal elements such as strategy, structure, systems, shared values, style, staff and skills. The mentioned elements of Manappat Group of Companies are discussed below reflecting their mutual alignment leading to an effective organisation.

Strategy

Manappat Group of Companies has adopted a combination strategy for obtaining continuous competitive advantage. The Group has adopted a mix of stability, expansion and divestment strategies over a period of time for different businesses. The strategy adopted for expansion of the hospitality business is predominantly based upon concentration strategy. Under this strategy, market development, product development and market penetration alternatives were considered. Multiple restaurants were set up at different locations in Oman thus, broadening the customer group catered by the business. In the trading business, Manappat Group has expanded through various vertical integrations into UAE, which were timely in terms of geographical expansions and also in terms of market expansion into green field areas. With regard to entry into the Human Resource Industry, the expansion was predominantly to leverage the internal recruitment capacity of the Manappat Group itself. HR division is established with the state of the art infrastructure which caters to external clients too. Manappat Group established their presence into the Fire Protection Industry in India, Oman and Saudi Arabia over a period of time through investment, divestment and internationalisation strategies. Manappat Group entered the trading business through several contractual agreements with suppliers of a range of products. The Group entered into a related diversification in India through engineering sector. Manappat Group has also diversified into the area of Robotics and Aerial Surveillance, an unrelated engineering field into a new geography.

Structure

The Group has well-organised teams. There is a top team which steers the group into various sectors and aligns businesses to the group's vision and mission. The top team consists of the group MD and Chairman along with the top management of five business verticals. The next ring consists of dedicated teams representing companies in different verticals. These teams are well organised with a clear line of accountability in place. The rationality for Manappat Group to have resorted to a combination of centralised and decentralised organisational structure is to ensure timely decision-making in a group which is spread across 5 countries, 5 industries and 11 companies. The centralised decision-making is a necessity for an effective control over the profitability of all the business units.

Systems

Manappat Group has established processes and procedures to ensure seamless functioning of the group. Each vertical has a process attuned to the industry requirements in order to support right decision making at right time. It is this timely decision-making capability of the conglomerate which has led to its growth, both vertically and horizontally.

Style

Mr. Ameer Ahmad has developed a culture of involving his employees in problem understanding, problem discussion and finding solutions. His managing style is a mix of democratic and MBWA (managing by walking around). This style fits in with his personality characteristic of being innovative with high need for achievement. Adopting this particular style of management has helped them find innovative solutions for the problems/issues faced by the organisation. Similar style trickles down across the length and breadth of the organisational structure.

Staff

Manappat Group is into Human Resources Placement business and specialises in providing temporary, contractual or permanent placements of high-calibre manpower from across the country. This vertical provides recruitment services to internal customers that is, within Manappat Group of Companies and also external customers across the country. The manpower recruited for the Group is well skilled and competent enough to deliver the services as per the organisational requirements. Most of the recruited personnel have technological skills which is reflective of Manappat Groups' predominance in the engineering industry.

Skills

The recruited employees have the required skills and abilities to perform and meet the organisational objectives. Regular training is imparted to the employees by Manappat Group to keep the employees capable of performing their tasks suitably.

Shared Values

Mr. Ameer Ahmad, the MD and Chairman of the group values honesty, trust worthiness and a sense of shared vision within the organisation. Contributing to the social responsibility of the employees, there are policies in place which ensure them to send money back home for family upkeep and also encourage the employees to save a month's salary to spend during holidays while they are with their families. The HR department of each company ensures that every new person inducted in the company is sensitised with the shared responsibilities. These norms are the guiding principles for employee behaviour towards a common goal.

The above seven elements are well aligned with each other to generate synergy within the organisation.

Conclusion

A fast-growing economy means a growing workforce and hence the emphasis on those management practices that increase effectiveness. Moreover, the high percentage of the expatriate workforce makes the working environment very different from the previous research settings.

Most of the research on management practices, competitive advantage, organisational effectiveness and productivity has focused on western organisations, and a need for research in the Arab context has been identified. It is expected to add to the richness of the management practices by exploring various aspects of performance in a unique working environment that is predominantly based on expatriate workforce and is in contrast to the traditional comparatively more stable work cultures. Improving management practice is also associated with large increases in productivity and output. Due to the intense competition, companies in GCC have been forced to take a systematic approach to management. Only by having strong and effective management practices in place, they would be able to replicate the standards of performance shown by American and Japanese companies operating across different regions, cultures and markets. Today, these companies are reaping the benefits of this effort in terms of higher productivity, better returns on capital and growth that is more robust.

References

Annan, K. (2014). Address to the World Summit on Sustainable Development. *World Summit on Sustainable Development*, 26 August–4 September 2002. Retrieved October 10, 2014, from http://www.un.org/events/wssd/

Augustine Babu Das. (2014). *Deputy Business Editor, GCC needs to diversify further to cut oil dependence*. Retrieved October 20, 2014, from gulfnews.com: http://m.gulfnews.com/business/gcc-needs-to-diversify-further-to-cut-oil-dependence-1.1335660

Bloom, N., Dorgan, S., Dowdy, J., & Van Reenen, J. (2007). *Management practice and productivity: Why they matter*. Retrieved from http://cep.lse.ac.uk/management/Management_Practice_and_Productivity.pdf

CIA. (2015). *The World Fact Book*. Retrieved May 27, 2015, from https://www.cia.gov/Library/publications/the-world-factbook/geos/mu.html

Creswell, J. W. (2009). *Research design: Qualitative, quantitative and mixed methods approaches* (3rd ed.). London: Sage.

Davies, A. J., & Kochhar, A. K. (2002). Manufacturing best practice and performance studies: A critique. *International Journal of Operations & Production Management, 22*(3), 289–305.

Etzioni, A. (1964). *Modern organizations*. Englewood Cliffs, NJ: Prentice-Hall.

Farooq, A., & Hussain, Z. (2011). Balanced scorecard perspective on change and performance: A study of selected Indian companies in Procedia. *Science Direct*, Elsevier, 1–13.

Fasano, U., & Zubair, I. (2003). *GCC countries: From oil dependence to diversification*. Washington, DC: International Monetary Fund.

Flynn, B. B., Schroeder Greswell, T., Childe, S., & Mull, R. (1998). Three manufacturing strategy archetypes—A framework for the Aerospace industry. In U. Bititci & A. Carrie (Eds.), *Strategic management of the manufacturing value chain* (pp. 53–61). Dordrecht: Kluwer Academic Publishers.

Fozia, M., Khan, F., Ahmad, & Farooq, A. (2016). *Indian management cases*. Mumbai: ET Cases.

General Secretariat for Development Planning. (2008). *The Qatar National Vision 2030*.

Government of Abu Dhabi. (2009). *Abu Dhabi Economic Vision 2030*.

Greswell, T., Childe, S., & Mull, R. (1998). Three manufacturing strategy archetypes—A framework for the Aerospace industry. In U. Bititci & A. Carrie (Eds.), *Strategic management of the manufacturing value chain* (pp. 53–61). Dordrecht: Kluwer Academic Publishers.

Gulf Cooperation Council (GCC). (2015). Retrieved May 28, 2015, from http://www.international.gc.ca/strategy-strategie/r8.aspx?lang=eng

Hayes, R. H., & Wheelwright, S. C. (1984). *Restoring our competitive edge: Competing through manufacturing*. New York: John Wiley.

Hertog, S. (2013). *The private sector and reform in the Gulf Cooperation Council*. Retrieved from http://www.lse.ac.uk/middleEastCentre/kuwait/documents/The-private-sector-and-reform-in-the-GCC

International Monetary Fund. (2014a). *Annual meeting of Ministers of Finance and Central Bank Governors, labor market reforms to boost employment and productivity in the GCC—An update*, Kuwait City, Kuwait.

International Monetary Fund. (2014b, October 25). *IMF Managing Director Christine Lagarde welcomes GCC countries strong economic performance identifies key reforms to sustain growth*.

Laugen, B. T., Acur, N., Boer, H., & Frick, J. (2005). Best manufacturing practices: What do the best-performing companies do? *International Journal of*

Operations & Production Management, 25(2), 131–150. Emerald Group Publishing Limited.

Manyika, J., Remes, J., & Woetzel, J. (2014, September). *A productivity perspective on the future of growth*. Retrieved October 15, 2014, from http://www.mckinsey.com/insights/economic_studies/a_productivity_perspective_on_the_future_of_growth

Muogbo, U. S. (2013). The impact of strategic management on organisational growth and development (A study of selected manufacturing firms in Anambra state). *IOSR Journal of Business and Management (IOSR-JBM), 7*(Issue 1 (Jan.–Feb. 2013)), 24–32.

Peters, T., & Waterman, R. H. (1982). *In search of excellence: Lessons from America's best run companies*. New York: Harper Collins.

Schonberger, R. J. (1986). *World class manufacturing: The lessons of simplicity applied*. New York: The Free Press.

The GCC Countries and the World: Scenarios to 2025. Section 2; *Executive summary*.

Voss, C. A. (1995a). Alternative paradigms for manufacturing strategy. *International Journal of Operations & Production Management, 15*(4), 5–16.

Voss, C. A. (1995b). *Manufacturing strategy: Process and content*. London: Chapman & Hall.

http://www.arabnews.com/news/economy/613961. *Private sector innovation to drive GCC projects*.

http://cep.lse.ac.uk/management/Management_Practice_and_Productivity.pdf

Josie Chun. http://www.careerfaqs.com.au/news/news-and-views/top-10-management-practices-of-effective-leaders/

http://www.indexmundi.com/factbook/compare/saudi-arabia.kuwait/economy

http://www.indexmundi.com/saudi_arabia/economy_profile.html

http://www.manappat.com

http://www.uaeinteract.com/business/economy.asp

CHAPTER 8

Diversification Strategies in the Gulf Agriculture Sectors

Salma Bani

INTRODUCTION

Gulf Cooperation Council (GCC) economic reform aims to diversify total oil dependency into more economic diversification, all of which aim to improve the competitiveness of other industrial sectors in order to achieve effective diversification. It has been seen that Gulf cooperation Council countries' economic diversification has affected diversification strategies and programmes, especially in the agriculture sector. The aim of this chapter is to critically assess the current diversification strategies and programmes in the agriculture sector in GCC and underline some key assumptions that could lead to the development of a new mode of diversification in the GCC context.

Food production in GCC countries is strongly influenced by natural environment. From nature endowment perspective, the biggest problem in GCC countries is availability of arable land combined with water scarcity. The total arable land in GCC is estimated to be 259 million ha; only

S. Bani (✉)
Ministry of Work, Municipality and Urban Planning,
Manama, Kingdom of Bahrain

1.7 is currently under cultivation, mainly with ground water irrigation. According to the United Nations, all the Gulf Cooperation Council (GCC) countries except Oman fall in the category of 'acute scarcity' of water. Also, being exceptionally arid has limited its contribution to GDP. Agriculture accounts for 1–4 per cent of the GDP of the GCC countries. It does not represent a significant component of the GCC economies. GCC governments have tried to boost agricultural output through productivity increases. However, due to shortage of fresh water, poor soil resources, low rainfall and high evapotranspiration in GCC countries, there are constraints in local agriculture production in meeting the food demand of the current and growing population.

GCC states do not have a comparative advantage in field crop production. They rely heavily on imports for their basic commodities and other foods. GCC import 80–90 per cent of food for their consumption. Also, the uncertainty caused by the supply shocks experienced globally in the last eight years for food items has appealed growing concern and development. This has raised serious concerns about food security in Gulf countries. Therefore, to close the gap between production and consumption, technology transfer and greater investment into agricultural modernisation are required. Thus, GCC, to reduce the deficit between food production and imports, need to achieve relative food security relying on local production of certain strategic items and to encourage agricultural investment and optimise the role of the private sector in developing the sector.

At the very centre of concern about overall economic development, there must be a concern for food, agriculture and people. Despite the fact that agriculture sector does not represent a significant component of the GCC economies, as agriculture accounts for 1–4 per cent of the GDP of the GCC countries. The future prospects of the agriculture sector in GCC will likely depend a great deal on government initiatives and support. Government provides subsidies to agriculture under the domestic support category. The main forms of agricultural support in the GCC include free mining of groundwater farms; seeds, fertilisers and other inputs are provided free of cost or at subsidised rates; individual governments conduct research, provide technical support to farmers for cultivation and irrigation, among others, and undertake public warehousing with an aim for food security; price support to farmers despite the high cost of production in the region.

Despite aiming for food security since a long time, GCC is able to produce only a quarter of the total food demand due to unfavourable climatic conditions and limited availability of arable land. As result of which, the high dependence on imports for the GCC is going to continue and this makes the issue of food security critical for the GCC.

Economic Diversification: Concepts and Trends

Economic diversification is generally taken as the process in which a growing range of economic outputs is produced. Economic diversification in its standard usage, either in terms of the diversity of economic activities or markets, is a significant issue for many developing countries, as their economies are generally characterised by the lack of it. They have traditionally relied heavily on the production of primary commodities that are predominantly vulnerable to climate variability and change (UNFCC 2015). Economic diversification aimed at increasing economic resilience and reducing reliance on vulnerable economic sectors. A good example is GCC countries, which are heavily reliant on hydrocarbons as a result of which economic diversification within GCC states is primarily understood as reduction of heavy dependence of the oil-based economy.

GCC countries' economic situation is unique; no other region in the world has such a small population in possession of such large hydrocarbon reserves. To varying degrees, GCC are seeking to reduce their economic dependence away from oil and gas; having economic policies that create a climate conducive of attracting a greater range of businesses is seen as imperative.

The concept of economic diversification has been on the agenda within the GCC for a long time. Since the 1970s diversification was the forefront of economic policy in the Gulf region as reason that oil revenues quickly crowd out any other economic activity. Beblawi (2011) stated that oil sector dominates the economy in the Gulf countries; it is almost a unique source of wealth. Therefore, heavy dependence on a single source of income makes GCC countries highly vulnerable. GCC understood the importance of diversifying their economy based on the abundant hydrocarbon resources. GCC state their challenge to diversify hydrocarbon resources varies depending on the specificities of each country. For example, it had achieved diversification within the oil sector; by expanding the oil-based and energy-intensive industries due to low costs of energy sources, the dependency of exports on the hydrocarbon sector has been strong and relatively stable over time. In addition, Gulf states have managed to establish strong refining and petrochemical industries as well as some heavy industries such as aluminium production. For example, Gulf countries have made significant achievement in development of smelters and aluminium primary production, producing around 3.7 million tons of aluminium according to numbers released by the Gulf Aluminium Council and expecting to reach 5 million tons in 2014, covering 13 per cent of global primary production (Gulf Aluminum Council (GAC) 2014). However, such economic orientation does not reduce dependence from oil and has little prospect of survival in the post-oil era. Economic diversification is also crucial for the employment policies of Gulf countries, especially in regard to the job creation for nationals. This is especially true for Saudi Arabia and Oman, which face a high unemployment rate, due to strong demographic pressures and current economic models. However, Oman is the only country among the GCC that has specific plans to privatise state-owned firms.

Non-oil sectors have had major impact on economic growth in all of the GCC economies. Kingdom of Bahrain generates more than 92 per cent of value added in the non-oil sectors. Significant efforts were made in developing new sectors which have high growing potential, such as aviation, tourism and hospitality, real estate, logistics and business services as well as introduction of smart or green technologies. However, most of the services are still closely linked with public sector, with the exception of Bahrain and UAE (Devaux 2013).

Diversifying sources of income needs a real partnership between the private and public sectors. Greater participation of the private sector is especially taken seriously in Oman and Bahrain.

According to Qatar National Development Strategy, the growth in non-oil sector in 2012–2016 is expected to reach 9.1 per cent. Qatari government has plans for massive infrastructure development along with further diversification such as manufacturing, construction, trade, communication, real estate and business services. Furthermore, Qatar's ambition is to promote itself as a high-end tourist destination through investment in infrastructure and through staging major business conferences.

GCC Agriculture Sector Challenges

Due to arid climatic conditions, natural sources of food production are limited in GCC countries. High temperatures limit yields for many stable food crops; soils are fragile and groundwater which can be renewed is inherently scarce and among the lowest in the world. Also, climate change is likely to tighten these constraints. As result of that, Gulf states do not have a comparative advantage in field food production especially stable food crops such as wheat and rice. Most of the water utilised for agriculture in the GCC came from non-renewable groundwater. Rainfall is well below that required for rain-fed stable food crops such as wheat which requires around 600–650 mm per year in hot climates (Laaboudi and Mouhouche 2012). As a result of that, agriculture exploits water use around 80–90 per cent of ground water, leading to alarming drops in the water table across the region (Table 8.1).

In response, agriculture in the region is being fundamentally reshaped by a policy shift from the food self-sufficiency goal pursued in the 1970s and 1980s to food security more broadly defined. Sustainable food self-sufficiency is not feasible for the GCC countries. As a result of which, all GCC governments have subsequently decided to move away from food self-sufficiency to food security policies. GCC governments must also encourage adoption of modern irrigation and dry farming, which can sustainably accommodate at least for some of the local demand. GCC governments are seeking also to outsource agricultural production by acquiring farmlands abroad, especially in countries that have unexploited

Table 8.1 The economic importance of agriculture in the GCC countries, 1997–2006

Country	Average (1997–2006) country contribution to GDP (%)	Average (1997–2006) % of economically active population
Bahrain	0.9	1.0
Kuwait	0.5	1.1
Saudi Arabia	4.4	9.1
Oman	2.2	35.4
Qatar		
UAE	2.9	4.6

Source: FAO, NCBC Research

land/water resources, and are geographically and culturally close. While the future prospects of the agriculture sector will likely depend a great deal on government initiatives and support, the presence of public-private partnership provides a wide range of opportunities for investors interested in the food security theme.

Conceptualisation of Sustainable Food Security

Various definitions of food systems and food security have been developed over time, which reflect particular worldviews expressed by both economists and food security analysts. Analysts have shifted from a focus on agricultural production towards including the question of access to and affordability of food into the notion of food security. Today both food utilisation and stability of food systems are, also, recognised as determinants governing the food security status of a household or a nation (Maxwell 2001; Ericksen forthcoming). Food security is not just a poverty issue; it is a much larger issue that involves the whole food system. Food security is the outcome of food system processes.

Food systems encompass all activities from production through to consumption, along with other key determinants of food security. The outcomes of these activate contribution to food security (food availability, food access and food use). The food system operates within and is influenced by social, political, economic and natural environments. A country is said to be food secure when its food system operates in such a way as to remove the fear that there will not be enough to eat. In particular, food security will be achieved when households have access to the food they want.

Food security arises when all people at all times have access to enough food that is affordable, safe and healthy and culturally acceptable and meets specific dietary needs, produced in ways that are environmentally sound and socially justified. Thus food security should be treated as a multi-objective phenomenon. Considering complexity of the food system, it is easy to see that many factors determine food security.

Food security historically referred to food supply and shortfalls in supply compared to requirements. However, the term has been broadened beyond notions of food supply to include elements of access (Sen 1981), vulnerability (Watts and Bohle 1993) and sustainability (Chambers 1989; Maxwell 1995).

Food security exists when 'all people, at all times, have physical and economic access to sufficient, safe and nutritious food that meets their dietary needs and food preferences for an active and healthy life' (World Food Summit 1996). This widely accepted definition points to the following dimensions of food security: food availability, food accessibility, utilisation and stability or sustainability.

Deriving from this definition, achieving food security requires that the aggregate availability of physical supplies of food is sufficient, that households have adequate access to real food supplies through their own production, through the market or through other sources, and that the utilisation of such food supplies is appropriate to meet the specific dietary needs of individuals. Therefore, food security needs to be ensured at national, household and individual level.

Food system activities are grouped into four categories. These include producing food, processing and packaging food, distributing and retailing food, and consuming food. Producing food includes all activities involved in the production of raw food materials. These range from the process of obtaining inputs such as land and labour, breeding animals, planting crops or obtaining young animal stock, caring for the growing food material and then harvesting or slaughtering it. A variety of factors determine these activities, from climate conditions to land tenure, input prices, agricultural technology and government subsidy provisions intended to protect or promote production (Fig. 8.1).

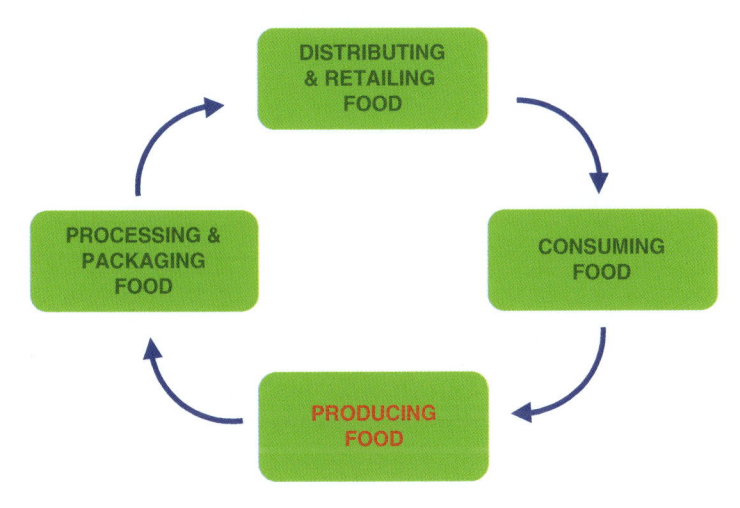

Fig. 8.1 Food system. Source: Bani 2014

Food security is the outcome of food system processes. In this study food security conceptual framework will be used to evaluate how government food policy interacts with the local food systems to produce food security. It analyses the impacts of these policies on agricultural development, and highlights the main achievements in terms of increasing the level of food self-sufficiency, particularly with respect to poultry, fruits and vegetables.

The primary outcome of any generic food system is food security, although in specific context food security may not be achieved because there are market and other institutional failures.

Food systems framework is useful for identifying entry points for changing undesirable outcomes through analysis of the drivers and activities that have resulted in these outcomes. The main categories of outcomes considered in this framework are food security. There are many ways in which these outcomes can be evaluated, depending upon the perspective or objectives of the evaluator, which are shaped by the political and social context. For example, in her paper (Bani 2014) on how to increase production, strategy of encouraging farmers to concentrate on growing locally consumed staple food is highlighted and emphasised. These strategies were related to different food security strategy outcomes.

Food system activities are grouped into four categories: producing food, processing and packaging food, distributing and retailing food, and consuming food. The first three categories constitute the food supply chain. Producing food includes all activities involved in the production of raw food materials. These range from the process of obtaining inputs such as land and labour, breeding animals, planting crops or obtaining young animal stock, caring for the growing food material and then harvesting or slaughtering it. A variety of factors determine these activities, from climate conditions to land tenure, input prices, agricultural technology and government subsidy provisions intended to protect or promote production.

Processing and packaging food includes the various transformations that raw food material such as vegetable, fruit and animal product (poultry) undergoes before it is sent to the retail market for sale. All of these activities 'add value' to the raw material in an economic sense, but these activities may also significantly alter the appearance, storage life, nutritional value and content of the raw materials. For example, wheat undergoes extensive processing and packaging before it becomes bread. The determinants of these activities are quite different from those pertaining to producing food.

Distributing and retailing food includes all activities involved in moving the food from one place to another and marketing it. Distributing is heavily influenced by transportation infrastructure, trade regulations, government transfer programmes and storage requirements. Retailing is influenced by how markets are organised and where they are located. Consuming food involves everything from deciding what to select through to preparing, eating and digesting food. Prices are influential, as are income levels, cultural tradition, preferences, social values, education and health status.

The outcomes contributing to food security are the following three, accessibility, availability and utilisation. Although highly influenced by food system activities, other drivers determine these outcomes as well.

Food availability refers to the amount, type and quality of food that a unit has at its disposal to consume. Access to food refers to the ability of a unit to obtain access to the type, quality and quantity of food it requires. Food utilisation refers to individual or household capacity to consume and benefit from food. Stability of food supplies refers to the long-term need to maintain consumption levels. Each of these can be further broken down as the following.

Food Availability

The three elements of food availability are production, distribution and exchange which contribute to food availability. Although familiar terms to food security analysts, their meaning has been modified slightly to fit the agenda of describing a food system holistically.

- Production: how much production? How much and which types of food consumed (by a given unit) are available through local production. The determinants of availability from local production include land holding sizes, resource tenancy arrangements, economic returns to labour, human capital and the control local producers have over their own products.
- Distribution: how the food for consumption is physically moved to be available, in what form, when and to whom? The determinants of distribution include transportation and infrastructure, public safety nets, storage facilities, governance, security and the enforcement of trade barriers and borders, summarily food logistics.

- Exchange: how much of the food available to a unit is obtained through exchange mechanisms such as barter, trade, purchase or loans rather than local production? Determinants of exchange include income levels and purchasing power, informal social arrangements for barter, local customs for giving and receiving gifts, markets, and terms of trade, currency value and subsidies.

Food Accessibility

The three elements that describe accessibility of food are affordability, allocation, and preference.

- Affordability: the purchasing power of households or communities relative to the price of food. The determinants of affordability include pricing policies and mechanisms, seasonal and geographical variations in price, local prices relative to external prices, income and wealth levels.
- Allocation: the mechanisms governing when, where and how food can be accessed by consumers. Markets are key determinants of food allocation; government policies often are designed to correct market failures by allocating food to remote areas or at lower prices.
- Preference: social or cultural norms and values that influence consumer demand for certain types of food.

Food Utilisation

The three elements of food utilisation are nutritional value, social value and food safety.

- Nutritional value: how much of the daily requirements of calories, vitamins, protein, and micronutrients are provided by the food consumed. Determinants of nutritional value include diversity of food consumed, type of primary protein, disease incidence, education, access to clean water and hygiene practices.
- Social value: all of the social and cultural aspects of consumption, for example, eating meals together may be an important part of kinship, it may be important to always have food for guests, or special foods may be an integral part of important holidays. Understanding the determinants of social value requires insight into the community and

household relations, as well as cultural customs, for example, in some places eating locally produced food is highly valued.
- Food safety: this encompasses the dangers introduced from the addition of chemicals during production, processing and packaging and food-borne diseases. Main determinants of this are the procedures, standards and regulations for food production, processing and packaging.

Food Stability

Stability of food supplies refers to the long-term need to maintain consumption levels. In the early 1980s, there was a shift in thinking about food security influenced by the concept of food entitlement. Analyses started to include the concept of stability or assured food access as a fundamental component. Therefore, there is growing acknowledgement of a scope for long-term food security interventions by ensuring access to food and by enhancing stability in consumption (see Pingali et al. 2005; Flores et al. 2005).

At the very centre of concern about overall economic development, there must be a concern for food, agriculture and people. The concept of sustainable food security combines the above three elements into a major objective that is fundamental to economic development. The issue of food security has become a major concern, on current global trends, particularly skyrocketing prices of basic commodities. Achieving sustainable food security will require more than improving farm productivity and profitability while minimising environmental impacts. The concept is broader than sustainable agriculture; it aggregates the goals of household food security and that of sustainable agriculture. Despite aiming for food security since a long time, GCC is able to produce only a quarter of the total food demand due to unfavourable climatic conditions and limited availability of arable land. As a result of which, the high dependence on imports for the GCC is going to continue and this makes the issue of food security critical for the GCC.

SUSTAINABLE FOOD SECURITY

The issue of food security has become a major concern, on current global trends, particularly sky rocketing prices of basic commodities. Achieving sustainable food security will require more than improving farm productivity and profitability. The concept is broader than sustainable agriculture; it aggregates the goals of household food security and that of sustainable agriculture.

Since the world hunger and poverty resolution, progress toward food security has been made, many nations, GCC countries agricultural production has increased. GCC governments have tried to boost agricultural output through productivity increases. However, agriculture accounts for 1–4 per cent of the GDP of the GCC countries. It does not represent a significant component of the GCC economies. Being exceptionally arid has limited its contribution to GDP.

Achieving sustainable food security will require more than improving farm productivity and profitability while minimising environmental impacts. The concept is broader than sustainable agriculture; it aggregates the goals of household food security and that of sustainable agriculture (Bani 2014).

Today both food utilisation and stability of food systems are, also, recognised as determinants governing the food security status of a household or a nation (Maxwell 2001; Ericksen forthcoming). Food security is not just a poverty issue; it is a much larger issue that involves the whole food system. A country is said to be food secure when its food system operates in such a way as to remove the fear that there will not be enough to eat. In particular, food security will be achieved when households have access to the food they want. Food security arises when all people at all times have access to enough food that is affordable, safe and healthy, culturally acceptable, meets specific dietary needs, produced in ways that are environmentally sound and socially justified. Thus, food security should be treated as a multi-objective phenomenon. Considering complexity of the food system, it is easy to see that many factors determine food security.

Food security historically referred to food supply and shortfalls in supply compared to requirements. However, the term has been broadened beyond notions of food supply to include elements of access (Sen 1981), vulnerability (Watts and Bohle 1993) and sustainability (Chambers 1989; Maxwell 1995).

Deriving from this definition, achieving food security requires that the aggregate availability of physical supplies of food is sufficient, that households have adequate access to real food supplies through their own production, through the market or through other sources, and that the utilisation of such food supplies is appropriate to meet the specific dietary needs of individuals. Therefore, food security needs to be ensured at national, household and individual level.

GCC domestic production meets only a small proportion of food requirements. The balance of food of 80–90 per cent of total food demand/consumption are imported. The high and increasing dependency on food imports in the face of a tightening global demand-supply balance exposes the Gulf economies to external inflationary risks.

The growing import dependence is coinciding with increasingly tight global food markets and elevated price volatility. Rising food prices since 2003 culminated in the 2007–2008 food price shock, which stoked inflation and exposed the quantity risk of GCC nations not being able to procure food due to embargoes by exporting countries. As a result of which, lack of economic diversification within the GCC means that food imports are financed through energy exports, leaving countries vulnerable to deterioration in the terms of trade between food and oil or the exhaustion of their reserves. Thus, GCC countries are exposed to two main threats: supply and price risk. Supply risk is relating to the availability of food imports, and price risk, relating to the affordability of food imports. Therefore, maintaining a diversified import profile allows GCC governments to manage supply and price risk by maximising alternative sources of supply.

GCC states do not have a comparative advantage in field crop production. It relies heavily on imports for its basic commodities and other food. With demand in the GCC expected to rise significantly, food imports to the region will increase by as much as 100 per cent. Hence, the need for agricultural investments for food security is a top priority. Also, GCC government should promote sustainable aquaculture, horticulture and poultry local domestic production.

Food security is linked to the availability of water, which is only going to go from bad to worse. Water availability is expected to reduce by 50 per cent by 2050 and hit widespread acute levels in 2025. Also, GCC population is expected to exceed 50 million by 2020 from its current 40.6 million. The biggest challenges GCC agriculture is facing are limited agricultural lands and shortage of water resources. GCC states continue to subsidise domestic agriculture as part of their food security strategy and to protect livelihoods in the remaining rural communities. GCC countries are likely to maintain domestic production of fish, dairy, and crops that are not water-intensive, such as dates. Thus, GCC governments should focus on sustainable agricultural techniques locally, such as hydroponics.

There are various options to achieve food security, including but not limited to local agriculture intensification using technological innovations, outsourcing food production and food import. A high food import risks food security when there are political instabilities, wars and famines in countries from where the food is being imported. It is, therefore, important to increase local production to reduce food import dependency. Thus, sustainable farming solutions become increasingly clear that coupling new technologies and research related to climatic and soil conditions will become critical factors in achieving food security.

GCC governments use a range of policies to manage price and supply risks. GCC populations benefit from a wide range of support measures designed to ensure food remains affordable.

Principal among these are price controls such as an implicit subsidy transferring wealth from food companies to food consumers. Other explicit subsidies include conditional transfers to help consumers purchase food, or measures such as import subsidies applied during times of high international prices.

Food prices are a significant driver of inflation within the GCC, and governments have responded with an array of expensive wider social expenditures not explicitly linked to food. Following the 2007–2008 food price crisis, governments hiked public-sector wages for national workers in addition to implementing price controls for key food commodities. Similar measures were taken in 2011 and 2012, alongside initiatives such as minimum wage policies, unemployment allowance, rent controls and further expansion of housing benefits for nationals.

In recent years, fiscally strong governments and agricultural corporations have increasingly begun to invest in land abroad for the purposes of food security. The GCC governments have become important participants in this process. Governments rather than corporate players are now increasingly shaping investments in foreign farmland, which in the past sought to benefit from lower production costs in developing nations. The role of the public sector is growing through direct investments and state-sponsored entities or public-private partnerships.

The limited land and water resource in the GCC countries pose a substantial technological challenge to increasing domestic food production.

The region's arid climate and constraints caused by severe biotic and abiotic stresses, including heat, salinity and lack of improvement cultivation limit the level of food self-sufficiency that can be achieved. Over the past few years, the GCC countries have begun to consider investing in farmland overseas, particularly in sub-Saharan Africa (SSA). The GCC countries have been investing primarily in Northeast Africa and South Asia. The GCC nations have tended to focus on countries that are geographically close and have established ties to the GCC. Sudan and Pakistan in particular have figured prominently in connection with these efforts. The established political and cultural ties are seen as a safeguard against the risk of embargoes. The GCC nations are not only investing directly but are also supporting the private sector in acquiring land overseas. A private Saudi firm, Planet Food World (PFWC), is reportedly planning to invest around US$3 billion in Turkey's agriculture sector with the goal of exporting farm products back to the GCC. PFWC has also invested in Ethiopia. Hail Agricultural Development Company (Hadco), formerly a listed company, but acquired by Almarai (2280.SE) in 2009, recently acquired around 8900 hectares of land in Sudan on a 48-year lease. Hadco is planning to invest in Turkey and Kazakhstan as well.

Three GCC financial institutions are planning to invest some US$9 billion in Turkey under an alliance named Vision3. The output of the farmland would be exported to Bahrain, and in exchange, the alliance would develop dams, irrigation networks and power stations in Turkey. The UAE is offering to develop infrastructure in Pakistan in return for ownership rights to the land in Pakistan and control over all production on that land. Pakistan has also offered Saudi Arabia farmland in exchange for oil supplies.

Diversification Strategy and Its Challenges in the GCC Countries

Due to shortage of fresh water, poor soil resources, low rainfall and high evapotranspiration in the GCC countries there are constraints in local agriculture production in meeting the food demand of the current and growing population. There are various options to achieve food security, including but not limited to local agriculture intensification using technological innovations, food import and outsourcing food production to countries, which have comparative advantage for agricultural expansion, leasing farmland abroad. In this chapter, emphasis will be given to various options to increase local agriculture production and to discuss alternate sound ways to achieve food security in the GCC countries. The Sultanate of Oman has pursued to find alternatives for oil and gas revenues by investing heavily in agricultural and fisheries sectors. It has good potential in diversifying sources of its national economy, especially its exploitation of its fisheries.

GCC countries have invested revenue from trade surpluses into domestic infrastructure and development projects. This has not been driven by fiscal necessity, but was a developmental option that aimed to achieve economic diversification, reduce the size of the public sector and strengthen the private sector. As a result of which, GCC countries enjoy the highest quality infrastructure and infrastructure-related services in the Arab region. Through economic diversification, GCC countries have invested oil revenue into infrastructure and achieved an advanced stage of development.

Public-private partnerships (PPPs) can be complex ventures requiring close supervision from the Government, and a serious commitment from both the private and public sectors. Governments entering PPP arrangements should first consider the existing legal framework, and the governance and supervisory frameworks for PPP projects. For this reason, it is essential to have a comprehensive preparatory phase to lay the groundwork for PPP projects and set up the appropriate institutions and the legal infrastructure required for it (PPIAF, World Bank 2013).

Therefore, with a sound institutional and regulatory framework, PPP will close the deals more quickly and face fewer problems during the implementation phase. Thus, managing a successful PPP programme requires a range of specialised functions, which not all governments have.

Political stability and effective regulatory frameworks for PPPs have become the essential comparative advantage defining the ability of a country to attract international investors and operators in infrastructure services. Given the mixed experience of implementing PPP projects in the region, attention should be paid to securing political support and to structuring projects in an economically viable manner. It is essential for countries to invest in capacity building in the field of public management, especially in assuring transparent and competitive procurement, and to set clear dispute resolution mechanisms. There have been several success stories of involving the private sector in financing infrastructure in the power and water sectors of oil-rich countries (Keenan 2011).

Setting up a comprehensive PPP programme, along with the legislative and regulatory framework, has been the key to success of PPP projects in those countries. Considering the ongoing transition in many countries of the region, establishing political stability proves to be one of the primary challenges to securing long-term investments in infrastructure assets. Therefore, effective legal, regulatory and contractual conditions are crucial to PPP success but can only exist if supported by an efficient institutional structure, which both facilitates PPP development and provides clear boundaries to protect the interests of all parties (European Commission 2003).

Regulatory framework is an important success factor for PPPs. Generally speaking, two approaches to regulatory frameworks for PPPs have been followed in the Arab region. Arab countries with systems informed by civil law tend to adopt cross-sectoral (or horizontal) laws and regulations on privatisation, PPPs and concessions. Countries that are more influenced by common law traditions, in particular GCC countries, tend to adopt sectoral regulations, and the corresponding authorities often have considerable discretion in the definition of non-contractual terms. To date, GCC countries have taken heed and adopted varying approaches consisting of establishing PPP units and undertaking legislative and regulation reforms. Although the very best practice can be introduced through laws, ultimately, legislation cannot be effective unless it is part of a holistic approach to creating an enabling environment, where PPPs can flourish.

GCC's nature and the availability of resources prevent the expansion of food production. Therefore, strategic for providing funds, credit and logistics to GCC investors to invest aboard in agriculture also to establish a strategic reserve for basic food commodities to meet the GCC needs for food and to avoid future food crises.

Food security is particularly important for the GCC countries because of rapidly increasing population, a dearth of arable land and the shortage of water. These factors are not going to change—so GCC need to mitigate them with strategic solutions planned well ahead of time. These strategies can only be achieved by close collaboration between public-private Public partnerships.

The GCC states are at the forefront of government-backed, private-sector investment in foreign land to expand their agriculture sectors. With sustainable policies and strategies, five factors should form the foundation of any international food security strategy.

With reference to food security, the GCC countries have strengthened their agro-security by the acquisition of large areas of farmland outside their own national borders and are investing heavily in major agricultural projects in Sudan, Ethiopia, Egypt, Turkey, Ukraine, Kazakhstan, Philippines and Brazil (Woertz 2013; Al Obaid 2010; Deininger et al. 2011).

Conclusion

It has been seen that Gulf Cooperation Council countries' economic diversification has affected diversification strategies and programmes, especially in the agriculture sector. The agriculture sector in GCC countries has appealed growing concern and development focus due to the uncertainty caused by the supply shocks experienced globally in the last five years for food items. Also, as a result of a combination of resource-related factors that limit production, including land scarcity, water scarcity and climate conditions, food security continues to be a challenge for the GCC with imported food accounting for 80–90 per cent of all food consumed. Therefore, as global food prices remain potentially unstable and the ability to produce locally remains constrained by GCC's resource endowment. GCC governments will depend upon successful economic diversification. Gulf states have strengthened their agro-security by the acquisition of large areas of farmland overseas and by investing in major agricultural projects in those countries.

In conclusion, the challenges of climate conditions, coupled with supply and price volatility in agriculture, have placed food security policy on the forefront of the national development agenda in GCC states. GCC, in order to overcome the deficit between food production and imports, need to achieve relative food security relying on local production of certain strategic items and to encourage agricultural investment and optimise the role of the private sector in developing the sector. GCC's agricultural policy is towards the right direction of creating impact on the role of local production system embracing diversified production base focusing on strategic option for a sustained growth of productivity and diversification of economies in general.

References

Al Obaid, A. (2010). *King Abdullah's initiatives for Saudi Agricultural Investment Abroad: A way of enhancing food security.* Expert Group Meeting on Achieving Food Security in Member States in a Post-crisis World, Islamic Development Bank, Jeddah, May 2–3.

Bani, S. (2014). Climate changes, water scarcity and food security complex. In S. A. Shahid & M. Ahmed (Eds.), *Environmental cost and face of agriculture in the Gulf Cooperation Council countries.* Gabrielle Kissinger: Springer publication.

Beblawi, H. E. (2011). Gulf industrialization in perspective. In J.-F. Seznec & M. Kirk (Eds.), *Industrialization in the Gulf: A socioeconomic revolution* (pp. 185–197). London: Center for Contemporary Arab Studies, Georgetown University/Routledge.

Chambers, R. (1989). Vulnerability, coping and policy. *IDS Bulletin, 20*(2), 1–7.

Deininger, K., Byerlee, D., Lindsay, J., Norton, A., Selod, H., & Stickler, M. (2011). *Rising global interest in farmland: Can it yield sustainable and equitable benefits?* Washington, DC: The World Bank.

Devaux, P. (2013). Economic diversification in the GCC: Dynamic drive needs to be confirmed. *Conjoncture.* BNP Paribas Paper, July–August 2013.

Ericksen, P. (forthcoming). *Conceptualizing food systems for research on impacts of Global environmental change (GEC).* GECAFS Working Paper No 1.

European Commission. (2003). Guidelines for successful public – Private partnerships.

FAO, NCBC Research. www.gulfbase.com/.../GCC_Agriculture_Sector_March2010.pdf

Flores, M., Khwaja, Y., & White, P. (2005). Food security in protracted crises: Building more effective policy frameworks. *Disasters, 29*(S1), S25–S51.

Gulf Aluminum Council (GAC). (2014). Retrieved from http://www.constructionweekonline.com/article-20714-gcc-aluminium-production-to-hit-5m-tonnes-by-2014/

Keenan, R. (2011). Public-private partnership (PPP), in the Middle East.

Laaboudi, A., & Mouhouche, B. (2012). Water requirement modelling for wheat under arid climatic conditions. *Hydrology Current Research, 3*(130). Food and Agriculture Organization (FAO). Retrieved from http://www.fao.org/nr/water/cropinfo_wheat.html

Maxwell, S. (1995). *Measuring food insecurity: The frequency and severity of coping strategies.* FCND Discussion Paper No 8. Washington, DC: International Food Policy Research Institute.

Maxwell, S. (2001). The evolution of thinking about food security. In S. Devereux & S. Maxwell (Eds.), *Food security in sub Saharan Africa.* London: ITDG Publishing.

Pingali, P., Alinovi, L., & Sutton, J. (2005). Food security in complex emergencies: Enhancing food system resilience. *Disasters, 29*(S1), S5–S24.

Public Private Infrastructure Advisory Facility (PPIAF). 2013. Annual report 2013. Washington, DC. Retrieved from http://documents.worldbank.org/curated/en/985511468339873006/Public-Private-Infrastructure-Advisory-Facility-PPIAF-annual-report-2013

Sen, A. K. (1981). *Poverty and famines: An essay on entitlement and deprivation.* Oxford: Clarendon Press.
UNFCC. (2015). http://unfccc.int/adaptation/workstreams/nairobi_work_programme/items/3994.php
Watts, M., & Bohle, H. (1993). Hunger, famine, and the space of vulnerability. *Geo Journal, 30*(2), 117–126.
Woertz, E. (2013). *Oil for food: The global food crisis and the Middle East.* Oxford: Oxford University Press.
World Food Summit. (1996, November). Food and agriculture organization. Rome Declaration on Food Security and World Food Summit Plan of Action.

CHAPTER 9

Destination Place Identity, Touristic Diversity and Diversification in the Arabia Gulf

Magdalena Karolak

Introduction

This chapter compares and contrasts the processes of destination place identity creation in the Gulf Cooperation Council [GCC] countries (with the exception of Saudi Arabia). It aims at examining whether these identities created for the purpose of leisure tourism are competitive enough to secure a flow of international tourists. This study starts with an overview of the development of the leisure tourism industry in the GCC over the last decade. For the purpose of the initial analysis, the research follows Ritchie and Crouch's Destination and Competitiveness Model (2003) and focuses specifically on two elements forming the model's foundations, namely, core resources and attractors, and other supporting factors. The analysis reveals that in order to attract tourists, GCC countries have to make large investments in superstructure and it is thanks to such developments that Dubai has been not only the most successful tourist destination among GCC countries but also has become the spotlight of the tourism industry on an international scale. The need to invest in superstructure coupled with a

---

M. Karolak (✉)
Zayed University, Dubai, UAE

© Gulf Research Centre Cambridge 2018
A. Mishrif, Y. Al Balushi (eds.), *Economic Diversification in the Gulf Region, Volume I*, The Political Economy of the Middle East,
https://doi.org/10.1007/978-981-10-5783-0_9

very broad array of tourism products each country aims to offer creates, in turn, a competition among GCC countries. And those GCC countries that do not possess a large capital to invest in tourism fall behind unable to offer comparable tourist attractions and thus receive less tourism receipts.

Secondly, this study assesses to what degree the selected GCC countries, namely, UAE, Qatar, Kuwait, Bahrain and Oman, have succeeded in creating competitive tourism strategies. The latter involve the creation of distinctive place identities, which are defined as the actual physical spaces as well as how they are perceived in the mind (place image). This approach entails that symbolism and meaning creation and recreation are thus inseparable from the material space (Kalandides 2012). Place identities are created through place branding strategies, which must, however, be accompanied by execution of ideas on the ground (Anholt 2003; Govers and Go 2009). As a result, it is necessary to compare the images communicated with the execution of the ideas in reality, which is the initial step of this chapter. Creation of images and meanings takes place in physical and virtual environments. By analyzing textual, visual and on-site materials, this study will provide the answers to the questions: Have the GCC managed to specialize and develop niche tourism strategies? Or is the Dubai tourism model simply copied? How successful have they been so far in attracting tourists? The aim of place branding is to attract tourism, investment, talent and trade (Kotler and Gertner 2002; Govers and Go 2009); thus, making such an analysis is especially important in light of the economic diversification strategies in the GCC.

The analysis also confirms that while GCC countries started to craft their tourism development strategies, each should focus on creation of a successful and distinct identity brand but also pursue regional strategies to maximize the opportunity stemming from the tourism industry in the Gulf region. Ultimately, by pointing out tourism strategy gaps, this chapter will provide recommendations on improvement of the tourism strategies adopted so far. In addition, it will provide new evidence to the study of semiotics in tourism in general.

Tourism as Means of Economic Diversification in the GCC Region

The six countries united under the umbrella of GCC are characterized by similar economic, social and political conditions. These countries occupy a vast area of the Arabian Peninsula, an arid and hot desert environment.

They share a monarchical system of rule, ranging from absolute monarchies to those that allow some form of political openness. In addition, their economies are characterized by a heavy reliance on oil and oil-related revenues. The latter factor has contributed to specific socioeconomic conditions characteristic of resource rentierism, that is, a condition when a state draws a significant share of its revenues from rents extracted from natural resources. Indeed, the discovery of oil in 1930s, initially in Bahrain and then in other GCC countries, has transformed the GCC societies as the flow of oil income prompted these rentier states to establish extensive welfare programs—providing their citizens with free healthcare, free education as well as subsidies on daily commodities—without taxing their population. Furthermore, oil revenues allowed rapid economic development with creation of modern industries and establishment of a vast range of services. Yet, oil dependence brought, at the same time, peculiar socioeconomic problems.

Rapid economic development that followed oil extraction exacerbated the demand for labor. GCC societies hardly had enough labor to warrant the need for growth; as a result, foreigners have been flocking to the region taking up various occupations, from manual labor to highly qualified professionals. The foreign population grew steadily and, in case of some GCC countries, outnumbered the citizens. This situation led to large amounts of remittances being sent out of the Gulf. In addition, it contributed to a split of labor market between the private sector, often requiring long working hours but modest benefits, dominated by foreigners, and the public sector dominated by GCC nationals. Although oil brought prosperity in the 1970s, its price fluctuation in the 1980s coupled with the Iraqi invasion of Kuwait and rising expenditures on arms, security and defense (Luciani and Beblawi 1987) affected GCC economies. Subsequently, high demographic growth and saturation of the public job market contributed to rising unemployment among GCC nationals. In addition, inflation combined with a growing consciousness of the decline of oil supplies brought further strain on the GCC economies and prompted the GCC authorities to establish strategies for future sustainable growth.

The beginning of twenty-first century marked a crucial turn since governments of the GCC countries made a commitment to sustainable development independent from oil resources and to competitiveness as requirements for future growth of the GCC region overall. In the past, economic reforms undertaken by the GCC had usually limited results.

They lacked a comprehensive approach that would combine transformation of "private sector participation, labor markets, financial markets and human resources" to yield significant results (Shochat 2008). They also lacked political will (Sick 1997). Contrary to past undertakings, the packages of economic reforms adopted in the 2000s by the GCC governments, branded usually as "Visions", offer a holistic approach aiming at a thorough transformation of economy and society. While it comes as no surprise that two decades ago, for most countries in the Middle East, international leisure tourism has been "either culturally undesirable or economically unnecessary" (Sharpley 2002), the economic reasons prompted GCC authorities to recognize tourism, among others, as an important factor for future stable economic growth (Koren and Tenreyro 2010).

The importance of tourism industry to the economic growth is well recognized. UNWTO assesses that foreign tourist receipts have become "an important pillar of the economies of many destinations", creating employment and development opportunities (2011). Indeed, in 2014 tourism created 1 out of every 11 jobs worldwide (UNWTO 2014) while providing jobs for a relatively high number of unskilled and semi-skilled workers (Ashley et al. 2007). Rossouw and Saayman (2011) pointed out that tourism contributes to increasing per capita income and government revenues that can be used for fostering growth of other economic sectors such as manufacturing. In 2014, tourism was responsible for generating on average 9 per cent of a country's GDP. Furthermore, Sharpley (2002) highlighted the fact that tourism redistributes wealth; spurs economic diversification; creates backward linkages to the local economy (i.e. farming, construction, transportation, etc.) and by utilizing economic resources, which are already there such as historic sites, it is a low-cost startup industry. Tourism tends also to have a positive impact on the employment of women and, as a result, has a positive role in enhancing their economic position (Ashley et al. 2007). These benefits are combined with the fast growth of tourism worldwide thus making it "a key driver for socio-economic progress". Indeed, UNWTO estimates that international tourist arrivals rose from 25 million in 1950 to 1.135 billion in 2014 and will continue to grow and reach 1.6 billion by the year 2020. In addition, international tourism generated 1.5 trillion US$ in export earnings. The benefits stemming from the tourism industry prompted governments to promote this option as means of economic development. Nonetheless, pursuing tourism as means of diversifying the economy requires a strategy that would enhance the competitiveness of the GCC region among other tourist destinations. It is especially important since GCC countries were "not normally associated with leisure/holiday tourism market" (Sharpley 2002); hence, promoting the region as a leisure tourism destination presents a set of challenges. The success of tourism in a country depends on "how tourism attractions develop value for tourists and how well destination resources are managed" (Gomezelj and Michalic 2008).

Among GCC countries, UAE "emerged as the forerunner in efforts to build tourism and market its attractions" (EIU 1993) as early as the beginning of the 1990s. It is especially true for the Emirate of Dubai, which successfully turned tourism into an important driver of the economy. Statistics indicate that in 2013 tourism accounted for 8.4 per cent of UAE GDP and 31 per cent of Dubai GDP alone (WTTC 2011/2013). As a result, UAE have become a global leader in the higher-end leisure market. UAE are ranked 28th among 139 countries covered by the Travel & Tourism Competitiveness Report 2013 issued by the World Economic Forum. The progress in development of tourism is noteworthy as UAE came "ahead of many of the ancient tourism destinations, despite the moderate natural resources of tourism sector" (Emirates News Agency 2011). Over the years, 2010–2020, tourism contribution is expected to have a steady share of 8.1 per cent growth in UAE GDP (Baumgarten and Kent 2010). Given the fact that using international leisure tourism as a vehicle for economic development proved to be successful in UAE, other countries in the region, with the exception of Saudi Arabia that specializes so far solely in religious tourism, embarked on similar ventures.

Yet, other GCC countries may not readily copy the success of Dubai as a tourist destination. Indeed, the tourist destination appeal results from a number of factors, which make it competitive, and so far no other entity has been able to reap the benefits stemming from tourism to the extend Dubai did. In Kuwait, tourism accounted only 3.5 per cent of GDP and created 4 per cent of total employment in 2013. In Bahrain, the proportion of tourism contribution to GDP amounted to 10.2 per cent, while tourism was responsible for creating 10 per cent of total employment. In Qatar, tourism contributed 6.6 per cent of GDP and 5.4 per cent of total employment. In Oman, tourism accounted for 6.4 per cent of GDP and 6.4 per cent of total employment. In UAE, tourism contributed overall 8.4 per cent of GDP and 9.1 per cent of total employment. UAE's touristic appeal is visible in the following data.

The data above shows that UAE has the highest tourism receipts out of GCC countries (Table 9.1), even when including Saudi Arabia in the picture, and the country has attracted the highest numbers of leisure tourists (Table 9.2).

The statistics confirm that UAE is a pioneer of leisure tourism in the GCC region. It is also significant that UAE has managed to establish itself as an internationally recognized tourism destination. The majority of tourists to the UAE come from the Middle East (33.5 per cent), Europe (30 per cent) and the Asia–Pacific region (26 per cent), while Bahrain that ranks second after UAE in leisure tourist arrivals receives the majority of

Table 9.1 Tourism receipts by country

Country	Tourism receipts in US$ billion			
	2008	2010	2015	2020
Bahrain	3.06	3.31	4.23	5.35
Kuwait	7.46	7.85	11	15.02
Qatar	3.79	4.35	7.28	11.80
Saudi Arabia	26.71	29.11	49.69	72.88
Oman	5.07	4.21	6.18	8.55
UAE	37.87	38.45	53.14	73.59
GCC	83.94	87.28	131.52	187.18

Source: Alpen Capital 2011

Table 9.2 International tourist arrivals (in millions)

Country	2013	2024 (prognosis)
Bahrain	9.1[a]	6.8
Kuwait	0.2	0.4
Oman	2.2	2.9
Qatar	1.3	2.2
KSA (religious tourism)	13.2	20.7
UAE	12.1	39.9
GCC (total)	38.1	72.9

[a]Data from the World Bank site (http://data.worldbank.org/indicator/ST.INT.ARVL)

Source: Alpen Capital 2014

tourist arrivals from the neighboring Saudi Arabia. UAE present, however, stark differences when it comes to tourist appeal of its particular emirates. The shares of the tourism contribution to the UAE economy were distributed in the following manner: 66 per cent for Dubai, 16 per cent for Abu Dhabi and 10 per cent for Sharjah (Alpen Capital 2014). Dubai has become the undisputed leader of UAE and GCC tourism market with 11 million guests checking in its hotels in 2013, while Abu Dhabi came in second with 8.8 million hotel guests. For the purpose of comparison, it is important to bear in mind that France, which tops the WTO list in terms of tourist arrivals, received 83 million visitors (2012), while the USA that came first in terms of tourist receipts received 139.6 billion US$ (2013). While it may not be possible for GCC countries to attain such results, studies suggest "there is still a gap between the opportunity that the GCC countries have in their tourism sectors and what they have achieved" (Atalla and Nasr 2013).

The success of a tourist destination depends on how competitive it is in comparison to other destinations. It is thus necessary to examine the factors contributing to destination competitiveness in detail in order to, on the one hand, understand the success of some destinations in the GCC region and, on the other hand, to also examine the necessary improvements to maximize the tourist attractiveness of the region.

Destination Competitiveness and GCC Countries

Various scholars examined the question of destination competitiveness (De Keyser and Vanhove 1994; Evans et al. 1995; Dwyer and Kim 2003; Ritchie and Crouch 2003), which is defined as the attractiveness of a tourist destination that makes it more appealing than others. Among the conducted studies, Ritchie and Crouch (2003) assert that:

> what makes a tourism destination truly competitive is its ability to increase tourism expenditure, to increasingly attract visitors while providing them with satisfying memorable experiences, and to do so in a profitable way, while enhancing the well-being of destination residents and preserving the natural capital of the destination for future generations.

Consequently, Ritchie and Crouch identified six dimensions of destination competitiveness model, which includes economic, political, social, cultural, technological and environmental strengths. Among these dimensions, they concluded, however, that sociocultural appeal of a destination is a determining factor in deciding its tourist appeal. As a result, the Ritchie and Crouch model of destination competitiveness and sustainability (below) lists as core resources and attractors, sociocultural aspects of a destination (Fig. 9.1).

Other authors also stress the importance of the resources a destination offers. Dwyer and Kim (2003) divide the resources into two categories: endowed (inherited) and created. Endowed resources include natural (mountains, lakes, beaches, rivers, climate, etc.) and heritage or cultural ones such as cuisine, handicrafts, language, customs, belief systems and so on. Created resources include tourism infrastructure, special events and the range of available activities, entertainment and shopping.

The success of a destination is built from the core resources that must be supported by other factors and resources, which facilitate the access to the core resources. It is important thus to examine these core resources of the GCC region in general before focusing on each of the countries separately.

Physiography and climate: GCC countries share similar climatic conditions. The sunny and warm weather presents an advantage during the fall-spring months for tourists coming from outside of the region. The summer becomes, however, unscrupulously hot with temperatures reaching at times 50°C and humidity levels nearing 100 per cent. The topography of the region ranges from sandy flatlands to sand dunes and mountains in the southern part of the Arabian Peninsula. The natural environment, although mostly desert, is dotted in places by oases. While some countries present a variety of these features, others like Bahrain present just one feature (salty, sandy flatlands). Oman boasts the most varied natural environment with high mountains, canyons and fjords in the Musandam Peninsula. The long coastlines of the Arabian Gulf offer the opportunities for bathing and diving. Nonetheless, in some places the coastline is completely built up and coral reefs have been destroyed by land reclamation (O'Shea 2007). The quality of the beaches remains also questionable as UAE's beaches are the only ones that are Blue Flag certified. Desert safaris are a popular activity in areas where sand dunes are formed, while mountains (especially in Oman) present the opportunity for caving, mountain climbing and sightseeing.

Culture and History: GCC countries share similar cultural characteristics. The daily lives of its inhabitants are deeply marked by the practice of Islam. The historic architecture, apart from religious structures, presents

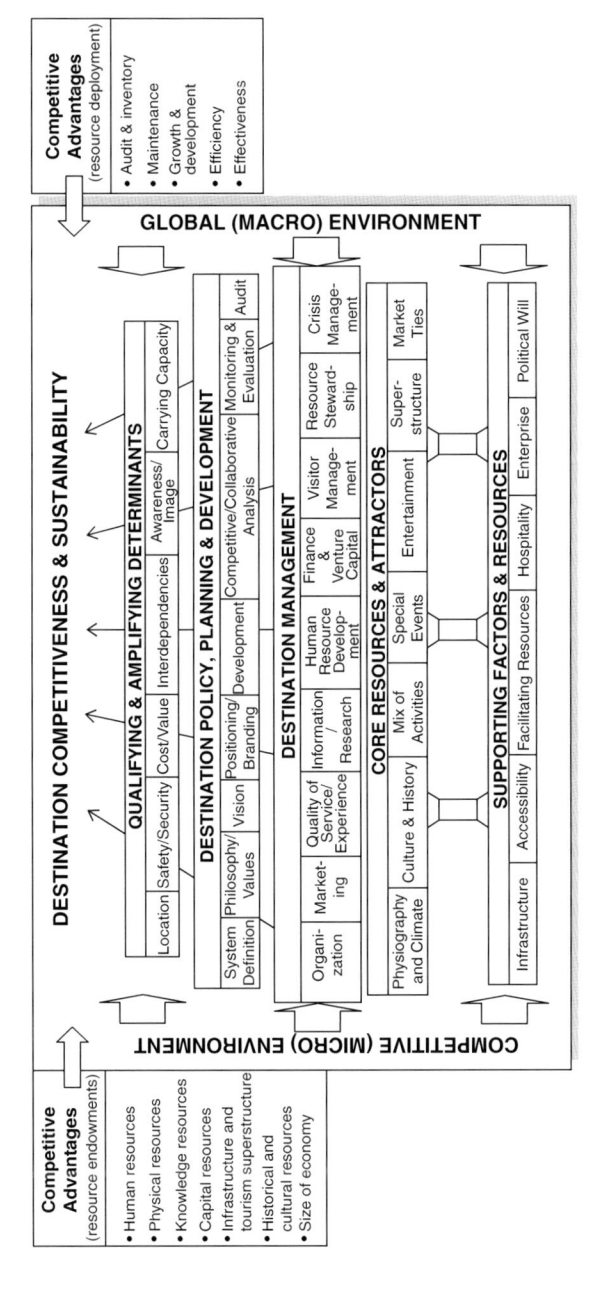

Fig. 9.1 Destination and competitiveness model. Source: Ritchie and Crouch 2003

similarities across the region with defensive structures such as forts and traditional houses fitted with wind towers. Traditional city districts inhabited in the past by the citizens have only recently been rediscovered and renovated as a testimony to the former life in the GCC. Such examples are Al Fahidi and Al Bastakiya areas located around the Dubai Creek or the houses of pearling merchants on the island of Muharraq in Bahrain. Despite its ancient history, the region is, however, characterized by a very low number of UNESCO World Heritage sites (Oman has four sites; Bahrain, two sites; UAE, one site; Qatar, one site; Kuwait, no sites). The existing historic sites, in addition, lack the overwhelming appeal and grandiosity of other monuments in the Middle East, for instance, those located in Egypt. This is one of the reasons why history museum displays are usually scant and focus on the life of Arabian Gulf inhabitants in the eve of the oil era. Bahrain is a notable exception being the site of an ancient civilization Dilmun. Its remnants are displayed in one of the most interesting national museums in the region: Bahrain National Museum. This overall deficiency of GCC is compensated by creation of new sites inspired by local architecture such as souks in Dubai and in Doha or religious structures. The recently completed Sheikh Zayed Mosque, for instance, provides an exquisite example of Islamic architecture on a gigantic scale and so does Sultan Qaboos Mosque in Muscat. The modern creations became the hallmark of the GCC and they will be discussed in the section devoted to superstructure.

Mix of activities. While the region seeks to diversify its tourist offerings, the core tourist activities center on beaches and shopping. As a result, major destinations in the Arabian Gulf share a number of common tourist activities such as desert safaris (KhorFakkan, Fujairah, Dubai, Muscat), forts (Muscat, KhorFakkan, Khasab, Salalah, Bahrain), souqs (Dubai, Fujairah, Muscat, Bahrain, Doha), beach leisure and water sports (KhorFakkan, Fujairah, Dubai, Bahrain, Doha, Kuwait), visits to famous hotels (Dubai, Abu Dhabi), dhow cruises (Dubai, Khasab, Muscat) and mountain scenic views (Fujairah, KhorFakkan, Khasab, Muscat, Sur).

Special events. Over the last decade, GCC countries hosted a variety of sport and cultural events. Bahrain has been the pioneer of Formula 1 racing in the Middle East with the opening of F1 international circuit in 2004 where Grand Prix races are held annually. Nonetheless, Bahrain's monopoly on Formula 1 races in the Middle East was broken in 2005 when Turkey opened its own F1 circuit in Istanbul. Moreover, Abu Dhabi became the closest competitor of Bahrain. Its Abu Dhabi Formula 1 Grand Prix was first held in 2009. Besides motor sports, GCC countries organize yearly boat shows (in Bahrain since 2009; also held in Dubai and Doha) and annual air shows (Bahrain since 2010; also held in Dubai and Doha). These events have mostly a regional importance. UAE and Qatar stand out as organizers of international sports championships. UAE hosts, among others, tennis, rugby, sailing championships and golf tournaments, while Qatar organized world handball championships and in 2022 will host the FIFA Football World Cup. Among the events recognizable on an international level, Dubai won the right to hold Expo 2020, the largest international exhibition showcasing technology. Thanks to this event, which was organized for the first time in London in 1851, Dubai aspires to increase its international tourist arrivals to 20 million in 2020.

Entertainment: This category includes all sorts of live performances, and the best-established cities in this regard are New York, London and Las Vegas. In the GCC region such forms of leisure are new developments. Yet, apart from hosting sporting events, GCC countries have also stressed promoting culture, which is reflected in the recent constructions of entertainment-related facilities. Indeed, recent years have witnessed increased investments in culture in the region with opening of theaters and opera houses. Doha (since 1982), Abu Dhabi (since 1981) and Bahrain (since 2012) already have national theaters. Muscat boasts its Royal Opera House (completed in 2011) and its cultural complex that will include a theater is under construction. Qatar opened doors of its Qatar Opera House as part of Katara Cultural Village completed in 2010, while Dubai inaugurated in 2016 an opera house near Burj Khalifa, the tallest building in the world. In addition, Dubai hosts theater performances in its multi-purpose Madinat Theatre. Such developments prompted GCC countries to establish for the first time national philharmonic orchestras. Opening of such new facilities fosters, in turn, organization of various events in an all-year-round schedule. Furthermore, festivals of culture that gather Arab and international artists are annually organized in Bahrain, Qatar and UAE. In Kuwait and Oman, culture festivals focus on the local heritage. Festivals include music, theater, poetry, art exhibitions and dance as well as academic lectures. In addition, GCC countries seasonally host a wide array of entertainment performances ranging from opera, classical music, musical, circus arts such as Cirque du Soleil, to popular music concerts and so on. The UAE entertainment scene remains the liveliest in the region with big-name artists including Dubai and Abu Dhabi in their world concert tours. The region has also become host to film festivals with Dubai International Film Festival attracting yearly world cinema premiers and international stars.

Superstructure: For Ritchie and Crouch, this concept encompasses a whole array of features such as hotels, restaurants, other built structures (especially those of unique architecture or history), attraction parks, museums and so on.

Construction of hotels is a prerequisite to receiving large numbers of tourists. The GCC region focuses on high-end hotel markets with four- and five-star hotels occupying a large share of the room supply. For instance, upper upscale and luxury hotels accounted for 28.6 per cent of Dubai's total existing supply in 2013 and 52.4 per cent of the additional projected supply. In Bahrain and Qatar, luxury hotels are estimated to cater over 75 per cent of all rooms. The region has attracted well-known international brands such as Hilton, Rotana, Sheraton, Kempinski, Royal Mirage and so on. There is clearly a need for middle- and budget-range hotels, which have become a new priority in UAE (Table 9.3).

Among the other types of superstructure elements, GCC region witnesses important investments in modern buildings, attraction parks and museums. Dubai is especially in the spotlight when it comes to construction with the tallest building of the world Burj Khalifa and other skyscrapers dotting the horizon. Other astonishing structures include, for instance, the largest man-made marina, a ski slope, an artificial palm-shaped Palm Jumeirah Island and so on. In addition, Dubai never ceases its extravagant projects and new developments, among others, Dubai Eye Ferris wheel, and the largest indoor shopping center in the world are in the process of development. Indeed, Dubai has become the place where everything has to be the biggest, the best and the most extravagant, an image that makes it stand out on an international scale. Cities like Abu Dhabi and Doha strive to catch up

Table 9.3 Hotel room supply in the GCC

Country	Room supply in 2013 (including apartments)	Rooms under development
Bahrain	16,265	3765
Kuwait	9111	982
Qatar	16,600	5968
Oman	14,396	3195
UAE	110,535	22,189

Source: Alpen Capital 2014

developing their own skyscrapers-filled skylines. In Kuwait City, recognizable by its twin Kuwait Towers, and Bahrain where Business Bay is under construction, the developments take more modest shapes in comparison to their neighbors. The Omani capital Muscat remains a fairly traditional city without any planned development of skyscrapers, which is part of its charm and planned preservation.

The region is experiencing a boom in museums. A total of five museums, for instance, are being built in just a one-phase development of Saadiyat Island in Abu Dhabi. They include branches of world-class art collections of the Guggenheim and the Louvre museums. Apart from UAE that aspire to become "the world's art and cultural hub" (Njeri 2009), this ambition is equally shared by Qatar. Qatar's royal family has been heavily investing in art through the Qatar Museum Authority. Qatar's new museums, Museum of Islamic Art, Arab Museum of Modern Art and National Museum of Qatar (development in progress) as well as contemporary art galleries in the Souk Waqif are not only exhibition spaces but also feature unique architectural designs.

Theme and amusement parks provide family-oriented entertainment. Thanks to the warm climate, modern water parks with fast slide rides are popular attractions of Abu Dhabi (Yas Waterworld), Dubai (Wild Wadi, Aquaventure on Palm Jumeirah), Bahrain (Lost Paradise; Wahoo) and Doha (an older Aqua Park with a more modest choice of attractions). Other parks include recognizable brands such as Ferrari World in Abu Dhabi. At the present moment, a film-themed park IMG Worlds of Adveture was opened in 2016 and the area will become in the future an amusement park complex featuring Pharaohs Theme Park, Giants World, Kids World, Global Village, Space & Science World, Space Hotel, Tourism Park, Film World, Desert World Theme Park, Snow World, Aviation World, Water Park, The Castles and Arabian Theme Park. Legoland, along with Motiongate and a Bollywood-themed parks, also opened their doors in Dubai in 2016.

Market ties: These refer to personal and professional/organizational ties that make visitors travel to a destination. Such ties can be strengthened through economic and political means. GCC is a political and economic bloc, which ensures intra-Gulf business travel. In addition, many GCC families have relatives in neighboring countries, which they visit for the purpose of family gatherings. On an international level, GCC are also hosts to conventions, conferences, international fairs and corporate meetings; yet their frequency and the volume of visitors may not be as important as that of Western countries. Even though GCC countries were initially associated with business travel, on an international scale, their rankings fall behind the average. The number of MICE (meetings, incentives, conferencing, exhibitions) organized in UAE and in Qatar ranks them at 47th and 74th positions, respectively, among 97 countries that were analyzed (Atalla and Nasr 2013), and it is estimated that MICE-related travel constitutes only 5 per cent of the total number of arrivals.

Supporting Factors and Resources in the Tourism Market

Ritchie and Crouch list six categories that are enablers of the core resources and attractors. This section will analyze the strengths and weaknesses of each.

Infrastructure: It refers to the state of general infrastructure and includes such facilities as transportation and communication services, sanitary systems and so on. In general, GCC countries present a high level of infrastructure development with fast and readily available communication services and high living standards. The national transportation networks vary depending on the country. Private transportation by taxis or rental cars is the backbone of transportation in GCC countries, even the very small ones like Bahrain. Public transportation remains scarce and caters often to low-skilled laborers in the cities. No railroads exist, while intercity bus connections depend on the country. Usually, if they exist, they do not easily link tourist attractions making independent travel difficult unless with a rented car. Information about connections is also limited. For instance, Oman National Transport Company's website schedule is under maintenance until the time of this publication (http://www.ontcoman.com/index.php). With regard to travel within the cities, public transportation in UAE offers an inexpensive but highly developed and reliable network of buses (Abu Dhabi, Dubai) and a state-of-the-art metro and trams (Dubai). Abu Dhabi, Dubai, Doha (Qatar) and Muscat (Oman) have also a network of Hop-on and Hop-off bus tours linking all tourist attractions within the city. In recent years, some GCC governments have taken on a role in regulating the private transportation service. For instance, in 2008 taxi drivers in Bahrain were made to use meters to curb the practice of overcharging newly arriving tourists.

Accessibility: This category refers to the ease or difficulty confronting tourists in traveling to the destination. Although GCC countries have a strategic location and overall accessibility by air, sea and land, air travel remains the most popular form of tourist travel to the region. In the last decade, GCC countries developed their own national airlines (dominated in the past by a joint cooperation of UAE, Oman, Qatar and Bahrain under the umbrella of Gulf Air airline) and expanded their airport capacities. Gulf airlines, especially Etihad (based in Abu Dhabi), Emirates (Dubai) and Qatar Airways (Doha) serve a vast network of international destinations and aim at turning their bases into international travel hubs where travelers not only connect to another flight but also may pass a day or two visiting the city in transit. National airlines in the region have become a vehicle for tourism promotion of their home countries in the regions they serve. The region noted also the establishment of low-cost airlines such as Air Arabia (Sharjah), FlyDubai (Dubai) and Jazeera Airways (Kuwait) operating on a smaller scale. This, in turn, created a stark competition between Gulf carriers that, in some cases, led to airlines struggling to continue their operations. A decline of the national airline Gulf Air may negatively affect the numbers of tourists incoming to Bahrain. In addition, the only low-cost Bahraini airline Bahrain Air announced bankruptcy in 2013. Due to the growing volume of passengers, UAE is home to the busiest airport in the world, Dubai International Airport (70 million passengers in 2014). Airport expansions and new airport constructions are taking place in the region, notably Dubai Al Maktoum Airport and new Muscat International Airport.

Due to visa regulations, the land routes between GCC countries are most often used by nationals, although the Oman-UAE border crossings are popular with GCC residents and tourists. The GCC network of roads that crosses through Saudi Arabia that has very restrictive entry regulations limits the possibility of further travel across GCC for the majority of foreigners. For Bahrain, however, the situation is slightly different. King Fahd Causeway is the preferred way of getting to the country and accounts for almost 80 per cent of the total number of arrivals to the islands (BEDB 2013). Intra-GCC rail networks are planned for development in the future. Sea routes are currently developed with the emergence of the Arabian Gulf cruise industry (Karolak 2015).

In terms of access to the country, GCC countries used to require all visitors (apart from other GCC nationals) to obtain a visa, often before traveling, which in the past limited the numbers of arrivals. Recent reforms aim at changing this state of affairs. In 2015 UAE implemented visa-free entry for EU nationals. The possibility of obtaining visas on arrival is another improvement. Bahrain has recently extended the list of nationalities that can obtain a visa on arrival to 64. In Qatar, Kuwait and Oman, that list is limited to 80 (since 2017), 52 and 54 nationalities, respectively. Yet, there are no multiple-entry tourist visas; thus, traveling between GCC countries may become challenging. Oman has, however, recently implemented a joint tourist visa facility with Dubai and Qatar that allows tourists to enter Oman visa free if directly entering from Dubai or Doha. Talks on a single GCC visit visa have been stalled.

Facilitating resources: They encompass a broad category of human, knowledge and capital resources, education and research institutions, financial institutions and various areas of the public service. All of these areas have an impact on the provision of customer service and attractiveness of the destination from the point of view of investors, including foreign ones. GCC countries rely on a high number of foreign workers in the customer service field; as a result, they do not face so far a shortage of staffing. Yet, within economic diversification strategies, nationalization of the job market is a priority. So far, GCC countries (with some exceptions such as Oman) fail to train and develop local tourism human capital, which will have a negative impact on the potential benefits stemming from the tourism industry in the future. The investment regulations and the ease of conducting business vary from one country to another. The establishment of free zones in the region allowed foreign companies to operate their service on an equal basis as local ones. Outside of a free zone, a foreign investor requires a local partner to establish a business. However, the economic activities allowed in a peculiar free zone may be limited. On the other hand, GCC is known as zero personal and corporate tax region, although this situation is about to change due to economic stagnation.

Hospitality: This category describes the friendliness and general level of hospitality displayed by the destination's host community. In the Arabian Gulf region, the century-old customs have put a high emphasis on hospitality and receiving guests is part of one's honor. In addition, the region is known for its political stability (with some exceptions in Bahrain that was affected by Arab Spring uprising in 2011). Despite the prevalence of Islamic traditions, some areas have adopted a liberal approach to tourism, necessary to cater to Western tourists' tastes. Dubai and Bahrain, for instance, have long relaxed the rules regulating the sale of alcohol, wearing bikinis and organizing clubbing events; prostitution, although illegal, is widely reported. Such approaches are not without their own problems. Manama was listed as "one of the top 10 cities to pursue vice and debauchery" (Al A'ali 2009) in a men's portal in 2009, while trespassing certain mores did land some Westerners in Dubai jails. Kuwait remains a dry country.

Enterprise: It relates to how entrepreneurship and new initiatives contribute to competitive destinations. The competition in this area depends on the country's overall approach to tourism as a source of income and the type and volume of tourists. In UAE, the number of travel and tour agencies is high, and they offer many alternatives in terms of local tour itineraries and prices. Similarly, hotels abound and offer various choices to tourists. However, Kuwait experiences a limited tourist base and competition is scarce. In Bahrain, despite high volume of tourist arrivals, sightseeing tours are limited due to the fact that the major portion of tourists are GCC nationals from Saudi Arabia coming to enjoy a more liberal lifestyle.

Political will: The political standing of national authorities has a decisive impact on development and facilitation of conducting any business. The tourism sector relies heavily on governmental rules and regulations and development of countrywide infrastructure. In the past, lack of a holistic strategy, planning and investments would stifle national tourism sectors. Some countries lacked national tourism authorities devoted to creating and implementing tourism strategies. Such was the case of Bahrain that only recently established a separate tourism authority. In addition, the lack of Gulf initiatives prevented developments of regional strategies. This situation is slowly changing. Dubai's Department of Tourism and Commerce Marketing (DTCM) adopted Tourism Vision 2020 for Dubai in order to capitalize on its successful Expo 2020 bid. Qatar Tourism Authority developed a national tourism strategy 2030. Bahrain created its first tourism strategy 2015–2018, which aims as rebranding the country as a "boutique destination", a move away from the current perception of the country as a playground for single Saudi Arab men in particular. Kuwait's 20-year tourism master plan adopted in 2004 focuses on increasing and improving domestic tourism as a priority. Oman has recently announced its 2015–2040 national tourism strategy. Their effects are to be seen in the future.

So far regional strategies include cooperation between Emirati and Omani governmental tourism agencies, which aim at facilitating the passage of cruise passengers. Abu Dhabi Ports Company along with Abu Dhabi Tourism and Culture Authority, the Department of Tourism and Commerce Marketing and Oman's Ministry of Tourism established a joint initiative Cruise Arabia at the end of 2013 in order to promote the Gulf region as an attractive and tourist-friendly destination. Qatar joined the initiative in March 2014. In 2014 Cruise Arabia started a promotion campaign to, on the one hand, strengthen the appeal of the Arabian Gulf among the already existing international tourist-sourcing markets such as European and North American and, on the other hand, to open new markets for tourist-sourcing such as India and China.

Place Identity: Methodology and Data Collection

In addition to what a country offers, a successful tourism strategy depends on the creation of a place identity. Tourism involves the production of destination identity, which is essential to attract tourists and increase market share (Dredge and Jenkins 2003). Given cultural and environmental similarities between the GCC countries, creation of such an identity is the core question of the study. The process is a complex one: "What is depicted or not depicted in destination image advertising, and on whose authority it is selected, involves a more complex question of what comprises the destination and who has the power to define its identity" (Fesenmaier and MacKay 1996). Creation of place identity involves "imagery as a political process that encodes and reinforces the dominant ideology of tourism culture, essentially a global process which manifests locally and explicitly involves the construction of place" (Ateljevic and Doorne 2002). Creation of such an identity takes place through the use of text combined with signs and images to add meaning to destinations, explain the destinations or the experience tourists can expect there; thus, semiotic language of tourism is deployed in the process (Tresidder 2011). Identities acquire meanings through the process of framing (Herbert 1995). Frames are the cognitive structures that we use to make sense of the world around us (Bateson 1972; Goffman 1974). Content analysis is well suited for retrieving frames from any written, verbal or visual form of communication (Cole 1988) and it may be complemented by critical discourse analysis. Content analysis concentrates on the text itself, without taking into account the context in which it was produced, that is, the social reality, the producer and the audience; discourse analysis stresses that social reality is constructed through meaningful interaction and it strives to examine how that reality was produced. It is clear that a text must be located in historical and social reality to be interpreted. As a result, discourse analysis complements content analysis and allows the researcher to interpret meanings. Hence, I will use the term content/discourse analysis in the following study, and the basic characteristic of discourse analysis, namely, its constructionist, inductive and subjective approach will be applied to data. The approach of this research is thus eclectic in nature, combining the content/discourse analysis of written text with that of images. This method is the most appropriate for the purpose of analysis given that "A place is a discourse—a way of constructing meaning [...]" (Govers and Go 2009).

Creation and consumption of place identities takes place in physical and in virtual environments (Molenaar 1996, 2002). As a result, data was collected, to begin with, online from governmental tourism websites, websites of local tourism agencies and national airlines, and the search purposely excluded international websites; and whenever it was possible on-site in national museums, at major attractions and so on. At that point, frames of place identity were extracted, analyzed and compared. It is important to keep in mind that place branding includes the marketing ties: (1) that support the creation of a name, symbol, logo, word mark or other graphic that both *identifies* and *differentiates* a destination; (2) that convey the *promise* of a memorable travel experience that is uniquely associated with the destination; and (3) that serve to *consolidate* and *reinforce* the recollection of pleasurable *memories* of the destination experience, all with the intent purpose of creating an *image* that influences consumers' *decisions* to visit destination in question, as opposed to an *alternative* one (Blain et al. 2005, cited in Govers and Go 2009).

Data Analysis

The analysis revealed a number of frames based on the imagery and text analysis, namely:

Frame 1: sea, sand and sun (beach and watersports, including outdoor waterparks)
Frame 2: leisure activities (arts, spas, shopping, indoor attraction parks and other activities)
Frame 3: active outdoor activities and natural scenery (desert safaris, mountain climbing, animal watching, etc.)
Frame 4: hospitality (hotels, resorts, dining, MICE)
Frame 5: local culture and heritage
Frame 6: modernity (architecture, innovation)

Table 9.4 illustrates the frames that were extracted in the analysis of the studied countries or entities. For the purpose of the comparative analysis, the researcher kept Dubai and Abu Dhabi as separate categories. The frames, which were highlighted, are the most important frames among others given their recurrence.

The analysis shows that so far Dubai and Abu Dhabi represent the most varied types of tourism attractors mirrored by the presence of all the frames. Other countries, notably Qatar, try to emulate this variety. Dubai has set the model of tourism development in the region (Balakrishnan 2008), and it is clear that Abu Dhabi and Qatar follow the success of Dubai's tourism industry. Qatar may as well soon add the themes gathered under frame 6 as the construction of its modern buildings and artificial islands progresses further. Similarly, Bahrain may follow by emphasizing this frame when the Bahrain Bay project is completed. In addition, Bahrain has already unveiled the planned creation of a "Natural Bahrain" theme for its 2015–2018 tourism strategy, which will fall under frame 3. However, the analysis also confirms that other GCC countries do not follow the same patterns. Oman aims at capitalizing on its rich heritage and natural environment, which are both low-cost tourism industry startups. The elements pertaining to frame 3 allow Oman to diversify its tourism offerings

Table 9.4 Frames analysis

	Frame 1	Frame 2	Frame 3	Frame 4	Frame 5	Frame 6
Dubai	√	√√	√	√	√	√
Abu Dhabi	√	√	√	√	√	√
Bahrain	√	√	*		√√	?
Kuwait[a]					√	√
Qatar	√	√	√	√	√√	*
Oman	√		√√		√	

√ existing frames
√√ dominant frames
* frames in the process of development
? frames that may be created in the future (based on current investment plans)
[a]Data collection in the case of Kuwait was limited in scope because the local authorities did not produce any web pages or printed material to promote Kuwait as a tourist destination. As a result, the author relied on information in Kuwaiti newspapers

Source: Author's analysis

with whale watching, turtle nesting watching as well as mountains and related geological structure activities (canyons, caves, fjords). These natural elements cannot be replicated in other areas; yet, UAE compensate this shortcoming by creating extravagant attraction parks, which offer, among others, encounters with wildlife. Oman, in addition, possesses a number of traditional cities that have preserved a unique character. In order to keep the traditional character, there are, for instance, restrictions on height of new buildings (King 2008). From this point of view and given its natural advantages, Oman seems to possess the unique features among GCC countries. Yet, the country aims at attracting primarily high-end tourists, while a diversification of the tourist base could help Oman promote its natural heritage. Many of Oman's natural attractions appeal to young people who may not be able to afford five-star-rated hotels and, hence, camp in nature instead. Budget hotels that follow international standards could increase the country's tourism receipts and help preserve the environment. Bahrain, a much smaller country and less endowed in terms of natural scenery, focuses on promotion of its ancient heritage and to a limited extent utilizes frame 2 elements such as dining, shopping and F1 races. Again, the focus in recent years has been put on high-end tourists, which may backfire if the country's offerings are not sufficient to attract such a tourist base. Kuwait, on the other hand, has a very limited selection of frames. While the country could also enhance the presentation of its heritage or promote itself as a shopping destination, this shortcoming stems clearly from lack of interest in development of tourism industry (Kuwait Times 2015). It should be especially highlighted that none of the countries has managed to clearly specialize in a particular type of tourism. A smaller number of frames present in the analysis is due usually to a lack of funds or lack of interest in the development of a particular tourism product.

Discussion and Conclusion

From the above overview, it is clear that GCC countries lack historical monuments comparable in scale to those located in other regions and they share similar natural resources. Consequently, GCC countries must mostly rely on created resources to attract tourism. Oman, as an exception, has been able to successfully capitalize on its natural environment as a tourism attractor, which cannot be matched by the environment in other GCC countries. Lack of diversity, in turn, creates a competition in GCC for more and more spectacular developments in superstructure in order to widen the array of tourist attractions and events. This is also the case of hotels since GCC countries aim at attracting high-end luxury tourism. Creation of new entertainment parks, museums, branded hotels as well as organization of sporting championships on an international scale requires heavy investments that are possible only in some of the GCC countries like UAE or Qatar. Other countries remain left behind due to smaller availability of funds (Bahrain) or lack of such a strategy (Kuwait). In the region, Dubai has become the spotlight of the worldwide tourism market, thanks to its ever-expanding and extravagant array of attractions. It set the model for the GCC region. Futuristic projects that are under development will no doubt ensure the tourist appeal of the emirate in the future.

Nonetheless, it is not surprising that when similar types of developments and events are created and organized in neighboring GCC countries, it limits their overall uniqueness. As a result, rather than copying those same types of developments, a country should determine which tourism products to prioritize, thus creating a specialized domain in which it is recognizable. It is especially true for the less wealthy GCC countries. Within the tourism sector, tourism offerings present various degrees of competition and of attractiveness. While heritage culture, sun and beaches and MICE are highly attractive and have a large market size, they are also very competitive products. Urban tourist offerings and modern culture have medium market sizes and are less attractive to tourists but they present moderate competition. In the zone of low attractiveness, nature and health and wellness have medium market sizes but moderate competition. Lastly, education presents a small market size, low attractiveness but also low competitively (Atalla and Nasr 2013). Within this framework, rather than competing for a full market share by offering all products at once, GCC countries should specialize in unique areas, which will make them recognizable in the region and worldwide, thanks to creation of a unique brand identity, and ensure their uninterrupted tourist appeal in the future.

GCC countries aim at economic diversification and they have recognized tourism as an important contributor to future economic growth. Consequently, each GCC country faces challenges and a stark competition from its neighboring states that aim at promoting themselves on the world tourist destination map. The all-or-nothing strategy pursued by some GCC countries (or entities) has resulted in lack of specialized niche tourism products and makes it difficult to compete for less wealthy GCC members unable to commit funds for the development of large-scale projects. So far, it is the appeal of the superstructure, which requires high capital investments, that has attracted the largest numbers of international tourist arrivals to Dubai. Yet, it is also clear that other GCC countries and other emirates in the UAE should focus on creating niche products for which they will be recognizable worldwide and which would be part of their branding strategies. Through successful branding, defined as "the conscious attempt of governments to shape a specifically designed place identity and promote it to identified markets" (Kavaratzis and Ashworth 2010), destinations become easily recognizable in the world. In addition, in the context of ever-growing competition, place marketing creates "uniqueness in order to improve the competitive position of the place marketed" (Kavaratzis and Ashworth 2010). Consequently, such destinations are able to attract tourism and foreign investments. Balakrishnan (2008) proposed a checklist to assess destination marketing strategy. It is composed of 6Ps:

- Purpose of the destination brand design and promise;
- People that will be affected, influencers and target of branding;
- Performance expected after a realistic audit;
- Products offered under the destination portfolio and their management;
- Positioning expected and ways to reinforce it and finally; and
- Process of ensuring the brand promises are delivered as effectively and efficiently as possible.

Such branding analyses are necessary to conduct in order to pinpoint the unique character of each of the GCC entities and develop a strategy for creating the necessary brand products supported by investments, and their implementation should be combined with well-managed promotion campaigns abroad. While examining Dubai, Balakrishnan found out, for instance, that it needed "a clearer, unified brand promise, and a few selected images" (2008). Place branding aims at creating a competitive identity, which should follow the motto "actions speak louder than words" (Anholt 2003; Govers and Go 2009), which means investments in tourism are needed to support a successful strategy.

All in all, while GCC have the potential to improve their tourist attractiveness, the level and the speed of growth of tourism industry will depend on a successful creation and implementation of destination brand place identities. In addition, further regional initiatives are needed to facilitate and strengthen the appeal of GCC as a tourist region overall and maximize the GCC capacity as a tourist destination. Furthermore, future studies are needed to assess the currently developed and implemented tourism strategies of particular GCC countries in light of brand identity creation as well as to assess the economic and the environmental sustainability of the proposed tourism models.

REFERENCES

Al A'ali, M. (2009). Hotels vice probe ordered by MPs. *Gulf Daily News*, December 23.

Alpen Capital. (2011). *GCC hospitality industry*. Retrieved June 15, 2012, from http://www.alpencapital.com/downloads/GCC-Hospitality-Report-13-April-per cent202011.pdf

Alpen Capital. (2014). *GCC hospitality industry*. Retrieved January 1, 2015, from http://www.alpencapital.com/downloads/GCC_Hospitality_Report_24092014.pdf

Anholt, S. (2003). *Brand New Justice: The upside of global marketing*. Oxford: Butterworth-Heinemann.

Ashley, C., Brine, D., Peter, L. A., & Wilde, H. (2007). *The role of the tourism sector on expanding economic opportunity*. Harvard: John F. Kennedy School of Government.

Atalla, G., & Nasr, A. (2013). *Reinventing tourism in the GCC: Building the tourism ecosystem*. Abu Dhabi—Beirut: Booz & Company.

Ateljevic, I., & Doorne, S. (2002). Representing New Zealand Tourism imagery and ideology. *Annals of Tourism Research, 29*(2), 648–667.

Bahrain Economic Development Board [BEDB]. (2013). *Bahrain economic yearbook 2013*. Manama: BEDB.

Balakrishnan, M. S. (2008). Dubai a star in the east: A case study in strategic destination branding. *Journal of Place Management and Development, 1*(1), 62–91.

Bateson, G. (1972). A theory of play and fantasy. In G. Bateson (Ed.), *Steps to an ecology of mind*. New York: Chandler.

Baumgarten, J.-C., & Kent, G. J. W. (2010). *Travel and tourism economic impact, United Arab Emirates*. London: World Travel and Tourism Council Research Report.

Cole, F. L. (1988). Content analysis: Process and application. *Clinical Nurse Specialist, 2*(1), 53–57.

De Keyser, R., & Vanhove, N. (1994). The competitive situation of tourism in the Caribbean area—Methodological approach. *Revue de Tourisme, 48*, 19–22.

Dredge, D., & Jenkins, J. (2003). Destination place identity and regional tourism policy. *Tourism Geographies, 5*(4), 383–407.

Dwyer, L., & Kim, C. (2003). Destination competitiveness: Determinants and indicators. *Current Issues in Tourism*, 6(5), 369–414.

Economist Intelligence Unit [EIU]. (1993). United Arab Emirates. *International Tourism Reports*, 3, 29–54.

Emirates News Agency. (2011, August 28). *UAE travel and tourism one of key contributors to GDP*. Retrieved April 16, 2012, from http://www.emirates247.com/news/emirates/uae-travel-and-tourism-one-of-key-contributors-to-gdp-2011-08-28-1.415393

Evans, M. R., Fox, J. B., & Johnson, R. B. (1995). Identifying competitive strategies for successful tourism destination development. *Journal of Hospitality and Leisure Marketing*, 31, 37–45.

Fesenmaier, D., & MacKay, K. (1996). Deconstructing destination image construction. *The Tourist Review*, 51(2), 37–43.

Goffman, E. (1974). *Frame analysis: An essay on the organization of experience*. New York: Harper & Row.

Gomezelj, D. O., & Michalic, T. (2008). Destination competitiveness—Applying different models: The case of Slovenia. *Tourism Management*, 29, 294–307.

Govers, R., & Go, F. (2009). *Place branding: Glocal, virtual, and physical identities, constructed, imagined and experienced*. Basingstoke: Palgrave Macmillan.

Herbert, D. T. (1995). Heritage places, leisure and tourism. In D. T. Herbert (Ed.), *Heritage, tourism and society*. London: Pinter.

Kalandides, A. (2012). Place branding and place identity. An integrated approach. *Tafter Journal*, 43.

Karolak, M. (2015). The cruise industry in the Arabian Gulf: The emergence of a new destination. *Journal of Tourism Challenges and Trends*, VIII(1), 61–78.

Kavaratzis, M., & Ashworth, G. (2010). Place branding: Where do we stand? In G. Ashworth & M. Kavaratzis (Eds.), *Towards effective place brand management: Branding European cities and regions*. Northampton: Edward Elgar.

King, D. C. (2008). *Cultures of the world: Oman*. Tarrytown: Marshall Cavendish.

Koren, M., & Tenreyro, S. (2010). *Volatility, Diversification and Development in the Gulf Cooperation Council Countries*. Kuwait Programme on Development, Governance and Globalisation in the Gulf States, Research Paper No. 9. London: London School of Economics.

Kotler, P., & Gertner, D. (2002). Country as brand, product, and beyond: A place marketing and brand management perspective. *The Journal of Brand Management*, 9, 249–261.

Kuwait Times. (2015). *Kuwait placed last in GCC tourism, 101 worldwide*. Retrieved March 15, 2015, from http://news.kuwaittimes.net/kuwait-placed-last-gcc-tourism-101-worldwide-al-anjeri/

Luciani, G., & Beblawi, H. (1987). *The Rentier state*. New York: Croom Helm.

Molenaar, C. (1996). *Interactive marketing*. Hampshire: Ashgate Publishing.

Molenaar, C. (2002). *The future of marketing: Practical strategies for marketers in the post-internet age*. London: Pearson Education.

Njeri, J. (2009). UAE sees good economic prospects in cultural investments. *Alrroya*, December 17.

O'Shea, A. (2007). Are coral reefs a history? *Gulf Daily News*, July 1.

Ritchie, J. R. B., & Crouch, G. I. (2003). *The competitive destination: A sustainable tourism perspective*. Wallingford: Cabi Publishing.

Rossouw, R., & Saayman, M. (2011). Assimilation of tourism satellite accounts and applied general equilibrium models to inform tourism policy analysis. *Tourism Economics, 17*(4), 753–783.

Sharpley, R. (2002). The challenges of economic diversification through tourism: The case of Abu Dhabi. *International Journal of Tourism Research, 4*(3), 221–235.

Shochat, S. (2008). *The Gulf Cooperation Council Economies: Diversification and reform: An introduction*. Kuwait Programme on Development, Governance and Globalisation in the Gulf States—Working Paper. London: LSE Centre for the Study of Global Governance.

Sick, G. (1997). The coming crisis in the Persian Gulf. In G. Sick & L. G. Potter (Eds.), *The Persian Gulf at the millennium: Essays in politic strategy, economy, security, and religion*. New York: St. Martin's Press.

Tresidder, R. (2011). The semiotics of tourism. In P. Robinson (Ed.), *Current themes in tourism*. Wallingford: CABI.

UNWTO. (2011). *Tourism highlights 2011 edition*. Madrid: UNWTO.

UNWTO. (2014). *Tourism highlights 2014 edition*. Retrieved March 1, 2015, from http://dtxtq4w60xqpw.cloudfront.net/sites/all/files/pdf/unwto_highlights14_en.pdf

World Travel & Tourism Council [WTTC]. (2011/2013). *Travel & tourism 2011*. Retrieved June 20, 2012, from http://www.wttc.org/site_media/uploads/downloads/traveltourism2011.pdf

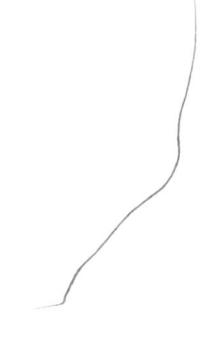

CHAPTER 10

Regional Integration, the Private Sector and Diversification in the GCC Countries

Ashraf Mishrif and Salma Al-Naamani

INTRODUCTION

Since the mid-1990s, the search for effective policy measures to develop and implement economic diversification strategies has been a key policy objective for all Gulf Cooperation Council (GCC) states. National visions and national development plans have spelled out a number of concepts and policy objectives aiming at shifting their economies from heavy dependency on oil and gas to economic growth driven by non-hydrocarbon sectors. Huge public investments are made in tourism, services, finance, petrochemicals, manufacturing, construction and real estates in order to support the diversification process. In fact, this classical approach to diversification has not yet changed the economic structure of the GCC countries as the majority of investments made in a few state-owned enterprises and the public sector remains the engine of economic growth.

This chapter explores a new line of inquiry into how the dynamics of regional integration in the GCC affect the economic diversification strategies of its member states. The key premise in here is that the dynamics and

A. Mishrif (✉) • S. Al-Naamani
King's College London, London, UK

© Gulf Research Centre Cambridge 2018
A. Mishrif, Y. Al Balushi (eds.), *Economic Diversification in the Gulf Region, Volume I*, The Political Economy of the Middle East,
https://doi.org/10.1007/978-981-10-5783-0_10

policy measures proceeding from the creation of various forms of integration, including free trade areas, customs unions and common markets, eliminate barriers to trade and investment and expand the size of the regional market. As explained below, statistics underscore a strong correlation between the introduction of the free trade area in 1983, the customs union in 2003 and the common market in 2008 and the number of small and medium-sized enterprises (SMEs) created in the GCC member states. Literature also shows that the rise in the number of SMEs in national markets has been associated with a noticeable expansion of their operations in the GCC regional market because of the new business opportunities offered by regional integration (Hertog 2008; Nechi 2011).

This chapter aims to fill a significant gap in literature on whether regional economic integration affects positively or negatively on the size and quality of the private sector, more specifically SMEs that form the backbone of the private sector in most GCC countries. The role of the private sector in economic diversification is examined, using a number of analytical tools to explain and measure the extent to which the elimination of tariffs and non-tariff barriers affects positively private enterprises. Such impact can be measured by the levels of reduction in the costs of doing business, which encourage SMEs to not only operate freely in their national economy but also seek business opportunities in neighbouring markets. This is tested by investigating the relationship between the introduction of the 2003 GCC customs union and the 2008 GCC common market and the growth levels in the number and enhanced absorptive capacity of SMEs in non-hydrocarbon sectors. Although the analysis focuses on Oman as a case study, it applies to most GCC countries due to the similarity in their economic structures, size of markets, economic policies and levels of economic growth. It acknowledges the political and economic difficulties that the GCC is facing to proceed further with a common currency and a monetary union (Alarab Newspaper 2013); but such difficulties could be overcome by harmonising the legal and regulatory systems that foster private sector development at the national and regional markets.

Perspectives on the GCC Regional Integration

The creation of a free trade area in 1983, only two years after the establishment of the GCC, underlines the importance of formulating a coherent regional economic structure for its small member states (GCC General Secretariat 2012a). The aim of the free trade area was to achieve full liberalisation of goods originating from the GCC and to facilitate business transactions among the GCC. This was consistent with global trends at the time that aimed at trade liberalisation and opening up national and global markets. The GCC regional market has become larger, more attractive to trade and investment and appropriate for specialisation in production order to offer a wider range of products for its growing consumer markets. The market is characterised by regional competition due to greater efforts to develop local commodities and more importantly substantial reduction in the cost of production. For example, there is no need for a local agent in order to complete a regional business transaction if the commodities originate in the GCC. There is reciprocal insurance, and also faster customs procedures and special lanes in all GCC ports for GCC citizens, which makes the movement in the region much easier (GCC General Secretariat 2012b).

Indeed, the free trade area eliminated most trade barriers among member states, but external trade barriers remained for non-members (Kerr and Gaisford 2007). The external common tariff affected those member states with self-enforcing arrangements in their trade relations—often have specific or limited relations—because of the fixing of tariffs of low cooperation; this effect is aggravated further by the availability of resources or factors in the import-rivals sector that could gain rents from specific skills of the sector (Staiger 1994).

In the meantime, the GCC market suffers from insufficient harmonisation in the economic policy of the GCC countries. Companies and sole traders do not receive relevant information about the other markets; this in turn discourages some of them to take risks due to lack of information and protection from the concerned authorities (Fisher 2009). Enterprises are required to obtain licences and to follow complex procedures in order to access new customers in other markets. They are also faced with high cost of transportation; in some cases, the cost of importing commodities from other GCCs is higher than those imported from foreign countries such as China. There are indirect taxes in some GCC states, which increase the cost of imported commodities. This is true when countries impose protectionist measures to support national products, thus affecting negatively competition in their local markets.

The introduction of the customs union in 2003 upgraded the level of integration and resulted in an increase in overall welfare of the GCC countries. Local GCC products received the same treatment no matter where the product originated in the GCC. There are tariffs for foreign commodities, estimated at 5 per cent for non-GCC local commodities at the port of entry and a 100 per cent tariff for products that affect health such as tobacco (GCC General Secretariat 2012a). The customs union minimised the barriers and increased commodity movement around member states, while allowing for effective utilisation of raw materials. This paved the way for the common market, increased interregional trade and fostered business relations among companies in the regional market, despite the fact that customs unions are very similar to free trade areas (Knickrehm and Hastedt 2003).

As for the welfare effect of the GCC customs union, one can argue that increase in welfare gains depends on several types of sources, including production specialisation, scale economies, terms of business or trade changes and rise in foreign competition, and hence enforces changes in efficiency and change in the economic growth rate (Lipsey 1960). In the case of the GCC, the welfare gains are not significant because of the postponement of implementation of some customs union articles more than once due to failure to devise effective mechanisms for the distribution of customs revenues among the GCC (Langenhove and Lombaerde 2007).

Without addressing this critical shortfall, the GCC implemented the next level of integration by stablishing a common market in 2008, hoping that this could pave the way for the monetary and economic unions. Theoretically, common markets embed the same rules as the customs unions, with the free movement of people, capital, goods and other factors of production among member states. However, the welfare gains may be larger in common markets than customs unions (Knickrehm and Hastedt 2003). In the GCC, citizens are eligible for free education and health services in all member states, as well as those working in either the government or the private sector in any member state. They are also entitled to undertake any kind of business activity and own property and to claim social security and retirement benefits.

In terms of trade, intra-regional trade among GCC countries rose dramatically and rapidly in value after the implementation of the GCC customs union in January 2003. Trade among member states increased from US$15 billion in 2002 to US$23 billion in 2003, after the first year of the union. The impact of the common market on trade was even greater than the customs union as trade statistics confirm that trade volumes of GCC countries reached US$121 billion between 2008 and 2013. This rise is clearly significant if taking into account that this figure was US$29 billion in 2004 (Al-Ali 2013).

However, the challenges to GCC regional integration are numerous. Chief among these challenges is the absence of a central body in the form of a GCC Commission with the power and authority to enforce decisions and follow up the implementation of decisions with GCC governments. There is a necessity for the existence of such body in the overall structure of the GCC, if the council is to follow the EU model of integration (Alhyat Newspaper 2014). This reinforces the claim made by the Bahrain Center for International and Economic Studies and Energy that some GCC countries do not effectively implement the policies and rules as stipulated by the GCC council. The authority of a GCC Commission could delegate specialised tasks to executive committees with more power, not acting only as advisory committees. Among these proposed committees is a specialised judicial tribunal to deal with dispute settlement in light of the growing number of trade and business disputes (interview with Abdul Rahim Hassan, Secretary General of the Federation of Chambers of the GCC, Alyaum Newspaper 2013).

Economic integration is also affected by lack of homogeneity among member states. There are differences in politics, laws and regulations of trade, as well as the procedures of running businesses. This hinders the desire of the companies to expand their activities in the regional market. The degree of harmonising the economic, political and legal contexts in the GCC needs to be deepened in order to overcome business transactions inadequacy and lack of expansion and internationalisation of SMEs in the GCC markets. No one can deny that all GCC member states follow the common market rules, but these are implemented in different ways, levels and periods, probably due to discrepancies in the income distribution among citizens, which is higher in Qatar and UAE than the rest of the region. Lack of commitment to speed up the levels of integration is also evident in the absence of electronic linkages among the member states and a single visa that could facilitate financial transactions and improve the business environment. Some analysts also highlighted the reluctance of some countries to accept the Article related to accommodating branches of banks and companies in their countries, and if they do accept, they allow only one, which is in conflict with the agreement of the GCC (Alyaum Newspaper 2013). These technical and bureaucratic challenges should be overcome if enterprises are to benefit from the Council's unique cultural affinity in terms of sharing similar culture, values and language and its geographical proximity to Asian emerging markets, European advanced economies and African untapped economic sectors. This provides companies with the opportunity to connect and expand in both the developed and developing countries. The GCC business community could further benefit from the proposed monetary union, with the aim of increasing the daily business transactions, facilitating transfer of capital and enabling the GCC to attain financial and monetary stability.

IMPACT OF GCC REGIONAL MARKET ON PRIVATE SECTOR ENTERPRISES

Statistical data show a huge surge in the volume of non-oil trade between 2000 and 2013. This is attributed to an increase in economic activities by many small- and medium-sized enterprises outside the hydrocarbon sector. Table 10.1 shows significant rise in total non-oil trade from US$12,785.26 million in 2000 to US$95,415.97 million. The country that experienced the largest surge in the non-oil trade is the UAE with a rise by US$23,151.54 million, followed by Oman with an increase by US$19,655.10 million. The lowest change was in Kuwait by US$4130.89 million and Bahrain by US$5350.32 million.

According to Jasem Al-Alwi, who is in charge of the common market management, regional trade among the GCC countries had increased to US$121 billion in 2014, an increase of more than seven times compared to 2000, but it only represents 7.1 per cent of the total value of foreign trade in the GCC countries (Argaam Newspaper 2015). If total non-oil trade among the GCC countries does not exceed US$95,500 million in 2013 when compared with the total trade among the GCC that is estimated at US$120 billion, then the total value of non-oil trade is less than 0.5 per cent of their regional trade. This did not deter Al-Alwi from arguing that the number of licences granted to GCC citizens to practise economic activities in other member states reached 40,753 until the year 2014, compared with 11,095 licences at the end of 2004. This means an increase in the number of licences granted to the GCC citizens in other states by 29,658 in a ten-year period. As indicated in Table 10.1 and echoed by Al-Alwi, trade data point out that each GCC country has its own major partner within the region, for example, Oman and UAE and Bahrain and Saudi Arabia. The availability of cheap energy across the entire region helps companies to move around with no concern over the production cost, if they are to operate in high-intensive industries or locate in an industrial zone with the aim of specialisation in production.

Table 10.1 GCC interregional non-oil trade, 2000 and 2013 (US$ million)

Country	Qatar 2000	Qatar 2013	Saudi Arabia 2000	Saudi Arabia 2013	UAE 2000	UAE 2013	Oman 2000	Oman 2013	Kuwait 2000	Kuwait 2013	Bahrain 2000	Bahrain 2013
Qatar			276.32	2454.39	320.54	8381.36	24.35	1570.68	27.76	1481.28	58.77	456.4
Saudi Arabia	276.32	2454.39			1508.95	8141.18	242.3	4623.43	719.13	2629.5	1268.09	5050.85
UAE	320.54	8381.36	1508.95	8141.18			1487.86	15,689.37	397.76	1692.18	243.66	1267.04
Oman	24.35	1570.68	242.3	4623.43	1487.86	15,689.37			50.48	777.67	40.28	385.55
Kuwait	27.76	1481.28	719.13	2629.5	397.76	1692.18	50.48	777.67			80.25	279.16
Bahrain	58.77	456.4	1268.09	5050.85	243.66	1267.04	40.28	385.55	80.25	279.16		
Total	707.74	14,344.11	3738.47	20,444.96	3638.23	26,789.77	1820.92	21,476.02	1247.62	5378.51	1632.28	6982.60

Source: Al Abd Alqadeer 2015

Although the various dynamics of GCC integration have been helpful in widening the regional market and supporting enterprises to internationalise into the GCC markets, business transactions of the SMEs and their participation in the GCC economies are not very huge (Ashrafi and Murtaza 2008; Kapurubandara and Lawson 2006). According to the Omani Ministry of Commerce and Industry (2012), Oman has around 121,000 SMEs, which contribute up to 20 per cent of domestic revenue. In Qatar, although the number of SMEs has risen from 8000 to 11,000, their contribution to GDP is between 15 and 17 per cent (Gulf Base Economic and Business News 2012). Bahraini SMEs contribute around 28 per cent of Bahrain GDP and employ 73 per cent of private sector workers. Of these 328,880 employees, 14 per cent are Bahraini citizens, while the rest are foreigners (Al-Rabeei and Scott 2011). In Bahrain, very small enterprises make up around 87.7 per cent of SMEs, which translates as 41,033 firms. Small firms make up about 10 per cent, or 4760 companies, and medium-sized enterprises make up 1.7 per cent, which works out at 808 organisations (Bahrain EDB 2013). According to Zawya (2012), 98 per cent of enterprises in Saudi Arabia are SMEs, with a contribution of up to 25 per cent of the country's GDP and 63 per cent of total employment. Emirates NBD (2012) estimates that there are 230,000 SMEs in the UAE. These contribute to almost 30 per cent of the UAE's GDP and hire more than 42 per cent of the labour force of the UAE. Al Saif (2004) estimates the number of businesses in Kuwait at about 25,000, of which 1 per cent hire fewer than 10 workers, 60 per cent employ 30 workers or fewer, 15 per cent have under 50 employees, whilst only 2.1 per cent employ 600 people or more. Only about 5 per cent of Kuwaitis work in the private sector, while 95 per cent work in the public sector.

Despite this huge number of SMEs compared to the large firms, their contribution in the economies and GDP remains low. This is recognised by the Secretary General of the Gulf Organization for Industrial Consulting (GOIC), who argued that GCC SMEs represent a very low percentage compared to their counterparts in the developed countries, which account for at least 50 per cent of GDP (Alyaum Newspaper 2013). Furthermore, the contribution of GCC SMEs in the employment is not high especially that the vast majority of them are owned or managed by foreigners. In fact, most GCC citizens prefer to have governmental jobs because it is highly paid, and there is greater job security. Even though some people find that work in the private sector or owning a business is more profitable, many youths in the GCC prefer to have a secure government job; some even argue that youths in Gulf States with a high-income level prefer not to have a job at all (Abdelhafiz 2015).

Business Environment and Non-oil Enterprises

The liberalisation of trade and investment regimes and elimination of most barriers to the free movement of capital, goods and labour have improved the business environment in the GCC countries. The implementation of the customs union and the common market has resulted in a business environment that is characterised by non-discrimination among national and foreign companies. EU experience shows that regional integration transforms the policy and economy of the member states and greatly affects trade among states within the integration area, as well as creating new rules, orientations and cooperative plans and strategies (Crowley 2001). For the GCC, integration can be seen as a united force politically and economically, with all member states gaining similar benefits. If they are willing to sacrifice their own national interests, they may be able to capture some of the positive outcomes of similar integration in the EU, where, for example, there has been the creation of a specialist, area-specific manufacturing industry. For example, EU member states manufacture airplanes; each of them specialised to manufacture a part (European Commission 2009), hence depending the degree of regional integration and allowing for greater cooperation among companies in the wider regional market.

Another benefit for companies from regional integration is the creation and development of an internal market. This internal market often leads to an increase in performance and productivity for SMEs and other firms. In the ideal world, member states properly follow the rules of their economic bloc, and this means taking social responsibility and protecting both the environment and intellectual property (Harris and Hasenknopf 1995). The expected outcome is better social and economic welfare, as well as an increased availability of cheaper products and more regional investments, which will consequently boost the employment level. According to the GCC General Secretariat, the net investment flows of the GCC rose from US$48 billion in 2009 to US$66.4 billion in 2010 and then to US$81.3 billion in 2011. Most of the investment flows came from private equity investment which rose from US$50.7 billion in 2009 to US$55.9 billion in 2010 and then to US$68 billion in 2011 (Akhbar Al-Khaleej 2010).

However, one can easily notice a huge difference between the GCC companies trading with foreign countries and trading among themselves. Data shows that about 5 per cent of local SMEs have joined in regional business transactions, and their proportion of export in the GCC area did not exceed 5 per cent of their total exports to the global markets (Al

Sadoun 2009). For example, total trade between the GCC and China rose to US$155 billion in 2012, more than 16 times the value of trade between them in 2001 (Gulf Center and Arabian Peninsula Studies, Kuwait University 2013). The trade volume between the Gulf countries and India increased by 29 times compared to 2001, at up to around US$159 billion in 2012. The fact that US$121 billion size of the interregional trade among the countries of the Council accounts only 7.1 per cent of the total foreign trade of the GCC underscores serious concerns about the structure of the Gulf economies and the capacity of their companies to increase their productivity and competitiveness nationally and internationally. The current conditions of the business environment and performance of the private sector enterprises should be taken into account when developing and implementing new integration policies. The private sector can no longer be ignored. It has to take the leading role in the overall economic and commercial activities, to be the main generator of national income and to provide job opportunities for the national workforce. Despite the ambitious plans of Oman to raise around 91 per cent of total investments from the private sector by 2020 (Argaam Newspaper 2015), one should be realistic when it comes to effectiveness of reforms and policy implementation.

Government Support to Private Enterprises

SMEs have significantly benefited from regional integration in the GCC. There are a number of programmes to encourage youth projects and start-up businesses. The development of the kind of enterprises and efficient utilisation of available resources could help to diversify and boost the economy. The initiation of supporting programmes for private sector companies is highly likely to increase the capacity of these companies and develop a new promising sector that is capable of utilising resources that are not exploited by public sector companies and contributing to sustainable economic development. In all GCC countries, there are many programmes offering support and funding to SMEs. Among these programmes are the Tamkeen Programme in Bahrain, the Kuwait Small Projects Development Company in Kuwait, the Raffd Fund in Oman, Social Development Centre controlled by the Qatar Foundation in Qatar, the Kafala Fund in Saudi Arabia and the Khalifa Fund in the UAE (2009). While the majority of these funds target the banking sectors in order to provide financial support to SMEs, they also aim to promote competition, encourage innovation, adapt new technology in the production process and increase export.

The effect of these programmes on the performance of private sector enterprises has been limited, particularly when compared with other supporting services provided to SMEs in other regions. If compared with the supporting initiatives to Indian SMEs, the outcome of GCC governments' initiatives is very modest, as Indian SMEs account for 50 per cent or more of the manufacturing industry (Das 2011). Government support goes beyond access to finance as in the case of the GCC, to include training, administrative, marketing, technological and technical assistance to SMEs. In addition to free or no corporate tax, the GCC government should provide other forms of incentives to encourage SMEs to operate in sectors or industries that are strategically important to economic development. New legislations aiming at promoting public-private partnership can encourage SMEs in participating in infrastructure projects and engage with larger firms in large projects.

SMEs' Contribution to the Development of Non-oil Sectors

The share of SMEs in the development of the non-oil sectors varies from one sector to another, depending on the degree of concentration of companies, government support and quality of infrastructure services. It could also depend on the ease of entry and exit in the sector, rate of returns on investment and the potential of the sector to grow. Available data shows variation in the average importance of the non-oil sectors in the GCC economies. Overall, the average share of the service sector in GDP in the GCC stands at 20 per cent, while the manufacturing sector contributes around 10 per cent, and agriculture records the lowest share at only 1.3 per cent. Table 10.2 confirms this sectoral distribution to GDP, where the service sector in Bahrain records the highest share at 24 per cent, while the agricultural sector in Qatar made the lowest contribution to GDP.

SMEs' contribution to sector development in Bahrain varies considerably from sector to sector and industry to industry. Data shows that 6.4 per cent comes from trade enterprises, 5.6 per cent comes from the manufacturing sector, 4 per cent from the construction industry, 3 per cent from real estate, 1.6 per cent from transport, 1.5 per cent from mining and 1 per cent from specialist education (Bahrain EDB 2013). Available

Table 10.2 The relative importance of non-oil sectors in GDP of the GCC countries (percentage)

	Services	Manufacturing	Agriculture
Bahrain	24	13	0.5
Kuwait	21	6	0.3
Oman	20	10	1.5
Qatar	15	9	0.1
Saudi Arabia	22	10	3.5
UAE	17	13	1.8

Source: Hussain 2014; Duha Al-Kuwari 2013

data on Kuwait shows that SMEs are classified into two major sectors: wholesale and retail trade. Restaurants and hotels make up around 40 per cent of SMEs, while the construction industry accounts for 33 per cent of the total number. The remaining 27 per cent of SMEs are industry, finance and services (Al Saif 2004). The Omani Ministry of Commerce and Industry (2012) confirmed that retail, wholesale and food firms make up almost 14 per cent, and manufacturing enterprises make up 17 per cent, while construction firms make up 13 per cent. The above data confirms that the service sector dominates in all the GCC states, whereas agriculture is very low in all of them. The contribution from agriculture is lower than 1 per cent in Bahrain, Kuwait and Qatar; Saudi Arabia is the highest with 3.5 per cent, which is still a very low percentage.

According to the Gulf Organization for Industrial Consulting database, the number of small- and medium-sized industries in the GCC was 12,684 manufacturing facilities, which accounted for 83.6 per cent of the total industrial enterprises in 2012. This shows that the percentage of the SMEs in the industry sector is very high but large industries still dominate the GCC markets, and there is a lack of participation of such SMEs in manufacturing. Investments in small industries of the GCC amounted to around US$14 billion, which is about 4.2 per cent of the total investment in the industrial sector of the GCC in 2012 (Alyaum Newspaper 2013). Such percentage is very low especially when GCC governments try to diversify their economies. Successful diversification in the industrial sector requires increasing the size of the industrial investment to nearly a trillion dollars by completing the establishment of industrial cities in progress and raising its contribution to the GDP from 10 per cent to 25 per cent by 2020. Apparently, this is an ambitious objective as GCC has yet been unable to make efficient exploitation of the SME sector in industrial development.

THE REGIONAL DIMENSION OF GCC ECONOMIC DIVERSIFICATION

This section explores the extent to which GCC economies are dependent on the oil sector and why there is a need for diversification from the hydrocarbon to the non-hydrocarbon sectors. It also examines the contribution of the private sector, more specifically SMEs, to the economic diversification strategy at the regional markets.

Diversification from Oil to Non-oil Sectors

The need to diversify GCC economies is now greater than ever before because of the fluctuation in international oil prices and heavy dependency of these economies on oil for their exports, revenues and GDP. In fact, some progress has been made in this direction as the share of the oil sector's contribution to real GDP declined from 41 per cent in 2000 to 33 per cent in 2014. Nevertheless, the pace of diversification is very slow, and the capacity of the GCC countries to diversify their domestic revenue base remains limited as the contribution of the hydrocarbon sector to budget remained high at 84 per cent on average between 2011 and 2015. Table 10.3 shows that GCC countries depend highly on oil. Qatar and Kuwait are the highest exporting states of oil in the region, with oil accounting for more than 90 per cent in 2011. Oman, Bahrain and the UAE, respectively, are the lowest. In terms of revenues, Kuwait is the most

Table 10.3 The relative importance of oil in GCC countries, 2011 (percentage)

	Export	*Budget revenue*	*GDP*
Bahrain	69	86	24
Kuwait	90	93	45
Oman	65	77	41
Qatar	91	80	46
Saudi Arabia	85	85	50
UAE	69	77	32

Source: Hussain 2014; Hvidt 2013

vulnerable to oil price fluctuation because oil accounts for 93 per cent of its budget. Oman and UAE are the least affected among the six countries, where oil accounts for 77 per cent of their budgets. In terms of contribution to GDP, Saudi Arabia has the highest dependence on oil, which accounts for 50 per cent in its GDP, while Bahrain is the lowest, with 24 per cent.

All GCC governments are under intensive pressure to accelerate the implementation of diversification policies as oil prices declined sharply from US$100 per barrel in mid-2014 to US$37 per barrel in January 2016. The impact of this decline is evident in almost all GCC countries; many of them have already announced budget deficits in the 2016–2017 financial year and beginning to introduce spending cuts in non-essential areas. Countries that are engaging in large-scale infrastructure projects as is the case in Qatar and Saudi Arabia are seeking new investments from the private sector and encouraging diversification in such sectors that are most appealing to private enterprises as manufacturing, finance, tourism, construction and real estate.

Although diversification is progressing at the national level, there is a need for coordination among GCC countries to maximise the impact of their efforts at the regional market. This may encourage a greater flow of commodities manufactured locally and strengthen the presence of products originated in other Gulf States regionally. Overall, GCC diversification of production could benefit from the dynamics of the common market to develop intra-industry trade and consequently increase trade transactions among GCC states. Indeed, the development of the GCC internal market because of the customs union, the common market and further liberalisation of the market may facilitate the internationalisation of SMEs within the GCC region. Internal market reforms mean increasing the competition level, hence forcing companies to invest heavily in capacity building, upgrading their operational systems and developing their human and technological capabilities in order to survive competition, grow and compete nationally and internationally. The internationalisation of SMEs provides an opportunity for enterprises to grow and diversify their business activities in the regional market, where they are more familiar with corporate culture, business environment and legal and regulatory systems. Private enterprises become more capable of developing plans and strategies for effective utilisation of resources, materials, capabilities and characteristics of the states, and the roles of the institutions concerned with foreign trade and investment. To enable enterprise to develop such capabilities, governments should work collectively to develop the infrastructural and industrial bases where companies can devise strategies aiming at production diversification.

CAN INTEGRATION FACILITATE DIVERSIFICATION?

The GCC countries have similar economic structures and hence share common aspects of economic diversification strategies and policies. They also share the same political and governance system, geographical and geological structure, climate, religion, history, traditions, language and customs. This provides a platform for collectively formulating and implementing initiatives and policy measures aiming at servicing the business sector. The most important dynamic provided by regional integration is the political context in which political, economic and business organisations and companies from the member states interact. The political will of the six GCC member states to develop a stable and secure environment reduces the political risk associated with operating in foreign markets. The GCC is the most politically stable part of the Middle East, with the exception of Bahrain that experienced a wave of uprisings after Arab spring, when compared to North Africa, the Levant and Iraq. The common internal and external threats facing GCC countries serve as a catalyst for collective action as seen in Yemen in the 2015 Decisive Storm. The treaties and agreements governing the GCC provide the institutional framework required for administrative, legal and regulatory reforms at the regional level. The agreements of the free trade area, the customs union and the common market have streamlined customs procedures and reduced the time of clearance of goods and services. Harmonisation of rules and procedures is vital for regional cooperation.

The second important dynamic of integration is the liberalisation of trade and investment regimes that resulted in significant improvement in the economic and business environment in these countries. World Bank's Doing Business Report 2015 confirms that UAE, Bahrain, Qatar and Oman top the list of Middle Eastern economies, while Saudi Arabia and Kuwait are in the eighth and ninth places in terms of ease in doing business. Table 10.4 shows a high ease of doing business in all GCC countries, as well as relatively developed regulatory and business environment. It illustrates the prominent position of the UAE economy at both regional and global rankings. Bahrain, Qatar and Oman are not far behind and could catch up with a second phase of political and economic reform. Saudi

Table 10.4 GCC economic ranking in the MENA context, 2015

	Ease of doing business		Start-up business	Dealing with construction permit	Getting electricity	Register property	Getting credit	Protecting minority investors	Paying tax	Trading across borders	Enforcing contracts	Resolving insolvency
	Global rank	MENA rank										
UAE	31	1	2	1	1	1	3	2	1	7	1	7
Bahrain	65	2	12	3	8	2	5	8	4	5	10	6
Qatar	68	3	7	2	12	3	12	10	1	10	12	1
Oman	70	4	15	6	6	5	10	6	13	6	7	2
KSA	82	8	10	4	2	4	1	5	3	13	8	17
Kuwait	101	9	14	16	16	6	5	3	6	12	2	10

Source: World Bank's Doing Business Report 2015

Arabia ranked first in ease of getting credit and Kuwait ranked second in enforcing contracts.

The positive effects of regional integration on Gulf business environment encourage enterprises to expand and diversify their business activities at home and beyond their local market. This is why GCC countries should develop a holistic approach when it comes to supporting private sector development in the region. Government agencies have to open up channels for high levels of coordination and communications in order to respond to the needs of companies operating in the regional market. GCC countries should consider creating a single authoritative organisation that takes the responsibility of coordinating national policies aiming at supporting the private sector and identifying economic sectors and business opportunities that could serve economic diversification strategies across the region. The aim of such organisation is to provide up-to-date information, establish business networks and communication channels for enterprises across the region and promote investment in new economic sectors that are strategically important for Gulf economies such as agribusiness, food and agriculture, chemicals, electronics, metallurgy, cement, water desalination, renewable energy and financial services.

INTEGRATION, DIVERSIFICATION AND THE PRIVATE SECTOR: THE WAY FORWARD

The common market provides new opportunities to increase interregional trade and investment in the GCC. Further liberalisation aimed at improving the business environment and the institutional structure of the national and regional organisations could enhance the efficiency and productivity of the private sector that could lead in the implementation of diversification policies. Theoretically, there is a strong correlation between successful regional economic integration and increasing the size and efficiency of the internal market in all member states of the regional bloc (Balassa 1967). Therefore, integration could act as a catalyst for change and development in the GCC markets, if member states are committed to the principles and objectives of the Council. Nevertheless, what relation or impact does regional integration have with the private sector and economic diversification in the GCC context?

Surveying literature produced by a number of ministries, government agencies and research institutions indicates a growing tendency in the GCC business sector towards utilising internal market reforms to diversify production and operations outside their traditional business (Omani Ministry of Commerce and Industry 2012; GulfBase Economic and Business News 2012; Bahrain EDB 2013; Canaan 2012; Al Saif 2004). This is because the free movement of labour, capital, goods and other factors of production often results in high levels of competition, high efficiency and growth in productivity. The internal market is beginning to benefit from a large number of cross-country infrastructure projects such as superhighways linking Saudi Arabia with Bahrain, Qatar, Oman and UAE (Times of Oman 2013; Khaleej Times 2013); this will be complemented by the completion of the new network of regional railways that connects all member states. The launch of advanced technology such as superfast broadband and connection of electricity grades between all member states (UAE and Oman in 2006; Saudi Arabia, Bahrain, Qatar, Kuwait completed in 2009; and UAE and rest of GCC in 2011) have increased interconnectivity and reduced significantly transportation costs. Despite the delays in creating a monetary union, the common market has already provided a strong base for the business community to prosper as GCC citizens have the right to employment in both public and private sectors, access to social insurance systems, land and property ownership and obtain loans from banks and industrial development funds, establishing limited and joint-stock companies.

The effect of integration on private sector enterprises could also be realised in easy access to neighbouring markets and possibility of opening branches where consumers and factors of production are cheaply accessible. The expansion of the market size often reduces the cost of interregional trade transactions and increases the number of service providers and suppliers. This is evident in the financial service sector where the establishment of Islamic banks such as Masraf Al-Rayan and Daman Insurance in Qatar in 2010 enabled citizens and firms from other GCC countries to utilise their services without having to move in Qatar (Oxford Business Group 2012). Private sector companies are now able to cultivate talent, innovation and expertise anywhere in the regional market, an advantage that could increase the competence and capabilities of their human resources (Scullion and Collings 2011). They could also gain more support when faced with threat from foreign competitors when it comes to monopoly or price differences. Article 8 of 2008 of the Common Market Agreement provides such protection through its clauses on consumers' rights, providers' obligations and disciplinary actions (GCC Legal Information Network 2014). Such legislations may help consumers to develop awareness of their rights and react to price differences. Legal protection can enable Gulf enterprises to compete easily in the regional market and merger to grow where possible to outstand competition from multinational corporations, with those having a good knowledge and experience in the regional market developing competitive advantages. The provisions on intellectual property rights, contract laws and corporate governance provide comfort to enterprises and, as shown in Table 10.4, have resulted in improvement in the ranking of GCC in the ease of doing business.

In fact, such improvement in the business environment, together with incentives and protection to private enterprises, is the key to successful economic diversification in the GCC. Efficient business environment can contribute to flexibility in business transactions and smoothness in running trade and investment operations. This provides the private sector with opportunities to develop production and services in and out of their home country. Such a free movement of factors is highly likely to contribute to establishing a degree of harmonisation within national economic policies (Grin 2003). Greater commitment and participation of the private sector could minimise pressure on the already overcrowded public sector and the government in employment and development, as well as reducing heavy dependency on oil and gas revenues. If given the right support, the private sector can lead to significant changes and adjustment in GCC economic policies, by shifting investments from traditional sectors such as infrastructure, energy and real estate to more advanced sectors such as technology and export that could have substantial impact on their economic development.

New economic policies aiming at increasing the role of the private sector in economic development could result in economic benefits such as enhanced innovation, healthy competition, new production brands, reduced prices, cost-effective services, more job opportunities and responding more rapidly and efficiently than the public sector to changing needs of the markets. In statistical terms, an enhanced private sector could overcome structural weaknesses in the GCC economy by increasing its shares in employment, where less than 1 per cent of citizens in Kuwait and UAE are employed in the private (Al Saif 2004), in industrial investment that accounts for only 4.2 per cent of the total investment in the industrial sector and in export, which is less than 10 per cent of total GCC export (Elasrag 2011). The success story of the plastic industry reflects the huge potential of the private sector to contribute to diversification. Efforts by

GCC countries to localise the plastic industry have secured around 157,000 jobs for the GCC citizens and are expected to increase the productive capacity of this industry to 33,300,000 tons by 2020 (Al Mashitaa 2015). Future investment is expected to more than double the number of plastic products from 13 to 29 by expanding in new industries such as airlines, transportation and food packaging and export its products to more than 150 countries around the world. Another success story is Dubai's utilisation of technology and information technology in the SME sector. A survey conducted by Mohammed Bin Rashid, Establishment for the Development of Small and Medium Enterprises, in 2013 shows that the percentage of companies using advanced information technology systems is the highest in the sector, with 26 per cent in services, 18 per cent in industry and 16 per cent in trade. This underlines the capacity of the SME sector to operate and contribute to the development of non-oil sectors. In the absence of highly efficient auditing systems in GCC countries, one could argue that the capacity of the private sector to make efficient use of resources could offer a new platform for GCC governments in reallocation of resources from inefficient industries to sectors that are more productive in the economy. Thus, the private sector is more capable than the public sector and the government in developing knowledge-based economy and achieving sustainable economic development.

Conclusion

The above discussion shows that economic diversification in the GCC has not gone far enough and that its success requires critical changes and adjustment in the economic policies of its member states in order to make efficient utilisation of the private sector and the dynamics of regional integration. The study also shows that policies aimed at developing regional integration, economic diversification and the private sector are entwined, and that their success depends largely on their efficient implementation. It is apparent that the slow progress in economic diversification and integration is caused by the absence of a single authoritative institution that has power beyond that of the General Secretariat to enforce change and monitor coordination and policy implementation in all member states. Analysis also underscores that the regional integration provides an appropriate platform to expand in the regional market and that efficient utilisation and allocation of resources could enable this sector to drive economic growth and attain the objectives of diversification. All this will certainly depend on the political will and the appropriate policies to support private sector development at the national and regional levels.

References

Abdelhafiz, M. (2015). Citizens: Government job—Stay with the guaranteed. *Annahar Newspaper*. Retrieved June 5, 2015, from www.annaharkw.com/Annahar/Article.aspx?id=347755&date=03092012

Akhbar Al-Khaleej. (2010). Secretariat of the Federation of GCC Chambers issued its semi-annual report, Gulf projects size declining from 2.4 to two trillion dollars. Retrieved June 12, 2015, from http://www.akhbar-alkhaleej.com/11877/article/407212.html

Al Abd Alqadeer, K. (2015). Cooperation and economic integration among the GCC countries: Achievements and obstacles. *Aljazeera Center for Studies*. Retrieved June 12, 2015, from http://studies.aljazeera.net/files/gccpath/2015/01/2015114111914285936.htm

Al Ali, H. (2013). Pattern of economic growth in the Gulf Cooperation Council (GCC). *Aljazeera Center for Studies*. Retrieved June 10, 2015, from http://studies.aljazeera.net/issues/2013/04/2013421104252798915.htm

Al Mashitaa, S. (2015). Gulf States exports 80% of the plastic production to 150 countries. *Arabiya News*. Retrieved June 10, 2015, from http://www.alarabiya.net/ar/aswaq/special-interviews/2015/02/26/%D8%AF%D9%88%D9%84-%D8%A7%D9%84%D8%AE%D9%84%D9%8A%D8%AC%D8%AA%D8%B5%D8%AF%D8%B1-80-%D9%85%D9%86-%D8%A7%D9%86%D8%AA%D8%A7%D8%AC-%D8%A7%D9%84%D8%A8%D9%84%D8%A7%D8%B3%D8%AA%D9%8A%D9%83-%D9%84%D9%80150-%D8%AF%D9%88%D9%84%D8%A9.html

Al Sadoun, N. (2009). Essays on economic integration among the Gulf Cooperation Council countries, Ph.D. thesis, University of Southampton, UK.

Al Saif, W. (2004). Creation: The experience of Kuwait small projects development company, Kuwait small business industry, Small Business Advancement National Center, Paper No. 80.

Al-Kuwari, D. (2013). Mission impossible? Genuine economic development in the Gulf Cooperation Council countries. Kuwait Programme on Development, Governance and Globalisation in the Gulf States, 33. The London School of Economics and Political Science, London, UK.

Alarab Newspaper. (2013). Gulf Monetary Council makes his way towards the single currency. Retrieved June 10, 2015, from http://www.alarab.co.uk/m/?id=5537

Alhyat Newspaper. (2014). "Study": Do not activate the resolutions of the "Cooperation Council" hinder the Gulf Common Market. Retrieved June 10, 2015, from http://alhayat.com/Articles/757966/ [Arabic edition].

Al-Rabeei, H. M., & Scott, J. (2011). Bahraini SMEs: Why think local? Think global challenges facing Bahraini SMEs and internationalisation, Small Business Advancement National Center.

Alyaum Newspaper. (2013). $14 billion is the volume of the GCC Small and Medium Size Enterprises. Retrieved June 11, 2015, from http://www.alyaum.com/article/3104247

Argaam Newspaper. (2015). Jasem Al-Alwi$ 121 billion size of the interregional trade among the countries of the council, representing 7.1% of the total foreign trade of the GCC. Retrieved June 10, 2015, from http://www.argaam.com/article/articledetail/485841

Ashrafi, R., & Murtaza, M. (2008). Use and impact of ICT on SMEs in Oman. *The Electronic Journal Information Systems Evaluation, 11*(3), 125–138. Retrieved from www.ejise.com

Bahrain EDB. (2013). Micro, Small and Medium Enterprises in the Bahrain economy. *Bahrain EDB* [Online]. Retrieved March 3, 2013, from http://www.bahrainedb.com/uploadedFiles/Bahraincom/BahrainForBusiness/8.%20AER%20-%20Articles%20-%20Micro,%20Small%20and%20Medium%20enterprises%20in%20the%20Bahrain%20economy.pdf

Balassa, B. (1967). *The theory of economic integration*. Green Wood Publishing Group.

Canaan, S. (2012). More than 833,000 small and medium Saudi women share only 8%. *Alriyadh News Paper*, KSA.

Crowley, P. (2001). *Beyond EMU: Is there a logical integration sequence?* ECSA-US Conference in Madison.

Das, K. (2011). *Micro and Small Enterprises in India: The era of reforms*. India: Routledge.

Elasrag, H. (2011). *Enhancing the competitiveness of the Arab SMEs*. MPRA Paper 30018, University Library of Munich, Germany.

Emirates NBD. (2012). Most friendly SME bank in the UAE. *Emirates NBD* [Online]. Retrieved March 3, 2013, from http://www.emiratesnbd.com/en/businessBanking/eNBDFriendlySMEBankInTheUAE.cfm

European Commission. (2009). Competitiveness of the EU Aerospace Industry with focus on: Aeronautics Industry within the framework contract of sectoral competitiveness studies; ENTR/06/054; European Commission, Directorate-General Enterprise & Industry, Munich. Retrieved from http://ec.europa.eu/enterprise/sectors/aerospace/files/aerospace_studies/summary_aerospace_study_en.pdf

Fisher, O. (2009). Small and Medium-Sized Enterprises and risk in the Gulf Cooperation Council countries: Managing risk and boosting profit, finance. *Financial Risk Management Best Practice*. Retrieved May 6, 2015, from http://www.qfinance.com/financial-risk-management-best-practice/small-and-medium-sized-enterprises-and-risk-in-the-gulf-cooperationcouncil-countries-managing-risk-and-boosting-profit?full

GCC General Secretariat. (2012a). GCC Custom Union. GCC General Secretariat. Retrieved June 5, 2015, from http://www.gcc-sg.org/indexfef9.html [Arabic edition].

GCC General Secretariat. (2012b). Gulf common market truth and numbers, Department of Statistics (5th ed.), December 2012, GCC General Secretariat [Arabic edition].

GGG Legal Information Network. (2014). GCC General Secretariat. Retrieved March 13, 2014, from http://www.gcc-legal.org/mojportalpublic/DisplayLegislation.aspxx?D3234

Grin, G. (2003). *The battle of the single European market: Achievement and economics 1945–2000.* UK: Kegan Paul Limited.

Gulf Center and Arabian Peninsula Studies, Kuwait University. (2013). Gulf states achieved the fastest growth rate of investments in the Middle East and Africa. Retrieved June 12, 2015, from http://www.cgaps.kuniv.edu/index.php?option=com_content&view=article&id=256:2013-12-22-09-36-45&catid=113&Itemid=1356&lang=ar

GulfBase Economic and Business News. (2012). SMEs' contribution to Qatar's non-oil GDP is lower, says QDB official. *GulfBase.*

Harris, G., & Hasenknopf, A. (1995). *European Union handbook and business titles.* Americans Group.

Hertog, S. (2008). Benchmarking SMEs policies in the GCC: A survey of challenges and opportunities. A research report for the EU-GCC Chamber Forum project.

Hussain, J. (2014). Economic diversification of the Gulf Cooperation Council. *Aljazeera Center for Studies.* Retrieved June 14, 2015, from http://studies.aljazeera.net/reports/2014/08/201481493035249222.htm [Arabic edition].

Hvidt, M. (2013). *Economic Diversification in GCC Countries: Past Record and Future Trends.* Research Paper, Kuwait Programme on Development, Governance and Globalisation in the Gulf States. London School of Economics and Political Science.

Kapurubandara, M., & Lawson, R. (2006). Barriers adopting ICT and E-commerce with SMEs in developing countries: An exploratory study in Sri Lanka. *CollECTeR '06,* 9 December, 2006, Adelaide. Retrieved March 13, 2008, from http://www.collecter.org/archives/2006_December/07.pdf

Kerr, W., & Gaisford, J. (2007). *Handbook on international trade policy.* Estey Center for Law and Economics in International Trade. Edward Elgar.

Khaleej Times. (2013). Saudi Arabia, Bahrain plan $10 bn rail link. July 12, 2013.

Khaleej Times. (2013). UAE to spend $25 bn on rail projects. September 6, 2013.

Knickrehm, K., & Hastedt, G. (2003). *International politics in a changing world.* Longman.

Langenhove, L., & Lombaerde, P. (2007). Regional integration, poverty and social policy. *Global Social Policy, 7*(3), 379–385.

LaPier, T. (1998). *Competition, growth strategies and the globalisation of services: Real estate advisory services in Japan, Europe and the USA, Routledge studies in international business and the world economy*. Routledge.

Lipsey, R. G. (1960). The theory of customs unions: A general survey. *The Economic Journal, 70*(279), 496–513.

Lu, J. W., & Beamish, P. W. (2001). The internationalization and performance of SMEs. *Strategic Management Journal, 22*, 565–586.

Ministry of Commerce and Industry, Oman. (2012). *New releases Oman industrial directory*. Oman Prelude Media Services.

Ministry of Finance Bahrain. (2015). The GCC common market, Bahrain. Retrieved May 5, 2015, from https://www.mof.gov.bh/images/uploadfiles/publication/Gcc-new.pdf

Mohamed Bin Rashid Establishment for the Development of Small and Medium Enterprises. (2013). Report of the case of small and medium businesses in Dubai. Retrieved June 12, 2015, from http://www.sme.ae/upload/category/SME_Report_Arabic.pdf

Motwani, J., Levenburg, N., & Schwarz, T. (2006). Succession planning in SMEs. *International Small Business Journal, 24*(5), 471–495.

Nechi, S. (2011). Determinants of trade flows among GCC countries: Potentials, Limitations and Expectations. *World Review of Business Research, 1*(5), 91–109.

Oxford Business Group. (2012). *Qatar Islamic Banks: Banking*. Retrieved from http://www.oxfordbusinessgroup.com/analysis/qatar-islamic-bankbanking-1

Pasquali, V., & Aridas, T. (2013). The world's richest and poorest countries. *Global Finance Magazine*. Retrieved May 17, 2014, from https://www.gfmag.com/global-data/economic-data/worlds-richest-and-poorest-countries

Peng, W. (2010). *Global business* (2nd ed.). Cengage Learning.

Qatar Report. (2007). *The report, Qatar 2007. Country profile*. Oxford Business group.

Rivera-Batiz, L., & Romer, P. (1991). Economic integration and endogenous growth. *Quarterly Journal of Economics, 106*(2), 531–555.

Sauad, S. (2013). Intra-regional trade, evidence from the UAE: A gravity model approach. *International Journal of Economic Perspectives*. Retrieved May 20, 2015, from http://www.readperiodicals.com/201309/3364230091.html#ixzz3aqxsrMcM

Scullion, H., & Collings, D. (2011). *Global talent management*. New York: Routledge.

SME Committee. (2010). SME Committee, Ministry of Industry and Commerce, Bahrain.

Staiger, R. (1994). A theory of gradual trade liberalization, "International Trade 9410003". *EconWPA*, revised 21 October 1994.

Sturm, M., & Siegfried, N. (2005). Regional monetary integration in the member states of the Gulf Cooperation Council. *Occasional Paper Series*, No. 31, June 2005.

The World Bank. (2015). Doing Business Report 2015: Going beyond Efficiency, World Bank Group, Washington, DC.

Times of Oman. (2013). Oman to spend $14.8 bn on roads, bridges and rail projects. September 25.

UNCOMTRADE. (2013). International trade statistics yearbook, 2012. Trade by Country. The 2012 international trade statistics yearbook, Vol. 1, *United Nations Statistics* [Online]. Retrieved October 3, 2013, from http://comtrade.un.org/pb/

Varghese, T. (2011). The small and medium enterprises in GCCs: A comparison between Sultanate of Oman and United Arab Emirates. *International Journal of Research in Commerce, Economics & Management, 1*(6).

Zawya. (2012). Saudi SME opportunity. *Zawya* [Online]. Retrieved March 3, 2013, from http://www.zawya.com/story/Saudi_SME_opportunity-ZAWYA20120919051002/

INDEX

NUMBERS AND SYMBOLS
2002 World Summit on Sustainable Development, 137

A
Abu Dhabi's Economic Vision 2030, 142
Achoui, M., 101
Acute scarcity of water, 164
Administrative regulation, 132
Agricultural development, 127, 170
Agricultural products, 126
Agricultural sector
　climatic conditions, 167, 168, 180
　economic importance, 167
　food self-sufficiency, 167
　GCC countries, 164, 180
Agriculture
　agricultural development, 127, 170
　agricultural sector, 23, 102, 219
Ahamed, A., 152, 153
Ahmad, A., 159
Akkas, E., 7

Al-Abduljabbar, A., 110
Al-Alwi, J., 214
ALBA aluminium smelter, 13
Al-Hinai, 21
Al Jouf Company, 126
Almarai, 126
Al-Naamani, 23
Al Saif, W., 216
Anas Al-Saleh, 39
Annan, K., 137
Arabian Gulf, 190, 192, 197, 198, 200
Asian Development Bank (ADB), 55
Azoulay, R., 30

B
Bahrain, 1, 9, 10, 13, 14, 20, 23, 28, 84–86, 91–94, 107, 138, 140, 141, 176, 177, 184, 185, 187, 188, 190, 192–199, 202, 203, 213, 214, 216, 218–223, 226
Bahrain Bay project, 202
Bahrain diversification strategy, 13–14

Bahraini Vision 2030, 11, 13
Balakrishnan, M. S., 205
Bani, 23
Beblawi, H. E., 5, 19, 165
Beer, S., 59, 62
Bilateral investment treaties (BIT), 120, 124
Bloom, N., 146
Boutique destination, 199
Buckley, P. J., 118
Budget
  budget deficits, 9, 10, 17, 28
  budget spending, 27, 28, 31–35
  GCC countries, 9
Build-Operate-Transfer (BOT), 30, 37, 38, 80
Business
  business climate, 14
  business environment, 18, 28, 35, 41
  business development, 166, 223
Business elite
  country's reform movements, 29
  labour nationalisation, 33
  public sector, 41
Business environment, 227
  GCC companies, 217
  internal market, 217
  trade and investment, 217–218

C
Capital Market Authority (CMA), 40, 42, 43
Career management, 152
Casson, M., 118
Central Planning Commission, 131
The Chronical of Higher Education, 100
CMA, *see* Capital Market Authority
Commercial Companies Law of 1960, 38

Commission for Economic Development, 131
Common Market Agreement, 226
Communication, 32, 52, 53, 59, 64, 102–105, 110, 112, 140, 149, 166, 196, 200, 225
Complexity
  organisational, 50–51
  structural, 63
  systemic approaches, 49
Consumer mentality, 109
Corporate governance, 42, 43, 144, 146, 227
Corporate social responsibility (CSR), 144, 146
CPM, *see* Cyclical Process Model
Creswell, 152
Crouch, G. I., 183, 189–191, 194, 196
CSR practices, 146
Cyclical Process Model (CPM), 61, 62
Cypher, J., 6

D
Daman Insurance, 226
Davies, A. J., 145
Davison, R., 61, 62
Destination
  climatic conditions, 190
  competitiveness model, 189–190
  culture and history, 190, 192
  entertainment, 193–194
  market ties, 195
  resources, categories, 190
  sport and cultural events, 192–193
  superstructure, 194, 195
  tourist activities, 192
Development
  educational, 99–102
  employment system, 108
  human resources, 111

investment, 99
Development Plan, 11, 13, 15, 24, 28, 131
Development process
  economic diversification, 4, 6, 10, 13
  economic sectors, 13
  environmental, 11
  export diversification and service industries, 3
  financial services, 13
  GCC, 2, 22
  human, 11
  PPPs, 21
  private and public sector, 13
  private sector challenges, 2
  public and private enterprises, 4, 5
  SMEs sector, 16
  social, 11
Development process
  economic diversification, 14
Dietz, J. L., 6
Digital Oman Strategy, 60
Diversification
  advantages, 132
  budgetary gaps, impact of, 9
  business community, 29
  definition, 4–6
  economic cycles, 2
  economic structure, 8
  energy markets, 10
  in energy sector, 5
  of exports, 5
  foreign direct investment, 132
  fossil fuels, 11
  GCC, 20–24
  GCC governments, 11–18
  knowledge-based economy, 3
  motivation of, 4
  oil revenues, 10
  oil sector, expanding, 2
  oil to non-oil sectors, 221–223

oil-dependency, 28
  private sector, 28, 30, 44
  public and private sector, 5, 7
  sovereign wealth funds, 7
Diversification policies, Kuwait
  BOT, 37, 38
  foreign business and FDI, 38–40, 42
  labour policies, 31–33
  market regulation, 42, 43
  privatisation, 35, 36
  subsidies policies, 33, 34
Diversification strategies
  Bahrain, 13
  economic diversification, 19
  industrialisation strategies, 18, 19
  Kuwait, 15
  Oman, 11–13
  Qatar, 14, 15
  Saudi, 17, 18
  UAE, 16
Double taxation treaties (DTT), 120
Dubai Land project, 142
Dubai's Department of Tourism and Commerce Marketing (DTCM), 199
Dwyer, L., 189, 190

E
E-business, 146
Economic diversification
  data sources, 78
  GCC countries, 78, 79, 163
  GCC states, 165–166
  need for, v
  non-oil sectors, 166
  oil sector, 165, 166
  PPPs, 79, 82, 93, 94
  Qatar National Development Strategy, 166

Economic diversification, Oman, 53
GCC's diversification activities, 51
income levels, 51–54
revenues, 54
SMEs, funding programmes, 53
SOEs, 52
systemic integration, 53
Economic reforms
diversification and sustainability, 30
Education
development, 99–102
education reform, 112, 113
education system, 3, 21
higher, 97, 110
labour force, 97
and labour market, 104–112
primary and secondary, 113
quality of, 97, 99, 110
Saudi, 97, 104, 112
E-government services, 60
Eighth Five-Year Plan (2011–2016), 12
Eighth National Development Plan, 108
El Kharouf, F., 4
Emaar, 142
Energy sector
labour-intensive, 5
public sector, 5
E-payment services, 60–61
Espinosa, 21
Establishment for the Development of Small and Medium Enterprises, 228
Etzioni, A., 144

F
Farooq, A., 22, 144
Fasano, U., 139
Fazli, S. F., 22
FDI, *see* Foreign direct investment

Fédération Internationale de Football Association (FIFA), 14
FIFA Football World Cup, 193
Finance, 209
access to finance, 219
financial sector, 7
Islamic finance, 7, 13
First Gulf War (1980–1988), 15
Five-year Development Plan (2010–2014), 15
Food accessibility, 169, 172
Food allocation, 172
Food availability, 168, 169, 171, 172
Food production and imports, 164, 180
Food safety, 171, 173, 174
Food security (FS), 125
agricultural development, 170
agriculture, 174
definition, 168
dietary needs, 168, 169
food prices, 176
and food supply, 168, 174
PPPs, 178, 179
productivity and profitability, 174
supply and price risk, 175
sustainable, 173–177
water availability, 175
Food stability, 173
Food system
categories, 169
definition, 168
distributing and retailing food, 171
outcomes, 170
processing and packaging food, 170
producing food, 170
utilisation and stability, 174
Food utilisation, 171, 172
Foreign business, 30, 38–42
Foreign direct investment (FDI), 6, 28, 83
definition and treatment of, 118

inward or outward, 118–119
multinational enterprises, 119
Foreign investment
  academic research, 118
  definition of, 118, 127
Foreign Investment Law, 2000, 129
Free Trade Zone (FTZ), 39, 40, 210–212, 223

G

GCC countries, *see* Gulf Cooperation Council countries
GCC countries
  control of corruption, 90
  economic growth, 93
  economies of, 139
  electricity, 84
  exports of goods and services, 89
  fuel exports, 89
  GDP of, 86, 87
  government effectiveness, 90
  government performance, 91–93
  infrastructure services, 86
  natural gas rents, 88
  oil rents, 87
  oil-dependent economies, 141
  political stability and absence of violence/terrorism, 90
  ports, 85
  regulatory quality, 91
  roads, 85
  rule of law, 91
  state-owned enterprises, 209
  sustainable development, 141
  telecommunications, 85
  voice and accountability, 91
  Water supply and sanitation, 84–86
  WDIs, 92
GDP, *see* Gross domestic product
General Telecommunications Organisation (GTO), 60

Generic food system, 170
Gross domestic product (GDP), 1–4, 6, 9, 12–19, 23, 33, 53, 61, 86–89, 98, 126, 129, 130, 139–144, 147, 164, 174, 186, 187, 216, 219–222
Group of Twenty (G-20), 125
Gulf Cooperation Council (GCC) countries, v, 1
  economic diversification, 2
  development strategies, 2
  diversification strategies, 3, 4, 11–18
  knowledge economy, 3
  sustainable development, 27
Gulf Organization for Industrial Consulting database, 216, 220

H

Hadi Property Investment, 127
Hafiz programme, 106
Hail Agricultural Development Company, 177
Hertog, S., 6, 30, 103, 139
Holwell, S., 58
Horizontal diversification, 141
Human development policies, 110
Hussain, Z., 144
Hvidt, M., 4, 5, 14, 17, 52
Hydrocarbons, v, 5, 8, 12, 14, 16, 18, 19, 22, 51, 106, 140–143, 165, 214, 221
  economic sector, 4, 8, 14, 22
  foreign direct investment, 16
  GCC, 19
  industrialisation, 18
  low-cost energy, 5
  Oman, 12
Hydrocarbon sector, performance of, vi

I

IMF, *see* International Monetary Fund
Information Technology Authority (ITA), 60
Infrastructure development, PPPs
  economic diversification, 93
  financial resources, 77
  GCC countries, economic diversification of, 78
  investment policies, 81
  PPPs, 94
  private sector, 82
  public sector, 81
  regulation, 82
Integration, 217
  common market, 19, 23, 210, 212, 217, 225
  customs union, 19, 23, 210–212, 217
  free trade areas, 210–212, 223
  internal market, 226
  liberalisation of trade and investment regimes, 223
  MENA context, 224, 225
  political context, 223–225
  private sector development, 225
  private sector enterprises, 226
  regional (*see* Regional integration)
  regional integration, 14, 19, 23, 24
  SOEs and SMEs, 49, 56, 57
Interdisciplinary approach, v
International Agreements
  bilateral investment treaties, 124–125
  multilateral agreements, 124
International Centre for the Settlement of Investment Disputes (ICSID), 124
International investment conventions (IIC), 120
International Monetary Fund (IMF), 2, 28, 118, 138

Internationalisation
  internationalisation of SMEs, 23, 213, 222
Inward FDI (IFDI), 120, 124, 128–130, 133

J

Jackson, M. C., 58

K

Kafala Fund, Saudi Arabia, 218
Kapetanovic, 16
Karolak, 23
Kaufmann, D., 90
KDIPA, *see* Kuwait Direct Investment Promotion Authority
Khalifa Fund, UAE, 218
Khalil, S., 126
Kim, C., 189, 190
King Abdullah Economic City (KAEC), 142
King Abdullah Project for Development, 2009, 112
Kingdom of Saudi Arabia (KSA), 117, 120–125, 128, 132, 133, 138
Knowledge economy, 3, 14, 22, 138
Kochhar, A. K., 145
Kuwait, 31–35, 138, 140
  business community, 29–31, 44
  discovery of oil, 29
  economic diversification, 28, 30 (*see also* Diversification policies, Kuwait)
  economic diversification and sustainability, 30
  oil dependency, 28
  parliamentary politics, 28
  private sector, 28, 30, 40
Kuwait Awqaf Public Foundation, 35
Kuwait Development Plan, 142

Kuwait Direct Investment Promotion
    Authority (KDIPA), 39
Kuwait diversification strategy, 15
Kuwait Economic Society report, 39
Kuwait Investment Authority (KIA),
    8, 35, 36
Kuwait Small Projects Development
    Company, 218
Kuwait Stock Exchange (KSE), 36–40,
    42
Kuwait Vision 2035, 15

L
Labour
    labour force, 19, 32, 33, 53, 97
    labour market, 14, 21
    labour skills, 6, 23
Labour market, 102–104
    educational system, 104
    harmony between education,
        104–112
    quality of education, 98
    Saudi (*see* Saudi labour market)
    in Saudi Arabia, 97
    Saudization programme, 99
Laugen, B. T., 145, 146
Lee, 150
Long-Term Strategy, 17
Looney, R., 19
Luciani, G., 29

M
Malik, A., 10
Management practices, 160
    business practices, 145, 146
    human resource planning, 151, 152
    leadership and governance (Style),
        150
    lean manufacturing (system), 149, 150
    organisational effectiveness,
        143–145
    and productivity, 143–145
    staffing, 151
Managing by walking around
    (MBWA), 159
Manappat Enterprise
    shared values, 159, 160
    skills, 159
    staff, 159
    strategy, 157, 158
    structure, 158
    style, 159
    systems, 158
Manappat Group of Companies
    engineering, 153
    food products, 153
    hospitality, 155
    human resources, 155
    trading, 153
Manpower and Government
    Restructuring Program (MGRP),
    32–33
Manyika, J., 143
Market regulation, 31, 42, 43
Masraf Al-Rayan, 226
McKinsey Global Institute (MGI),
    143
McKinsey's 7S Framework, 22
    implementation model, 147, 148
    independent variable, 147–148
    management practices, 148
    strategy, 148
    structure, 148
MENA countries, *see* Middle East and
    North Africa countries
Meta-systemic functions, 65, 70
MGRP, *see* Manpower and
    Government Restructuring
    Program
Middle East and North Africa
    (MENA) countries, 6, 224
Midgley, G., 58
Ministry of Economics and Planning,
    123, 131

Ministry of Education, 21, 98, 101, 104, 110
Ministry of Higher Education, 110
Ministry of Transport and Communications (MoTC), 60
Mishrif, A., 7, 16, 21, 23, 106
Model
  allocation state model, 2, 7, 19
  economic model, 17
  production-based model, 20
Moore, P., 29
Morakabati, Y., 5
Mubadala Development Corporation, 17
Multilateral Investment Guarantee Agency (MIGA), 124, 125
Muogbo, U. S., 144

N
National Broadband Strategy (NBS), 61, 63, 65
National Economic Strategy, 13
National strategic projects(NSPs), 49, 56, 70, 71
National visions
  assessment of, 2
  development plans, 24
  diversification strategies and policies, 3, 11
  GCC government policies, 19
  public sector, 19
  sustainable development, 3, 11
Nationalization, 107, 111, 198
  labour, 30–33
"Natural Bahrain" theme, creation of, 202
New product development (NPD), 146
Ninth Development Plan (2010–2015), 104, 111
Ninth Development Plan (2010–2014), 141

Ninth Five-Year Plan (2017–2021), 12
Nitaqat policy, 108
Non-hydrocarbon sectors
  private investments in, vi
Non-Kuwaiti companies, 39
Non-oil sectors
  GCC economies, 220
  industrial development, 220–221
  manufacturing sector, 219
  SMEs' contribution, 219–221
Non-verbal behaviour, 149
Nutritional value, 170, 172

O
Oil
  discovery of, 185
  economic cycles, 2
  export revenues, 1, 4, 17
  fall in prices, 4, 5, 7–10, 24, 106
  prices, rise of, 1–3
Oman, 1, 8–10, 13, 14, 20, 23, 28, 60, 61, 84–86, 88, 91, 93, 107, 138, 140, 144, 153, 155, 158, 164, 166, 178, 184, 187, 190, 193, 197–199, 202, 203, 210, 214, 216, 218, 221–223
  economic diversification in, 51–54
Oman Broadband Company (OBC), 60, 61
  Business Model, 64
  operations of, 69
  value integrator, 68
  VSM and recursion analysis, 64, 65
Oman diversification strategy, 11–13
Oman Oil Company, 55
Oman Vision 2020, 11
Omani Ministry of Commerce and Industry, 216, 220
Omanisation' policy, 52, 53
Organizational design, SOEs, 55
Organizational effectiveness

INDEX   243

definition, 144
economic performance, 143
and productivity, 143–145
Organization for Economic
   Co-operation and Development
   (OECD), 118
Organization structure systems, 149
Outsourcing, 6, 20, 146, 176, 177
Outward FDI (OFDI), 120, 128–130, 133

P
Paris Agreement, 11
Peters, T., 148
Place identities, 184, 201
   content/discourse analysis, 201
   creation of, 200–203
   data analysis, 201
   frames analysis, 202
   marketing, 201
   natural heritage, 203
   tourism websites, 201
Planet Food World (PFWC), 177
Plastic industry, 227, 228
Policy
   education and labour market, 105
   youth unemployment, 106–108
PPPs, *see* Public-private partnerships
Private enterprises, 4, 10, 20
   case study, 152–157
   corporate structure, 156
   economic development, 17
   economic diversification, 14
   economic liberalisation, 20
   GCC, 4, 7, 22, 23
   large-scale infrastructure projects, 21
   Oman, Sultanate of, 155
   production process, 6
   Saudi Arabia, 157
   SMEs, 218, 219

systemic approach, 21
   United Arab Emirates, 155
Private sector, 35–43, 218
   asset ownership, 80
   civil liberty and political freedom, 3
   customer-focused services, 81
   delivering services, 79
   economic development, 227
   economic diversification, 3, 5, 7, 9, 11, 16–18, 20
   economic growth model, 2
   exports, 6
   import substitution industries, 5
   infrastructure service, 82, 83
   innovation systems, 13
   low wage, 14
   Omani, 11–12
   policies and regulations, 91
   PPPs, 4
   SMEs, 12
Private sector enterprises, 6, 7, 137, 214–216, 219, 226
   impact of GCC regional market on, 214–216
Privatization, 18, 20, 22, 30, 35–37, 121
Privatization system, Saudi Arabia
   private sector, 124
   Resolution No. 1/23 in 2002, 123, 124
   Supreme Economic Council, 122–124
Productivity, 10, 22, 23, 32, 52, 61, 85, 103, 107, 138, 146, 147, 160, 164, 173, 174, 180, 217, 218, 225, 226
   organizational effectiveness and, 143–145
Public Authority for Minors Affairs, 35
Public enterprises (PEs), 54
Public Institution for Social Security, 35

Public sector
  asset ownership, 80
  economic diversification, 5, 7
  energy sector, 5
  GCC, 20
  infrastructure services, 81, 88
  large-scale infrastructure projects, 21
  oil and natural gas sectors, 78
  PPPs, 4, 81
  private enterprises, 10
  UAE Vision 2021, 11
Public-private partnerships (PPPs), 4, 21, 178, 179
  benefits of, 80–82
  comparison of, 80
  definition, 79–82

Q
Qatar, 1, 8–10, 12, 23, 84, 86, 88, 90–99, 138, 140, 142, 144, 166, 184, 187, 188, 192–200, 202, 204, 213, 215, 216, 218–224, 226
Qatar diversification strategy, 14–15
Qatar Foundation, 218
Qatar National Development Strategy 2011–2016, 14, 166
Qatar Tourism Authority, 199
Qatar Vision 2030, 14
Quality management, 145, 146

R
Raffd Fund, O., 218
Rashid, M. B., 228
Reform
  education-labour market problem, 112
  of labour laws, 108
  leadership levels, 111

Regional integration, 228
  economic diversification strategies, 209, 210
  economic integration, 213
  free trade area, 210–214
  GCC market, 211, 213
  private sector, 228
  SMEs, 216
Regulation
  infrastructure development, 82–84
  Jakarta water concessions, Indonesia, 83
  PPPs, implementation of, 79
  private sector, 83
  regulatory framework, 82
Research and development (R&D), 3, 16, 130
Revenues
  export revenues, 2–4, 12, 13, 15, 17, 19, 35, 221
  government revenues, 3, 4, 12, 19, 33
  oil and gas, 227
Reynolds, M., 58
Ritchie and Crouch's Destination and Competitiveness Model, 183
Ritchie, J. R. B., 189, 191
Rondinelli, D. A., 55
Rossouw, R., 186

S
Saayman, M., 186
SAGIA, *see* Saudi Arabian General Investment Authority
Saudi Agricultural Investment Abroad, 126
Saudi Arabia, 157
  coding process, 120
  education system, 98–102
  labour market, 97, 98

primary and secondary data sources, 120
Saudi Arabia Monetary Agency (SAMA), 122
Saudi Arabian General Investment Authority (SAGIA), 22, 121, 122, 125, 128, 133
Saudi Basic Industry Corporation (SABIC), 130
Saudi Cabinet, 121, 122, 131
Saudi diversification strategy, 17–18
Saudi human development strategy, 109
Saudi investments, 125–127
Saudi labour market
  administrative sectors, 102
  agricultural sector, 102
  private enterprises, 103
  skills and training, 103
Saudi regulatory system
  FDI, 120–125
  SAGIA, 122
  Saudi Supreme Economic Council, 121, 122
Saudi Supreme Economic Council, 121, 122
Saudi Vision 2020, 111
Saudi Vision 2030, 17, 20, 133
Saudization programme, 98, 99, 111
Schonberger, R. J., 145
Schwaninger, M., 67
Second Gulf War (1990–1991), 15
Seventh Five-Year Plan (1996–2011), 12
Sharpley, R., 186
Shepherd, D. A., 62
Shura Council, 131
Small and medium enterprises (SMEs), vi, 5, 6, 12, 16, 21, 23, 49–72, 102, 210, 213, 216–222, 228
Social Overhead Capital (SOC), 54
Social value, 171, 172

Sornarajah, M., 119
Sovereign wealth funds (SWFs), 1, 7, 8, 18, 24, 126
State-owned enterprises (SOEs), 5, 49
  business entities, creation of, 54
  creation of, 70
  definition, 54
  governance structures, 54, 55
  governance system and state-ownership, 55, 56
  non-commercial services, 56
  operational activities, 68, 69
  organisational design, 55
  private sector, 56
  systemic integration, 56
Strengths, weaknesses, opportunities, and threats (SWOT) analysis, 148
Sultanate of Oman, 153, 155, 178
Supervisory Control And Data Acquisition (SCADA), 64
Supplier strategy, 146
Supreme Economic Council, 123, 131
Sutcliffe, K. M., 62
SWFs, *see* Sovereign wealth funds
System thinking approaches
  classification, 58
  definition, 57–60
  traditions of systems, 58
  VSM, 59, 60
  waves of, 58

T
Tabuk Agriculture, 126
Tax on business, 32
Telecommunication Regulatory Authority (TRA), 60
Total factor productivity (TFP), 144–145

Total preventive maintenance (TPM), 145
Tourism, 52, 209
 development strategies, 184
 economic diversification, 204
 economic growth, 186, 187
 GCC economies, 185
 growth of, 205
 heritage culture, 204
 historical monuments, 203
 international leisure, 186
 international tourist arrivals, 188
 oil and oil-related revenues, 185
 Oman, 187
 Saudi, 111
 UAE economy, 188, 189
Tourism market
 accessibility, 197
 entrepreneurship, 199
 facilitating resources, 198
 hospitality, 198
 infrastructure, 196–200
 political will, 199
 regional strategies, 199
Tourism Vision 2020, 199
Tourist destination
 competitiveness model, 189
 Dubai, 187
 marketing strategy, 6Ps, 205
Travel & Tourism Competitiveness Report 2013, 187

U
UAE diversification strategy, 16–17
UAE Government Strategy 2011–2013, 16
UAE Vision 2021, 11, 16
Unemployment, 17, 21, 53, 99, 105–112, 166, 176, 185

United Arab Emirates (UAE), 138–140, 155–157
United Nations Conference on Trade and Development (UNCTD), 118

V
Vertical diversification, 141
Viable System Model (VSM), 49, 59, 60, 64, 66
Vidgen, R., 21
Visions, 2, 186
 Bahraini Vision 2030, 11, 13
 Kuwait Vision 2035, 15
 national (*see* National visions)
 Qatar Vision 2030, 14
 Saudi Arabia Vision 2030, 17, 20
 UAE Vision 2021, 16
Vision3, 177
Voss, C. A., 145

W
Washington Convention, 124
Waterman, R. H., 148
World class manufacturing (WCM), 145
World Energy Council, 125
World Petroleum Council, 125
World Trade Organization Report, 53
World Trade Organisation (WTO), 17, 60
Worldwide Governance Indicators (WGIs), 90, 93

Y
Youth unemployment, 106, 107, 109
 benefits package, 107
 consumer mentality, 109
 demographic indicators, 109
 economic diversification, 107

employment system, 108
Hafiz programme, 106–109
job opportunities, 106, 107
Nitaqat policy, 108

Z
Zakat House, 35
Zawya, 216
Zubair, I., 139